Mediating
Mobility

VISUAL ANTHROPOLOGY IN THE AGE OF MIGRATION

Steffen Köhn

WALLFLOWER PRESS
LONDON & NEW YORK

A Wallflower Press Book

Wallflower Press in an imprint of
Columbia University Press
publishers since 1893
New York
cup.columbia.edu

Cover image from Laura Waddington film's *Border* (2004) © Laura Waddington.

A complete CIP record is available from the Library of Congress.

ISBN 978-0-231-17888-4 (cloth : alk. paper)
ISBN 978-0-231-17889-1 (pbk. : alk. paper)
ISBN 978-0-231-85094-0 (e-book)

c 10 9 8 7 6 5 4 3 2 1
p 10 9 8 7 6 5 4 3 2 1

Mediating Mobility

Nonfictions is dedicated to expanding and deepening
the range of contemporary documentary studies.
It aims to engage in the theoretical conversation
about documentaries, open new areas of scholarship,
and recover lost or marginalised histories.

Other titles in the **Nonfictions** series:

Direct Cinema: Observational Documentary and the Politics of the Sixties
by Dave Saunders

Projecting Migration: Transcultural Documentary Practice
edited by Alan Grossman and Áine O'Brien

The Image and the Witness: Trauma, Memory and Visual Culture
edited by Frances Guerin and Roger Hallas

Films of Fact: A History of Science in Documentary Films and Television
by Timothy Boon

Building Bridges: The Cinema of Jean Rouch
edited by Joram ten Brink

Vision On: Film, Television and the Arts in Britain
by John Wyver

Chavez: The Revolution Will Not Be Televised – A Case Study of Politics and the Media
by Rod Stoneman

Documentary Display: Re-Viewing Nonfiction Film and Video
by Keith Beattie

The Personal Camera: Subjective Cinema and the Essay Film
by Laura Rascaroli

Playing to the Camera: Musicians and Musical Performance in Documentary Cinema
by Thomas Cohen

The Cinema of Me: The Self and Subjectivity in First Person Documentary
by Alisa Lebow

Killer Images: Documentary Film, Memory and the Performance of Violence
edited by Joram ten Brink and Joshua Oppenheimer

Documenting Cityscapes: Urban Change in Contemporary Non-Fiction Film
by Iván Villarmea Álvarez

Documents of Utopia: The Politics of Experimental Documentary
by Paolo Magagnoli

Contents

Acknowledgements

This book would not have been possible without the continuous support of numerous individuals over many years. Fist of all, I wish to thank Prof. Matthias Krings, Prof. Anton Escher and Prof. Karl N. Renner for providing a stimulating work environment and for their continuous intellectual and moral guidance and encouragement. I further want to thank Nanna Heidenreich, Laurent van Lancker and Antje Weitzel for sharing texts, films and knowledge with me; and Sandra Sievers for helping me obtain many of the films I analyse throughout my work. In addition, I wish to thank my good friends and colleagues Felix Girke, Judith Beyer, Gerd Becker, Laura Münger, Florian Walter, Eva Knopf and Danilanh Lathnotha for reading chapters in their various drafts and for providing insightful criticism and comments. The artists Sylvain George, Raphael Cuomo, Maria Iorio, Bouchra Khalili, Elias Grootaers, Alex Rivera, Ursula Biemann and Zineb Sedira (and her gallery Kamel Mennour) were so generous as to share their work with me, and their unique approach to filmmaking was a constant source of inspiration to me in my practical and theoretical work. For friendship, collaboration (and the occasional distraction when needed) I express my infinite gratitude to Johannes Büttner, Henrika Kull, Leonardo Franke, Helge Peters, Lola Abrera, Barbara Breitenstein and Irina Breitenstein. Thank you for being you!

I have presented versions of chapters at various international events. These include the 12th EASA conference in Paris-Nanterre, the workshop 'Mobile Images – Images of Mobility' at the University of Cologne, the 'Arts with(out) Borders' conference at the University of Bern, the 17th IUAES world congress in Manchester and the 35th DGV conference in Mainz. I am grateful to the conference organisers, panel conveners and participants at these events for the opportunity to test my ideas and for their engagement with them. This book has evolved over many years. Parts of chapter three have been published as 'Organising complexities: the potential of multi-screen video-installations for ethnographic practice and representation' in *Critical Arts: South-North Cultural and Media Studies* 27:5 (2013). Another section of the same chapter was included in 'Screening Transnational Spaces', *Anthrovision* 2:2 (2014). I am grateful to the publishers and editors for their permission to reproduce this material here.

The fieldwork for this project was funded by the Research Unit Media Convergence and the Center for Intercultural Studies at Johannes Gutenberg-University Mainz, as well as by the Film and New Media Fund for Emerging Filmmakers Rhineland-Palatinate and I wish to thank these institutions for their support. I am especially grateful to Paola Calvo for creating such wonderful images and to my family for their enduring support, without which I could never have completed this work. My deepest gratitude, however, goes to those people that granted me so much insight into their lives and shared so many intimate moments with me during the fieldwork and filmmaking on which this project is based. Opara Onyekachi, Shahbaz Aakthar and Ilham Regadda in Melilla, Halidi Yahaya Soidikh and Sitti Aboudou in Mayotte, and Serpil Çelik, Axel Hartfiel, Mercedita de Jesus, Patricia Rendon and your families, may you cross all the borders and overcome all the barriers you are faced with in your lives!

Anthropology, Migration and the Moving Image

I n June 2015, the performance art group Center for Political Beauty staged their latest intervention right in the political heart of Europe. For *The Dead are Coming*, they brought the corpses of illegalised migrants who drowned at the continent's external borders to the German capital Berlin in order to rebury them at exactly the place where, according to the group, the most important decisions against Europe's humanity are taken. This public action was based on intensive research the collective conducted on the harrowing conditions under which the bodies of those who die on their way to Europe are treated at the continent's border regions. The group visited secret mass graves and cooling chambers in Greece and on Sicily where they found the dead anonymously piled up in trash bags. They were able to identify some of the victims and managed to contact their relatives with whom they opened the humiliating graves, exhumed the bodies and planned the reburial of the deceased migrants. Their transfer to the German capital was not only meant to bring the migrants' journeys to an end but also to generate attention and put pressure on European leaders to make them face a growing humanitarian crisis. The group first organised the burial of a 34-year-old woman from Syria, who drowned near the Italian shores, in an Islamic cemetery in Berlin's south-western Gatow district. This happened before the eyes of the international media but in the absence of her surviving husband and three children, who are in Germany and seeking asylum but were not allowed to travel to Berlin due to a law that prevents asylum seekers from moving freely within the country while their applications are being processed. A couple of days later, they gave the body of another 60-year-old Syrian a final resting place in Berlin and then called for a 'March of the Determined' during which they announced their intention to bury more bodies right in the forecourt of Angela Merkel's Federal Chancellery in the midst of the city's government district. With these burials, the Center also aimed to lay the foundations for

Fig. 1: The Center for Political Beauty's plan for a memorial 'To the Unknown Immigrants'.
Courtesy: Alexander Lehmann.

an unprecedented burial ground: a memorial for the victims of Europe's border policy under a grand arch dedicated 'To the Unknown Immigrants'. This memorial site would make the German chancellor, the cabinet and visitors of the chancellery literally walk over dead bodies. The group's announcement naturally caused a stir in the German political and media sphere. While the 'march' was approved by the authorities as a demonstration, the group was not allowed to transport any remains nor bring the excavators they claimed to have hired. Together with over 5,000 protesters, they transported an empty wooden coffin along the demonstration route towards the chancellery instead and thus reframed the demonstration as a funeral procession. A number of the demonstrators then overthrew the site fence around the freshly sown grass in front of the nearby Reichstag building and, with their self-made crosses and candles, immediately transformed the lawn into a massive symbolic graveyard. In the following weeks, more symbolic graves appeared in several German cities and even other countries like Switzerland, Austria, Sweden and Bulgaria,[1] while #TheDeadAreComing was trending on Twitter.

The Center for Political Beauty's campaign was an act of bringing to public visibility conditions that were largely unrepresented in most European media and repressed by the governments of Central Europe's economic powerhouses. Particularly Germany had done everything in its power to pass on its responsibility. With the Dublin Regulation, Germany profited for many years from an EU law ruling that asylum claims have to be processed in the member state where the applicant first enters the EU. This naturally put immense pressure on the Union's external border regions like Italy and Greece, where the majority of asylum seekers arrive and where states, due to the continuing economic crisis, are least able to offer them support and protection. Since the installment of the Dublin Regulation, European leaders have continuously failed to reach agreement on a quota system that would distribute arriving migrants more evenly across EU member states. Thus, the conditions the group documented at the EU border regions, where over-challenged local authorities find themselves left alone with the situation, are unsurprising. The collective's act of physically bringing the bodies of deceased migrants from the continent's margins right into its centre of political power therefore challenges a politics of invisibility upheld by European politicians who fear the anti-immigration fervour currently strengthening nationalist parties throughout the continent; a politics of invisibility that even disguises the sheer number of people who die every year at the fortified borders of Europe, people whose names nobody knows and whose relatives nobody informs. The drastic means by which the artist group gave visibility to these anonymous dead, however, did not go uncontested. Sonja Zekri for example even condemned the public exposure of the dead in the German newspaper *Süddeutsche Zeitung* on 16 June 2015 as 'political pornography'.

The Dead are Coming and the debates it created get to the core of the questions this book wants to address: how are we to understand the relationship between visibility and the political in the public discourse surrounding migration? How can we visually represent people who are barred from political representation, and how might such visual representations then gain political

Fig. 2: The symbolic graveyard in front of the Reichstag building. Courtesy: Nick Jaussi.

momentum? Migration nowadays is eminently iconic, and this applies not only to those forms labeled 'illegal'. Its public perception is profoundly shaped by mass media representations. Since the summer of 2015, the rising number of refugees and migrants coming to the European Union, across the Mediterranean Sea or Southeast Europe, has led to what the media have termed a migrant crisis as most European states find themselves either ill-prepared to handle the situation or react with downright hostility (it might therefore make much more sense to say that these migrants are experiencing a European Crisis). This situation has been accompanied by a worldwide escalation in media coverage of migrants. As the *New York Times* on 4 September 2015 noted with horror, many of these images are uncannily reminiscent of Europe's 'darkest hours'. Particularly from eastern European EU member states like Hungary and the Czech Republic images reach the world that show people locked into trains, armed police officers supervising crowds of people, and toddlers being passed over barbed wire fences. Political entities like individual EU member states have reinforced their border regimes on the symbolic level by operating with such strong imagery. Images thus have become an integral part of the political regulation of migration: they help to produce the categories of legality versus illegality, they foster stereotypes and mobilise political convictions.[2] The aim of this study, however, is not only to think about the images that circulate with reference to migrants, or to draw attention to those that accompany, show or conceal them. My quest is instead to think about migration *with the help of images*. As an anthropologist and filmmaker, I seek to link visual practice to theoretical reflection, discourses within the social sciences to aesthetic concepts. As we increasingly experience the world mainly through visual representations, the very acts of seeing and of making visible attain a tremendous theoretical and political relevance. I thus explore the epistemological and ontological assumptions they produce, but also their potential to make us perceive global processes in their complexity. Politics, Jacques Rancière says in his *10 Theses on Politics*, 'before all else, is an intervention in the visible and the sayable' (2010: 37). Yet in social science and the humanities we tend to disregard the political impact our representations might create. Arjuan Appadurai has recently demanded that we should not reduce our work to merely describing the present. He wants us to imagine possibilities and possible futures rather than give in to the probabilities of externally imposed change (2013: 213). As anthropologists, migration scholars or documentary filmmakers we thus have to seek for new, transformative forms of visibility that do not merely reproduce the visual discourse of the government or the corporate mass media but rather challenge the given political order by uncovering what is purposefully made invisible, articulating what has not yet been said and picturing viable alternatives to the status quo.

A WORLD DISPLACED

According to the United Nations High Commissioner for Refugees, the number of people who were forcibly displaced from their homes by violence or persecution was pushed to a staggering 59.5 million in 2015, more people than at any time since UNHCR records began (UNHCR 2015). In the Arab world, revolutions were followed by civil wars that were followed by reigns of terror. The conflicts in Syria, Iraq, Sudan and Afghanistan, the rise and expansion of the Islamic State, the unrest in eastern Ukraine and the continued destabilisation of developing nations in parts of sub-Saharan Africa and South and Central Asia have forced people to migrate as they seek to escape war, poverty and repressive regimes. Yet they frequently meet increased security at the Global North's militarised borders as neoliberal globalisation propels the uninterrupted flow of goods and capital but violently disrupts the movement of people. The divisions of economic and political power between a prosperous north and an impoverished south, between Europe and Africa and the Middle East and between North America and its Southern neighbours, however, do not only intercept the journeys of refugees but are in themselves for many people a reason to migrate. One could indeed argue, as Ambalavaner Sivanandan has, that 'the economic migrant is also a refugee, because the forces of global capitalism and its financial institutions such as the World Bank and the International Monetary Fund have eroded the integrity and economies of Third World (and even Second World) states' (2000: 13). Many wars, famines and even natural catastrophes result from the political, economic and ecological devastations globalisation has wreaked in recent decades (see Klein 2007). While Syria's neighbour Turkey now hosts more than two million refugees, most EU member states are still tightening their asylum regulations and fortifying their external borders (with Hungary now securing its border with Serbia with a four-metre-high, 110-mile-long fence). As there is no legal way to apply for asylum from outside the continent and due to the visa controls at the airports, the only ways into the EU are the extremely dangerous passage via the Mediterranean Sea or the exhausting land route via the Western Balkans across reinvigorated land borders.

Meanwhile in the US, a comprehensive immigration reform is essentially dead for the foreseeable future and the last bill that nearly made it to the House floor in January 2015 was solely concerned with further improving border security while legalisation for the roughly eleven million undocumented migrants in the country is out of sight. Mexico in recent years has rapidly transformed from a sending country into a transit state for the migration from Central America to the US. Yet transit through the country has become more and more hazardous, with female migrants becoming particularly highly vulnerable and being subject to serious and frequent violence. The most notorious and highly publicised incident was the San Fernando massacre that occurred in August 2010, when 72 migrants were found dead in the village of El Huizachal in the municipality of San Fernando, Tamaulipas state. They were killed by the Los Zetas drug cartel for failing to pay for their kidnapping ransom and refusing to work as hitmen for the cartel. Armed and violent robberies as well as kidnappings by organised crime groups thus make the route through Mexico one of the most perilous transmigration routes in the world, before migrants even reach the heavily guarded US/Mexico border.

This global geopolitics of exclusion forms the pressing context of this book. It draws on the in-depth analysis of over twenty films and video installations by contemporary video artists, experimental filmmakers and visual anthropologists, as well as on a trilogy of moving image works that I produced myself between 2009 and 2015.[3] The works I discuss investigate contemporary border zones and the transnational spaces (both physical and virtual) they have brought about. They map the living conditions of 'illegal' migrants in the French coastal town of Calais, the Spanish exclaves of Melilla and Ceuta and on the island of Mayotte in the Indian Ocean, one of the EU's so-called 'outermost regions'. They follow migrant journeys through the Sahara desert, across the Mediterranean or the US/Mexico border. They evoke migrant experiences in detention centres and the streets of Western metropolises. They explore mediated memoryscapes as well as migrant media practices. I will take these works as points of departure for a theoretical exploration of film's potential to communicate the bodily, spatial and temporal dimensions of the experience of migration. Yet beyond their engagement with these particularities of migrant lifeworlds, the films and videos I discuss also examine urgent questions regarding the interrelation between politics and poetics, mobility and mediation and the ethics of probability and possibility. My analysis therefore also ties into recent scholarship exploring the fresh impulses to be gained by working from within the shared ethnographic space that has opened up between anthropology and contemporary art practice. In particular, I investigate the innovative documentary strategies emerging in that very space, strategies that critically negotiate the pitfalls of representation involved in any attempt to render visible the accelerated movements of lives across the globe.

MIGRATION AND THE DILEMMAS OF ANTHROPOLOGICAL KNOWLEDGE PRODUCTION

I want to begin my discussion with some reflections on the shifting modes of anthropological knowledge at stake in the study of migration. I will identify the complex dilemmas that its research and representation pose on the level of ethics, methodology, epistemology and theory. In the realm of anthropology, human mobility has long been a central research area. Yet the recent proliferation and acceleration of transnational migrations and the question of what they mean for different peoples and societies has become a major issue in recent decades, contributing to an 'anthropology of migration' (for example, see Glick Schiller *et al.* 1992; Papastergiadis 2000; Castells and Miller 2009; Vertovec 2010). Yet the advent of an 'age of migration' (Castells and Miller 2009) has also constituted a challenge for anthropological theory as it raises new epistemological problems and requires new research methodologies. Anthropologists have wrestled with the question of how to adequately come to terms with these new transnational movements and relations. The *'terrain vague* of globalization' (Demos 2010: 14) thus calls for new modes of representation. As Slavoj Žižek (2015) notes, refugees, be they fleeing from war or poverty, are the inevitable outcome of a globalised economy whose hunger for oil or minerals, including coltan, cobalt, diamonds and copper, has abated many of the civil wars that haunt the contemporary Global South. He further reminds us that sweated labour is a structural necessity of captitalist globalisation and many of the refugees currently entering Europe will become part of its growing precarious workforce. Contemporary migrations thus are to a large degree, either willingly or unwillingly, produced and patterned by the demands of a globalised capitalism that is ambiguous and contradictory in its nature (see also Sassen 1998; McNevin 2011). Its very complexity, which sets people, goods and ideas in motion, has, as Frederic Jameson already argued in the early 1990s, rendered the languages of analysis and description insufficient; we are faced with a 'system so vast that it cannot be encompassed by the natural and historically developed categories of perception with which human beings normally orient themselves' (1992: 2). As global capitalism's 'mechanisms and dynamics are not visible', they 'stand as a fundamental representational problem – indeed, a problem of a historically new and original type' (ibid.). Jameson's perceptions corresponded in many aspects with anthropology's so-called crisis of representation that was widely felt during the 1980s. At that time, the experience of decolonisation raised serious doubts about the legitimacy of the anthropological enterprise. Poststructuralist thought had challenged the interpretative authority of Western science and unmasked scientific knowledge as sustaining global power inequalities (see, for example, Foucault 1970; Said 1978). The publication of Bronislaw Malinowski's field diaries (1967) had forever destroyed the belief in the ethnographer as an objective observer. The Western 'master narratives' for explaining reality seemed to have collapsed (see Lyotard 1984) while at the same time the world was becoming ever more complex. This new present, 'that eludes the ability of dominant paradigms to describe it, let alone explain it' (Marcus and Fischer 1986: 12), left anthropology with a deep uncertainty about the adequate means of its representation.

Further, despite the enormous output of books and articles in academic journals, the social sciences are not the only producers of knowledge concerning migration. Big supranational think tanks or research institutions like the International Organization for Migration (IOM), the International Centre for Migration Policy Development (ICMPD) or the Consortium for Applied Research on International Migration (CARIM) employ their own researchers and collect statistical evidence pertaining to migrational 'facts', 'trends' or systems. These organisations, working outside of any political or parliamentarian monitoring, raise an influential voice in policy debates. They define which forms of migratory movement are unwanted and to be considered 'illegal' and hence support the political regime that governs migration (see Düvell 2001). Anthropologists thus have to cope with the moral dilemma that knowledge about migration is seldom neutral and can indeed play into the hands of state authorities (see De Genova 2002; Black 2003). 'Clandestine' and 'undocumented' forms of migration are inevitably invisible and therefore constitute a highly sensitive subject for scholarly research. An emerging critical approach to migration studies (see Karakayali 2008; Hess and Kasparek 2010) thus carefully avoids the production of economist or functionalist theories of human mobility that could be misused for the sake of regulation and control. It rather postulates the 'autonomy of migration' (Papadopoulos and Tsianos 2007). This perspective by no means implies that one should consider migration in isolation from the fields of society, culture and economy but rather understands it as a creative force, a productive social movement within these very structures. It seeks to look at 'migratory movements and conflicts in terms that prioritize the subjective practices, the desires, the expectations, and the behaviours of migrants themselves' (Mezzadra 2011: 121). However, anthropologists' representations inevitably also enter the minefield of a distorted media discourse. Corporate mass media often produce distorting, ideological images of migration that influence political debate. Anthropologists therefore not only have to implement nonhierarchical modes of knowledge production that come as close as possible to migrants' subjective experiences, they also have to develop a deliberative discourse that attends to the lived reality of migration. In chapters one and two of this book, I will show how innovative visual approaches can challenge stereotyping mass media representations and bring the spectator into close sensual proximity to migrants' lifeworlds. This perspective brings into focus the embodied and material aspects of migration, the meaning of global processes for the individual. It meets the challenge of representing what, in many cases, is unrepresentable: the traumatic experiences of many migrants, the need to remain invisible or to 'disappear' from official tracking mechanisms and surveillance (see Doy 2005).

Yet migration also poses an epistemological challenge to anthropology as it implements new spatial and temporal formations. Since their research participants have become mobile, anthropologists are faced with 'traveling cultures' (Clifford 1997) and 'global ethnoscapes' (Appadurai 1996). In the light of globalised capitalism, cultures can no longer be explained as homogenous, enclosed systems outside of global relations. Hence, the discipline's traditionally fixed site of research, its theoretical equation of culture with place, has had to give way to multi-sited forms of enquiry and to theoretical concepts that account for the complexity of transnational connections (see Marcus 1995; Falzon 2009). Contemporary migration brings anthropologists and their subjects not only close to each other in space (for example, in the big European and North American metropolises) but also in time. This new 'intense proximity' (Enwezor *et al.* 2012) defies anthropology's tendency to situate the cultural worlds it describes in a timeless realm, a pre-modern time *before* time. Johannes Fabian (1983) famously referred to this mode of thinking along the old colonial distinctions between centre and margin as the 'denial of coevalness'. Chapters three and four of this book thus explore filmic strategies that account for the spatial and temporal simultaneity migration brings about. They investigate how film can chart new transnational networks and, hence, how the medium might foster a theoretical reexamination of anthropology's spatial and temporal concepts. In my conclusion then, I investigate how these new forms of cinematic knowledge production might gain political momentum. Drawing on Jacques Rancière's thoughts on the politics of aesthetics, I discuss how engaged filmic approaches may disturb the ruling distribution of the visible and the sayable and implement new forms of expression into the consensual public discourse.

In recognising the difficulties inherent in attempts to (re)present such a global phenomenon, this book lays necessary groundwork for the politics and poetics of migration studies. I will argue that the medium of film has the potential to push the boundaries of conventional representation. I am going to show how film can implement alternative modes of knowledge, how it can offer us those innovative methods of 'cognitive mapping' that Jameson called for; methods which 'enable a situational representation on the part of the subject to that vaster and properly unrepresentable totality, which is the ensemble of society's structures as a whole' (1991: 51). Only recently, social scientists have started to participate in the expanding circulation of visual representations of migration. Alan Grossman and Àine O'Brien, who have provided a first overview of work done in this field, praise visual media practice as facilitating 'a deeper understanding of the lived, contradictory and at times ephemeral conditions shaping the lives of migrant subjects' (2007: 6). Hence, in what follows, I will discuss how film can bring us close to the experience of migration and how it can convey our entanglement in large-scale global processes. My argument aims not only at describing a new representational aesthetics of globalisation, but also at a broader reevaluation of the potentials of the medium film for anthropology.

So far, I have discussed migration in a rather broad sense. This is, of course, not to imply that there is a universal or generic 'migrant experience', nor to dispute the broad variety of particular migratory movements. On the contrary, I hope that all the works I draw upon make clear that migrations are distinct processes and that the experiences and lifeworlds of migrants are socially and historically specific. The films, videos and cinematographic installations I discuss engage with (or emerge from) the experiences of legal and 'illegal' migrants, political refugees and diasporan communities. Throughout this text, I take up Nicholas De Genova's suggestion (2002: 420) and deploy quotes whenever I use the term 'illegal' to refer to migrants or migration in order to emphasise that illegality is not some natural condition but a label, a status imposed on individuals by the law. Furthermore, I agree with him that the distinction between legal and 'illegal' migration is rather tenuous. This attribution can change easily due to certain kinds of (non)behavior or (non)action. In many states like the US or Spain, periods of law enforcement alternate with legalisation programmes, always depending on which government is in power. As will become obvious, the 'illegal immigrant' thus mainly exists as a stereotype, that is, an image. Another problematic distinction is that between the 'economic migrant' and the political refugee or asylum seeker. In contrast to the 'illegal migrant' the political refugee is (since the Geneva Convention of 1951) a juridical category that provides (at least temporarily) a certain amount of security and protection by the state. However, many states do their best to limit the access to this privileged status. In reality, there often is a complex web of reasons for an individual's decision to migrate. Forced and voluntary (economic) migration are therefore not that easy to distinguish between. What the media discourse about 'bogus asylum seekers' also oversees is that initiating an asylum process for many border crossers is the only means to win some time and not be deported right away. Hence, the asylum process produces two political and juridical identities: it accepts some persons as political refugees and thus as objects of humanitarian care while it denounces others as 'illegals'. As a last terminological consideration, I dismiss the term 'immigration' as it implies a unilinear teleology that is at odds with the spatial and relational complexity of contemporary migratory movements (see Glick Schiller *et al.* 1995). The paths of migration are not one-way roads but transnational cross-links, allowing the exchange of people, goods and ideas across the barriers of nation-states.

SITUATING VISUAL KNOWLEDGE: ART AND ANTHROPOLOGY

The moving image works that my argument is based on offer access to new concepts of time, space and perspective, as well as to modes of engagement with the material and embodied dimensions of migration I find essential to adequately describe the transnational movement of human beings. This body of work does not, however, exclusively originate from within the institutions of visual anthropology, nor necessarily from an academic background at all. It could rather be situated in a context that Catherine Russell (1999) has emphatically called 'experimental ethnography': that is, experimental or essayistic documentary films and videos that engage in areas of anthropological enquiry and therefore have the potential to expand the horizon of visual anthropology. In much contemporary art, we have witnessed in recent years a veritable resurgence of documentary approaches. Documentary work now dominates the global biennial scene as well as theoretical debates. Julian Stallabras (2013: 14f) ascribes this re-awakening of documentary to the over-reach of neoliberal power, the revival of imperialism and the long and continuing 'war on terror' that since 9/11 has covered the globe with new zones of conflict to which contemporary artists want to bear witness. In the light of this 'return of the real' (Foster 1996), it is no surprise that many artists who seek social and political engagement have begun to explore the potential of ethnographic methodologies to research and observe social worlds and situations. In this so-called 'ethnographic turn' in current art production, artists such as Sharon Lockhart, Lothar Baumgarten, Susan Hiller, Alfredo Jaar, Ursula Biemann or Gillian Wearing have, since the mid-1990s, started to adopt (or interrogate) methods of ethnography such as interviewing and participant observation and do fieldwork in cross-cultural contexts. This is also fostered by an ongoing trend in the production of art towards site-specificity, in which curators and institutions commission artists to work in collaboration with local communities (see Coles 2001). Thus, art increasingly has come to occupy, as George Marcus and Fred Myers predicted, 'a space long associated with anthropology, becoming one of the main sites for tracking, representing, and performing the effects of difference in contemporary life' (1995: 1). Hal Foster further links this 'ethnographic turn' to the rise of conceptual art, which has made the autonomy of art a contested ideal. He expresses a critical attitude towards this appropriation, as he sees it based on a series of misrecognitions in which both sides have ignored how differently methods, traditions and paradigms were established within each field. Yet Foster oversees that conceptual art has also challenged the romantic ideal of the artist as genius. Many artists have ceased to produce mere self-referential objects and entered the immaterial sphere of cultural discourses, offering what Miwon Kwon has called 'critical aesthetic services' (1997: 103). As curators have become major players in the art-circuit, many exhibitions nowadays are organised around current political and social issues, often accompanied by symposia that assemble political activists, social scientists, artists and art critics alike. Therefore, the division of roles between artists and academics as well as the disciplinary borders between the art world and academia have increasingly become blurred. This has also created a grow-ing demand for art that is infused with cultural theory. Artists have begun to translate theoretical concepts into aesthetic ones, take up a critical interest in media imagery, develop their work in dialogue with curators and form research alliances with social scientists, activists or other experts within a given field (see Lind and Steyerl 2008).

Within anthropology, this continuing appropriation by contemporary art-ists has likewise led to an impulse to push anthropological practice to new boundaries. Anthropology's advocates of this approximation (for example, Grimshaw and Ravetz 2005; Schneider and Wright 2006, 2010, 2013; Ingold 2011a; Schneider and Pasqualino 2014) argue that engaging with the sensual and material practices of art can offer the discipline new ways of seeing and working with visual materials. Their new concern with the particularities of sensory experience has led many scholars to recognise the limits of textual rep-resentation and become increasingly interested in how these might be overcome. The recent sensory turn in anthropology (see Pink 2009) has therefore brought about a renewed engagement with artists' explorations of human perception (as exemplified in the works of Arnd Schneider, Tim Ingold and others). The Sensory Ethnography Lab at Harvard University, for instance, has become one of the most visible outlets for creative work and research that is conducted through audiovisual media and thus transcends purely verbal systems of signifi-cation. Associated anthropologists like Lucien Castaing-Taylor, Véréna Paravel, Stephanie Spray, Aryo Danusiri (whose work I discuss in chapter three) or J. P. Sniadecki all consciously employ analogue and digital media to explore the af-fective fabric of lived existence. They combine intense ethnographic fieldwork with artistic strategies that are often derived from experimental and structural filmmaking to create immersive cinematic experiences that inject a good deal of visceral imagery into conventional anthropological representation.

There are, of course, historical precedents to these approximations between art and anthropology. James Clifford (1988) reminds us that there already once was a space for profound interaction between anthropologists and artists of the avant-garde in the Paris of the 1920s and 1930s. After the barbarisms of World

War I, looking at other cultures implied, for both groups, a search for alternatives to (or transgressions of) their own civilisation that had just revealed its monstrous face. Marcel Mauss's seminars at the newly opened Institut d'Ethnologie or George Bataille's journal *Documents* provided intellectual encounters that eventually resulted in common projects like Marcel Griaule's and Michel Leiris's famous Dakar-Djibouti expedition with its interest in cosmological concepts and other states of consciousness and its research and representation practice strongly influenced by surrealism. 'Surrealist ethnography' for Clifford was thus about approaching a reality experienced as shattered and in crisis by the creative means of juxtaposition, by applying modernist artistic techniques of collage and fragmentation to cultural representation, thereby subverting customary classification systems and hierarchies. The legacy of this historical constellation can be traced for example in the work of ethnographic filmmakers like Jean Rouch (see Stoller 1994) or in textual experiments like the montage-style ethnographies of Michael Taussig (1987, 2004).[4]

In this respect, our own time of globalised disaster and emergency is not that dissimilar. As Jean-François Chevrier (2005) argues, contemporary artistic investments in the documentary have to be understood in the light of the shattering of established paradigms of truth during global crisis. This has pushed questions of politics and its representation to the fore, questions that now are of prime concern for many contemporary artists. Against this backdrop, transnational migration has naturally become an important subject of a considerable amount of artistic exploration that is still in the process of emergence today. This work is accompanied by an exciting scholarly discourse on the aesthetic foundations of these artistic formations (see Marks 2000; Naficy 2001; Aydemir and Rotas 2008; Bal and Hernández-Navarro 2008, 2012; Gutberlet and Helff 2011; Mathur 2011; Demos 2012a, 2013; Heidenreich 2015). T. J. Demos (2013) traces the current conjunction of art and migration back to the diasporic art of the 1980s and the nomadic art practices of the 1990s. Partially as a response to the social unrest in Britain in the 1980s, young artists like Mona Hatoum (whose video *Measures of Distance* [1988] I will analyse in chapters two and four), the Black Audio Film Collective or Isaac Julien began to create an aesthetics of exile that was influenced by emerging debates on postcolonialism, multiculturalism and identity politics. When globalization fully unleashed after the fall of the Berlin Wall in 1989 and the subsequent integration of the former communist states into the global capitalist system, this new phase in the geopolitical transformation of the world at the same time led to a transformation of the art world and the modes of art production. Local art scenes became connected to the Western markets and a globalising biennial system rapidly placed many non-Western artists on the world stage. The 1990s thus became the decade of the 'nomad artist' who embraced dislocation and celebrated the transgression of borders and cultures. Rirkrit Tiravanija, for example, installed his nomad kitchens where he cooked free Thai food in museums and art spaces around the globe; Gabriel Orozco created universal sculptures out of found objects that are purified of any local or political character; and the Belgian-born, Mexico City-based artist Francis Alÿs travelled for *The Loop* (1997), his contribution to the bi-national *InSITE* art festival, from Tijuana to San Diego without crossing the US/Mexico border. Heading south, he took the longest possible route once around the world. For Demos, such celebrations of the nomadic, however, ultimately failed to acknowledge the extend to which borderless travel is a privilege of the few (particularly in a post-9/11 security-state environment) and how quickly the nomad became a role model for the transnational capitalist 'free market' ideologues.

Today's generation of artists has become very conscious of such false promises, particularly as they have witnessed the EU rapidly turning from a borderless zone into an isolationist 'Fortress Europe'. As Demos notes (2013: 15) they have relinquished the false universality of the nomadic to turn instead to an exploration of the ethnographic details of migrant living conditions and the political and economic structures that shape them. As of late, some research projects, exhibitions and conferences have consequently begun to investigate migration by combining artistic and scientific research. In 2007, Mieke Bal and Miguel-Ángel Hernández-Navarro organised two conferences entitled 'Encuentro' in Amsterdam and Murcia that brought artists, social scientists and cultural theorists together. They were complemented by the video art exhibition '2Move' that examined the relationship between the mobility of people and the mobility of images. In this context, Bal developed the concept of 'migratory aesthetics' as a mode of thinking about migration through visual forms.[5] She has since taken up such a practice of 'visual thinking' herself and begun to produce films and video installations in addition to her output of academic publications. Besides Bal's and Hernández-Navarro's work, there have been other recent exhibitions and research ventures that have been very influential for this present book, such as 'Maghreb Connection: Movements of Life Across North Africa', initiated by artist Ursula Biemann, and 'Transit Migration', a collaboration between researchers from the Institute for Cultural Anthropology in Frankfurt, the Institute for Theory of Art and Design at HGK Zürich and independent filmmakers, media activists and artists. Both provide further examples for how artistic and academic discourses can stimulate each other. 'Maghreb Connection' originally took shape as a curatorial enterprise, comprising artistic production and research on trans-Saharan migration to Europe over a period of eighteen months. Its focus was profoundly transnational, with participants from the Maghreb countries and Europe working in Niger, Morocco, Egypt or the Italian island Lampedusa. The results where presented in a travelling exhibition, a conference and a bilingual (English/Arabic) publication (see Biemann and Holmes 2006). 'Transit Migration' was founded within the framework of the larger 'Projekt Migration', a five-year project funded by the German Kulturstiftung des Bundes, that aimed at re-examining the changes brought about by migration within European societies, thus revising a national self-image to incorporate migrant histories. 'Transit Migration' focused on the formation of a European border regime and explicitly on its representation and representability (see Transit Migration Forschungsgruppe 2007). Both projects, hence, tried to establish new forms of exchange between theory and practice and consider art as a legitimate form of knowledge production. Another crucial point of reference is the exhibition 'Transient Spaces – The Tourist Syndrome', presented in 2010 at Berlin's Neue Gesellschaft für Bildende Kunst and at Kunstraum Kreuzberg/Bethanien. The show raised questions of global mobility and analysed how the seemingly antithetical movements of migrants and tourists shape our contemporary social landscape. Further, the correlations between politics and aesthetics have recently been addressed with much rigor by Okwui Enwezor's 2015 show for the Venice Biennale, termed 'All the World's Futures'. While his 'Documenta XI' in Kassel in 2002 was one of the first large-scale exhibitions to explore the postcolonial condition through the prism of art practice (and was extremely influential for the proliferation of documentary forms of video art), Enwezor has now curated a show that examined the current morphologies of globalisation with regards to art's potential to produce, transform and transmit knowledge across the conflicted terrain of today's world. What unites the artists participating in all these research and exhibition endeavours is that they consciously face the dilemma of merely reproducing the conditions of inequality of which they give testimony in their work. This has led them to invent critical documentary strategies that give presence and recognition to lives that are without political representation. Instead of repeating the corporate media's objectifying images of victimhood, they thrive for new modellings of affect that invite their audiences into a position of proximity towards the complexities of the migrant experience. They use various aesthetic strategies to destabilise their spectators' corporeal, spatial and temporal orientation in order to make dislocation a shared experience between subject, artist and audience. This position of proximity then creates an autonomous space in which the current separation of roles between the citizens and the excluded can be called into question and different political configurations become visible. Thus, it forms the fundament for an ethics of possibility that may make us taste alternatives to the current arrangement of things.

POLITICAL THEORY AND AESTHETIC PRACTICE

The artistic practices I have described above have inspired much theorisation and many terms: socially engaged art (Thompson 2012), activist art (McLagan and McKee 2012), relational aesthetics (Bourriaud 1998) or participatory art (Bishop 2012). These concepts all seek to define a newly emerging space where cultural production engages the social and political sphere and in which political action can sometimes take on aesthetic characteristics, in which politics is not only artistically represented but activated and performed. What we see emerging here is a complex yet mutually responsive meeting of politics and aesthetics. At the same moment, many scholars in political theory and political science have equally begun to show interest in themes that have traditionally been considered to belong to the realm of the aesthetic and thus started to explore the relationship between visual representation and political thought. On the one hand, this is an obvious reaction to the fact that our perception and understanding of our globalised world now is, above all, conveyed through visual media. Our experience of the conflicts of our time, be it around questions of autonomy, sovereignty or nationality is shaped foremost by visual representations and much contemporary politics is therefore conducted through popular visual culture (see Weber 2008). Recognising the extent to which images have become autonomous participants in the construction of social meaning, Roland Bleiker (2012) advocates a more aesthetic form of political thinking. He proposes an aesthetic engagement with world politics based on an understanding of aesthetic sources as offering valuable insights that conventional social scientific modes of enquiry are unable to account for: for example, the emotional consequences of political events for individuals or the perspectives of those who remain excluded from the political game and whose interests are unrepresented in the prevailing arrangement of power.

Yet how can we further understand representation in its double sense as depiction and advocacy? Ariella Azoulay (2008, 2012) has recently proposed a political ontology of visual representation that fosters an understanding of images as active agents in social relations. Drawing on photographs of Palestinians in the Israeli-Occupied Territories, Azoulay describes how images may offer a space of citizenship for those who do not belong to or do not receive protection by the sovereign power of a nation-state . She sees a 'civil contract' inscribed in the medium of photography in which the photographer, the photographed and the viewer of the photograph all participate. As no photographer can claim the ownership of what appears in the photograph nor determine its sole meaning, the photographed persons may use their image to claim the rights they are denied by the state. The viewers are addressed by photography as 'universal spectators' who are bonded in a form of civic duty with the photographed and thus are invited to take responsibility for 'witnessing the insufferable' (2008: 18). For Azoulay, this collective act of witnessing first photography and then film have brought about is not a passive, static activity. Rather, it reaches across national boundaries and transcends borders as virtually anyone can join in a social concern for others. Visual representation may thus offer those who are excluded from political representation a first chance to articulate the ways in which they have been dominated. It enables them to 'present their grievances, in person or through others, now or in the future' (2008: 86). For Azoulay, one becomes a citizen through photography not merely by being photographed but by virtue of being visible in a world in which visual media give public recognition to potentially everyone, in which (given the ubiquity of cameras as tools for the masses) photography always is a 'potential event' (2012: 22). Photography thus allows its citizens to make themselves appear in public, come before it and enter a dialogue with the public by means of images. The processes of being and making visible therefore implement a dynamic field of political relations. Azoulay here draws on Hannah Arendt's ideas on the emancipatory qualities of visibility that also form a theoretical backbone of this present text and that I will further elaborate in chapter one. There, I will show in detail how visual practices condition the belonging to or exclusion from a political community and the ways in which such (non)membership is constituted audio-visually. In Arendt's political theory, political action presupposes visibility in what she terms the space of appearance, a space of plurality in which individuals venture to generate something new through speech or action. As they do so in public, among many other people, and exposed to their gaze, they critically negotiate the *res publica*, the common interest. Image making, for Azoulay, is a political action in an Arendtian sense, as it adds

> a new way of regarding the visible, one that previously did not exist or that, at least, existed in a different manner. This gaze is based on a new attitude toward the visual. It constitutes in an approach toward items, situations, customs, images, or places that, before photography came into existence, were not held worthy of contemplation in and of themselves. This approach or attitude now exists in contexts of plurality, among people, in a public sphere, contexts within which every participant not only contemplates what can be seen but is also, herself, exposed and visible. Such regard for the visual departs from the disciplinarian gaze or the pattern of communicating prerecognized messages. It approximates at least the central distinguishing features of action: it includes the aspect of a new beginning, and its ends are unpredictable. (2008: 96)

Azoulay contests the dichotomisation of the political and the aesthetic, an opposition she traces back to Walter Benjamin's (1936) famous critique of the aestheticisation of politics by fascism (that he claimed should be countered by Marxism with the politicisation of art). Since Benjamin, the 'aestheticisation of politics', the accusation that a work of art is 'too aesthetic' in its representation of situations of social crisis like violence or suffering is a recurring critique in the discourse about politically engaged art. For Azoulay, however, documentary images can never be 'too aesthetic', because they always document the relationships and the negotiations between the photographer and the subjects, they always depict the political context in which they were created. They always bear, as visual anthropologist Lucien Taylor puts it, the 'scars of the encounters that produced them' (1996: 79). Likewise, reducing the image to the aesthetic decisions of the artist, also a recurring trope in the discourse of art that routinely ascribes all effects produced by a work of art to the intentions of the artist as its sole creator, limits our understanding of these complex relations inscribed in every image and denies the depicted an active role in the production of its meaning. For Azoulay, photography is always the product of an encounter between citizens and her analyses of images from the history of photography explore in fascinating detail how the photographed have continuously used the 'event of photography' to contest the injustices done to them in public in the form of a civil address. Azoulay thus collapses the binary between the space of the political, that, for her, is inherent in every encounter between human beings (2012: 101) and the space of aesthetics, making these two spaces one. As I noted, this politico-aesthetic space for her establishes a deterritorialised community that is much more encompassing than the citizenship distributed by the nation-state and whose political relations are not mediated by a governing power. Azoulay's political project is thus to denounce the idea that national citizenship is the ultimate realisation of citizenship. Rather, she sees citizenship as an 'interface that enables people who inhabit different spheres of existence to share a common world despite marked differences in the conditions of their existence' (2012: 105).

A recent work of art that evokes such a common world shared by an art audience and the politically excluded while putting the prevailing equation of citizenship and nationality into question is Nigerian artist Emeka Ogboh's *The Song of the Germans* (2015), an installation commissioned for Okwui Enwezor's Venice Biennial exhibition 'All the World's Futures'. Ogboh recorded the voices of 'illegal' African migrants who reside in Germany but are denied formal residency, singing a stanza from the German national anthem. The singers perform the anthem each in their own native tongue; in Ibo, Yorouba, Bamoun, More, Twi, Ewondo, Sango, Douala, Kikongo and Lingala. In the immersive installation, these recordings are played continuously (each singer is on a separate speaker), with a new arrangement each time: one singer starts the piece, then the others join in at different points in the song, slowly building up to a full chorus. The migrants perform a song of belonging to a nation that actively excludes them from a proper political status. Yet with their beautiful voices, they make the values of 'unity and justice and freedom' that the lyrics of the German anthem praises and also calls 'us' to strive for insistently their own. They act as if they were equals within the political community the song conjures up. In the middle of the installation a book is placed on the visitor bench that contains photos from the recording session as well as the lyrics of the song in each language, hence inviting the audience to also join in the choir. Ogboh's installation thus proposes a new community, one that transcends the exclusive borders of national belonging. It deploys the context of the exhibition in order to rehabilitate, or indeed to create, a common 'civil space' (Azoulay 2012: 87) and evokes art as a site of civil imagination.

Azoulay's concept of visual citizenship has been taken up by other scholars who have begun to analyse how 'audiovisual practices condition, exacerbate, impede, or render (in)consequential the rights, privileges, duties, and entitlements among people who are included and excluded, seen and unseen, heard and silenced in journalistic practices, in direct action campaigns, in commercial advertisements, in the built environment, and so on' (Telesca 2013: 339); and I situate my own attempt to rethink the ways in which audio-visual practices mediate political action and vice versa within this emerging discourse. I examine the complex processes by which 'illegal' migrants are made anonymous in the public sphere and invisible under the eyes of the ruling law, and point to the potentials inherent in the medium of film to extend the possibilities of what can be seen, whose claims can be heard and whose story told.

The distribution of what is visible, audible and sayable in public discourse has been rigorously analysed in recent years in the work of the French philosopher Jacques Rancière, who traces the possibility of political participation (and the exclusion from it) back to individual sensual perception. Rancière's argument is in fact an acknowledgement of the aesthetic nature of politics because he sees the conflictive rearrangement of society's symbolic order (that for him is politics proper) as inscribed in an individual's sensory apprehension. Thus, it shapes existing forms of visuality and modes of representation and therefore preconfigures how we perceive (and actually what we can perceive of) the social world. Rancière's writings depart from a commonsensical understanding of aesthetics and politics as he redefines both terms, as well as their relationship toward each other. For Rancière, aesthetics does not simply refer to the study of art, beauty or taste. Rather, it extends well beyond the realm of art.

It encompasses all symbolic modes of expression that a community deploys to act and communicate in a meaningful way. It is a process, signifying as well as sensory, that frames what can be seen, said and thought; a 'system of *a priori* forms determining what presents itself to sense experience' (2006: 13). What is visible in a common space, what can be expressed in a shared language, what is permissible to say or to show, is governed by the 'distribution of the sensible': an implicit law, a sensible order that partitions what Arendt has called the 'common world'. Aesthetics establish the modes of perception through which we can apprehend the world and thereby defines the access to its places and the forms of participation that are possible in it. Sense perception and experience thus are not subjective domains but highly political matters. The distribution of the sensible includes and excludes at the same time as it determines 'who can have a share in what is common to the community' (2006: 12). Aesthetic practices, then, are acts of making visible the interventions in the general arrangement of the sensible. They are configurations of experience that emerge from the field of society, interact with it and possibly change its parameters as they might introduce novel ways of perception and induce new forms of political subjectivity. Rancière rejects the common understanding of politics as the struggle over, exercise of or division of power; the confrontation between interests and opinions, or the search for a consensus. He asserts that real politics is not practiced by constituted parties. It has no natural subjects and no proper place. All these attributions, rather, adhere to what Rancière calls the 'police': the established order that determines the distribution of the parts and roles in a society, assigns everybody their place in the structure of the social body and preconfigures an individual's or a group's possibilities of being, acting and communicating. The 'police' is not necessarily a mode of repression; it is not identical with the state apparatus. It installs, however, a particular distribution of the sensible which then appears as the status quo, as the natural order of things. Politics, then, is a term Rancière only reserves for an 'extremely determined activity antagonistic to policing: whatever breaks with the tangible configuration whereby parties or parts or lack of them are defined by a presupposition that, by definition, has no place in that configuration – that of the part of those who have no part' (1998: 29f). Political action proper thus reconfigures what has been defined by the police order. It reveals its arbitrariness and contingency and undoes its perceptual divisions. It is an act of dispute that implements the 'part of those who have no part': the subaltern who 'cannot speak' (Spivak 1988), whose articulations are not considered discourse but mere noise in the ears of those in power. Hence, the only object and principle of politics is the equality of every speaking being. However, equality, Rancière says, is itself undetermined. It has no essence, no given, only an assumption 'that needs to be discerned in the practices of implementing it' (1998: 33). Aesthetic practice for Rancière is not the same as political action and its effects will never be political in the same way as, say, those of a strike or a demonstration are. The ultimate objective of politics is to postulate equality and attempt to implement its validity in a world that negates it whereas art may give us a sensible insinuation of its full realisation. The Center for Political Beauty, for example, has, with its public action *The Dead are Coming*, discussed at the beginning of this chapter, created a strong image for such an egalitarian promise that seems almost too beautiful to become true: a memorial in the centre of Berlin's government district that commemorates those who died on their way to Europe, founded by a society that respects the dignity of all human beings, and not just its own citizens.

Bouchra Khalili's *Words on Streets* (2013), the second chapter of her *Speeches Series,* is a work of art that reorganises the fields of visibility and audibility in yet a different manner to allow 'those who have no part' in the current political order to step out of the shadows of the nation-state. For her video, the Moroccan-French artist has collaborated with migrants she encountered in the Italian city of Genoa whom she filmed delivering intimately personal and self-conscious narratives of displacement that take on the form of manifestos. They address issues of citizenship, nationality, identity and belonging, describe their experiences of xenophobia, racism and legal and social exclusion, and thus articulate their relationship to the country they now call their home. The Peruvian Malu Guttierrez, for example, describes her struggle for a legal status in the city that welcomed her once as a dancer touring the country, a second time as a migrant, yet still does not welcome her a third time as a citizen. Finally, she states, she will 'win this right not because I love this country or know the language or the constitution but because ten years will have passed of paying taxes and that's what the law says'. Simohamed Kaabour a young Moroccan narrates how he was formally sworn in as a citizen seventeen years after coming to Italy as a child and how the official welcomed him to the country as if he just arrived. Djilly Sylla, a Senegalese in his fifties, recalls his involvement with political activist groups during the 1990s when he fought for migrant workers' rights and how these movements gradually lost their momentum. The migrants all deliver these stories about their minority positions in Italian, the language of their new place of residence. Khalili films their performances in (empty) public places throughout the city, which she thus reclaims as contemporary manifestations of the agora, the place in which citizens negotiate the public interest. She consciously places her video in the Italian tradition of civil poetry that traces back to Dante and had been revived by poet and filmmaker Pier Paolo Pasolini. The choice of Genoa as a setting is itself loaded with meaning as the city has one

If I were Italian,
I could move throughout all countries without a visa

Fig. 3: Addressing citizenship and belonging in *Speeches – Chapter 2: Words on Streets*. Courtesy: Bouchra Khalili and Galerie Polaris, Paris.

of the largest migrant populations of the county and was the site of the protests against the infamous G8 summit in 2001, a key event in the formation of the new left in Europe. As Djilly, the last of the speakers in Khalili's video, explains, it is also the place where Italy's first self-organised and autonomous migrant advocacy group was founded. The spoken autobiographic texts have been developed in close collaboration between Khalili and the migrants. Through them, they become the chroniclers of their own lives as they refashion their experiences in the form of a condensed narration that, given the theatricality of the setting and the mode of presentation, borders on fiction (understood with Rancière as the friction between the factual and the symbolic). Thus, in rethinking their own existences in front of her camera, they are already changing them. The 19-year-old Alice Chan, who grew up in Italy as a child of Chinese parents confesses that she has no consciousness of herself: 'But I'll certainly confront these questions in the future, as I'll confront myself.' As they stage their egalitarian participation in the public realm, Khalili's protagonists convince themselves and others of their equality through the act of public speech. *Speeches – Chapter 2: Words on Streets*. thus offers an aesthetic experience in the Rancièrean sense as it demonstrates equality and provides a sensible form to experience it.

THE PERSPECTIVE OF PHENOMENOLOGY

The aesthetic-political ontologies of Arendt, Azoulay and Rancière all describe the act of viewing not as a passive activity that is opposed to action but stress the mutual interdependence between the seer and the seen. For Arendt, gaze and speech are constitutive aspects of the 'vita activa', the life of action. For Azoulay, spectatorship constitutes an empathetic encounter between the viewer of an image and the lives and suffering of the depicted, an encounter that inherits a deeply ethical dimension and entails a civic appeal. Rancière sees in the opposition of viewership and action that is proclaimed by avant-garde artists like Debord or Brecht, or contemporary purveyors of 'relational aesthetics' and participatory art who all want to force the audience out of its presumed passivity a return of Plato's old warning of the images on the cave wall. Why, he asks, shall we identify looking with passivity, unless we presuppose that 'to view means to take pleasure in images and appearances while ignoring the truth behind the image' (2009: 12)? For Rancière, an art that fashions itself as a vehicle for the spectator to become active itself perpetuates an unequal distribution of the sensible in which the artist possesses all the knowledge about the social world while the audience is inferior and in need to be schooled. Rancière's 'emancipated spectators', in contrast, actively co-produce the meaning of what they see, hear and feel and thus constantly demonstrate that there are many equitable ways to interpret reality.

These accounts of viewing as active and compassionate, as a dialogic encounter and as constitutive for our embodied 'being-in-the-world-together' all resonate with phenomenological descriptions of 'the thickness of flesh between the seer and the thing' that is 'not an obstacle between them, it is their means of communication' (Merleau-Ponty 1968: 18). The perspective of phenomenology offers an understanding of audiovisual mediation that is attentive to the perceptive processes media involve the spectator in, and thus brings into view the meaningfulness of an embodied viewing experience. Throughout this book I will therefore describe how film allows for a sensual proximity to and sensory participation with the experiences of others and the detailed features of their lifeworlds. As it directly addresses two sensory channels (and others, as I will show, by evocation), film provides access to other, non-abstract, sensuous forms of knowledge that encompass emotions, bodily perception, sensory experience and the mimetic faculty, all subjects that are of renewed concern for much contemporary anthropology. In what follows, I will therefore engage with a range of approaches that can be termed phenomenological. I relate Vivian Sobchack's phenomenological description of the film-viewing experience to anthropological approaches to experience, embodiment and the senses. I examine how a phenomenological understanding of space and place can reveal how global relations are necessarily inscribed in local lifeworlds, and I deploy a Husserlian understanding of time-consciousness to explore migration as a temporal experience. As Paul Stoller argues, the study of migration can benefit immensely from a phenomenological perspective, as 'transnational complexities require a more sensuous approach to ethnography, an approach in which local epistemologies and sensory regimes are more fully explored'; he goes on to 'suggest that sensuous descriptions improve not only the clarity and force of ethnographic representations but also the social analysis of power relations-in-the-world' (2004: 820). The phenomenological qualities of film therefore inherit an important ethical potential as they bring us into an empathetic position towards the other and make abstract political processes become understandable in their effects on individuals and their lifeworld. The analytical language of phenomenology thus provides me with a vocabulary that attends to the corporeal, the visible, the sensible and the connectivity of the spaces in-between that the theories of Arendt, Azoulay and Rancière cannot fully account for. Yet I use these authors to politicise phenomenology's description of our sensory access to the 'flesh of the world' and the ways it can be evoked by audiovisual media. I describe how it is exactly the sensory and empathetic qualities of film that make it act, inspire solidarity, constitute new political communities and thus potentially translate politics into sensible form.

**

The complex questions about politics and poetics raised so far I have tried to tackle not only theoretically, but also in my cinematic practice. Throughout my argument, I will therefore return to the trilogy of films that I have produced on the contemporary European border regime and the indefinite geographies of globalisation. These cinematic works will hopefully exemplify my ideas on film as a sensory and intellectual form. They constitute the ethnographic part of this present study but they also put forward an anthropological argument by audiovisual means. *Tell Me When....* (2011), a mid-length ethnographic documentary film, *A Tale of Two Islands* (2012), a two-screen cinematographic installation and *Intimate Distance* (2015), a webcam-video triptych, explore the sensory lifeworlds of 'illegal' migrants stranded in the Spanish exclave of Melilla, the postcolonial space that comprises the French island of Mayotte and its African sister island Anjouan in the Indian Ocean, and the webcam communication patterns of transnational families dispersed between the EU and the Philippines, Turkey and Colombia.

However, before I elaborate further on these projects, chapter one will set the stage by analysing why we have to extend the anthropological discourse about migration to the visual realm. It offers an anatomy of the often ideological and distorting representation of migrants in the mass media. I investigate the role 'illegal' migrants are assigned in the public sphere by engaging with Hannah Arendt's lucid thoughts on the relationship between visibility and political power. Arendt's writings are not only helpful to understand the links between visual and political representation. They also expose the distinct political (non)status the 'refugee' has received in Western nation-states. Unlike citizens, 'illegal' migrants cannot act in public, in the space of visibility and appearance. They are subjected, rather, to concurring regimes of exposure and concealment. On the one hand, this makes them overtly visible as 'naked lives' that are politically abandoned and thus open to the access of the state. Yet, at the same time, it obscures them from public view and hence from political debate. Their hyper-visibility in mass media discourse (in the figure of the 'illegal intruder') thus stands in stark contrast to their invisibility as individuals. For filmmakers and anthropologists participating in the discourse on migration, this entails the danger of unwillingly reaffirming the perspective of the state and reproducing its modes of surveillance and control. Hence, I discuss artistic forms of visual intervention that expose the politics of in/visibility at stake in the representation of migration.

In the subsequent chapters, I go on to describe innovative approaches to ethnographic filmmaking that challenge the painful indeterminacy of migrants in public discourse. In an essay entitled 'New Principles of Visual Anthropology', David MacDougall has identified four distinctive areas of anthropological concern 'for which visual media have demonstrated expressive affinity' (2006: 271). These categories of relevance, about which film can indeed communicate differently, will further guide me through this work as they allow for a different perception of the experience of migration.

Chapter two deals with what MacDougall calls the *corporeal* aspects of social life. I discuss the current anthropological interest in the notion of 'experience', specifically conceptions of experience offered by phenomenological or existential approaches. I explore film as a methodology for the study of experience, as the medium presents a unique ability to communicate about this subject. Film uses experience both as its content and its mode of reference. Building on phenomenological theories of film spectatorship and on anthropological theories of sense perception, I describe how film can incorporate embodied experiences and further evoke them in its audience. I argue that film thus goes beyond visual representation, offering us instead a form of direct contact and a pathway to the other senses. I provide a close examination of films that try to convey migrants' embodied experiences, allowing for a multisensory participation on the side of the spectator, a mode of reception not so easily achieved by writing. In discussing my film *Tell Me When...* I show how this conception of the medium's evocative qualities has informed my own approach to filmmaking. I began to work on this project in 2009 in the Spanish city of Melilla on the North African coast, an exclave that is surrounded by a huge fence, seven miles long, separating EU territory from the Global South in order to keep away migrants seeking their fortune in Europe. *Tell Me When...* focuses on the experiences of three migrants who have made it across the fence and are now trapped in limbo. It thus conjures up what MacDougall praises as the *personal* dimension visual anthropology is able to express: the perspective of individual social actors and their worlds, their unique individuality and personalities. Opara is from Nigeria. For two years, he has lived in the detention camp at the outskirts of the city. He doesn't want to surrender to his situation and fights for the respect of the Spanish population. He is also an active member of the city's small Pentecostal church. Shahbaz from Pakistan has lived in the camp for three years. Through his mobile phone, he organises a complex network of relationships to his family at home and to friends who have already reached the European continent. The pictures and Hindi pop songs he has saved on his phone provide him with an emotional connection to home. Ilham is from Morocco. Like many other Moroccans, she lives illegally in the city. For years she has fought for legal status. She lives on the street or stays occasionally with friends, and does small jobs to survive. With one foot on European soil, all these people can do is wait either for their papers or their final deportation. My approach to making this film was heavily influenced by my interest in phenomenological anthropology. Yet I sought to understand my protagonists' experiences in Melilla not only as embodied, but also as emplaced. By exploring the concreteness and phenomenological reality of this particular place, I also wanted to bring into focus the larger political situation they found themselves in. Such an expanded notion of experience provides the background for an investigation of the complex spatial and temporal coordinates of migration I then carry out in the next two chapters. There, I try to relate my ideas about the sensory participation of the spectator to the medium's formal ability to express abstract thought, thus exploring how the cinematic undercuts the divisions between subjective and objective viewpoints.

In this vein, chapter three focuses on space and place, the *topographical* in MacDougall's terms. It discusses how contemporary migration demands a new spatial paradigm from anthropological theory. I will assess the new spatial formations that transnational migration and its political regulation have brought about: border zones, non-places like camps or transitory spaces. As a key concept, I will describe the possibilities of montage as an analytical tool for charting our globalised present. By revealing the invisible interconnections between places, transcultural forms of montage (see Suhr and Willerslev 2013) pose a challenge to realist representations. I discuss recent multi-screen video installations that articulate these complex relations by expanding the modernist techniques of montage and juxtaposition into space. I describe how my own cinematographic installation, *A Tale of Two Islands*, evokes the invisible EU frontier between two of the Comoros Islands in the Indian Ocean while at the same time it examines the potentials of multi-channel video for the organisation and dissemination of anthropological knowledge. The work is based on multi-sited fieldwork that was conducted on the French island of Mayotte and its neighbouring island Anjouan that belongs to the Union of the Comoros. Geographically, both islands are part of the Comoros archipelago in the Indian Ocean. Politically, Mayotte and Anjouan both belonged to the French colonial empire until 1974 when referendums were organised on both islands so that inhabitants could vote for or against independence. Whereas a great majority on Anjouan (as on the other two Comoros islands, Mohéli and Grande Comore) chose to depart from France, the Mahorans wanted to remain under the protective and wealthy French administration. While Mayotte has since been integrated into the French state and the European Union, the Union of the Comoros is politically unstable and ranks 169th out of 187 countries in the 2012 Human Development Index (UNCDF 2013). While for centuries both islands formed a cultural unity and inter-insular trade, migration and family relationships where the norm, the new maritime border now is firmly controlled by the French *Police aux Frontières* and the citizens of the Union of the Comoros require a visa to enter Mayotte. Due to the severe economic imbalances between Mayotte, an artificial enclave that offers social security, wages and education of European standards, and the other Comoros Islands that form one of the poorest nations in Africa, many Anjouans try to migrate clandestinely to Mayotte in search of a job and a better future. *A Tale of Two Islands* thus explores the possibilities of spatial montage to evoke the complex postcolonial situation originating from this political separation. By simultaneously charting the lifeworlds on both islands on two opposing screens, the work places its audience on the very border that separates them. It thus gives the spectators access to multiple perspectives, allowing them to draw their own connections between both synchronised films.

Chapter four is about questions of time, the *temporal* for MacDougall. Migration is not only a matter of space, but also a matter of time as it involves a variety of temporal experiences, when past, present and future constantly seem to shift. Time can be a prison, like in the European detention centres where wait-time and a politically motivated denial of coevalness are used as a weapon against unwanted migration. The migrant's time thus often passes asynchronously to the time of mainstream society (see Mathur 2011). Film can represent these heterochronies by its ability to create what Gilles Deleuze (1989) has called 'time images'. This chapter thus engages with cinematic explorations of memories, the incontemporaneities of globalisation and what is absent in the present. Hence, it describes the hitherto unexplored potential of time-image cinema for ethnographic film. In discussing my film *Intimate Distance*, I explore the webcam communication practices of transnational families and how such new digital technology facilitates feelings of proximity and synchronicity, of temporal co-presence over spatial distance. I am particularly interested in how such instantaneous forms of mediated communication shape their users' temporal experience. *Intimate Distance*, the concluding part of my trilogy, is a collaborative project for which I asked people who live in transnational relationships and who make intensive (and creative) use of the communication software Skype to stay close to their faraway loved ones, to record their webcam conversations. Mercedita (who goes by her nickname Dittz) came to Europe in 2004 as an OFW (Overseas Filipino Worker) and worked as a nurse and domestic helper in the household of an Italian family in Bologna. The Philippines are one of the few countries that actively encourage their population to work abroad, knowing that the remittances this creates form a huge part of the country's GDP. More than a million Filipinos every year leave to work temporarily abroad through overseas employment agencies or government-sponsored initiatives. Nearly half of these are women who predominantly find work in the caregiving industry. Dittz, like many other female OFWs, left her children Hydee and Hadji, aged fourteen and eight at the time, with their grandparents. While most OFWs initially plan to stay only a few years abroad, their families often grow to depend on the money they send back home. Dittz and her husband (who is also an OFW) originally planned to bring their children along, yet they finally decided that their chances for a career are better if they sponsor a good education for them at home. As Dittz can only afford a trip to the Philippines every other year, she has had to mother her children from afar, first via infrequent and expensive landline phone calls, then via mobile phone, and finally via Skype. Webcam has now become the most important means for her to deepen her relationship with her children.[6] Patricia, my second protagonist, has lived in Germany for ten years but she still has strong ties to her hometown, Barranquilla in the north of Colombia, where she founded a community radio station. She still joins the editorial meetings via webcam or produces programmes from her new home in Leipzig, Germany. As she can only rarely find the time and money for a trip home, she uses Skype extensively to stay in touch with her mother and especially with her younger sister, Milena and her two nephews, Alejandro and Juan Pablo. Patricia's own daughter, Camilla, who spent the first seven years of her life in Colombia, also frequently joins the online family reunions. Serpil and Axel have been living in a long distance relationship between Istanbul and Berlin since they met during a diving holiday in Turkey three years ago. They plan a common future in the German capital, but Serpil has a well-paid job as a dentist in a hospital in Istanbul and has so far not managed to receive a working visa for Germany. While getting married would be an option to solve the visa problem she is still a little reluctant to give up her life and career and move to Berlin. Meanwhile, Axel has already found a flat for them and rents out one of the rooms to tourists through the social networking service Airbnb until Serpil finally moves in with him. Until then, their relationship is lived out mainly via Skype and they spend several hours a day in front of the webcam. Whereas Axel works from home most of the time, Serpil uses Skype on her mobile phone to spend the hours she is stuck inside public transport with Axel. The two have developed many little rituals involving the webcam, like co-sleeping in front of the camera or having meals together. I used the video footage generated by my protagonists to edit a film that demonstrates how feelings of intimacy and distance are continuously renegotiated in the synchronic social space that is set up by this kind of webcam-based communication. The resulting work is a meditation on the potentials and the limits of digitally mediated proximity.

In my conclusion then, I examine the politics within the aesthetics of ethnographic filmmaking I have laid out in the chapters before. Drawing on the writings of Jacques Rancière, I discuss 'engaged' modes of anthropology and analyse the potential political impact of its representations. Taking up Rancière's concept of 'dissensus', I describe how anthropological representations may ultimately become the sites of radical possibility, spaces where new configurations of power might be imagined and played out. Film, I argue, might be uniquely suited for inscribing equality into a world that denies it, as it can offer us some of our most tangible experiences of dissensus that challenge what is sensible, thinkable and thus possible.

CHAPTER ONE

Migrant In/visibility

his chapter discusses the visual discourse surrounding migration and the politics of in/visibility inscribed in it. In the last two decades, we have witnessed an increasing acceleration of both the migration of people and the circulation of images. The power and meaning of images and visual representations has since become an urgent question of academic concern. For this reason, I want to take a closer look at the images of migrants and their representation in the public sphere. The huge attention migrants have received in mass mediated discourse has recently become a focus of research within cultural and media studies, as well as for scholars of an emerging interdisciplinary field of visual culture (see Mitchell 1994, 2004; Wenk and Krebs 2007; Bischoff *et al.* 2010; Falk 2011). These approaches have offered a critical iconology of the visual stereotypes and clichés in which migration is frequently portrayed. They reveal the assumptions these representations entail and explore the practices of social exclusion inscribed in them. To fully understand the entanglement of visual representations with political processes, however, I argue that one has to not only analyse the discursive content of these depictions but also those very acts of visualisation that render migrants visible. Visibility and invisibility have to be understood first of all as political modes of existence. In this chapter, I therefore build upon Hannah Arendt's political theory that allows us to apprehend representation in both visual and political terms and that dissects the relationship between visibility and power. I show that the existence of migrants in the public sphere is constituted by a dialectics of in/visibility, of both concealment and exposure. The prominent visibility migrants receive in the media as stereotypes effectively renders them invisible as individuals. There further exists a disturbing connection between media representations and the state's politics of surveillance and control of migrants. Their visualisation is thus potentially dangerous for many migrants as it conflicts with their need to remain invisible. In what follows, I will unfold the ethical, epistemological and theoretical challenges at stake in the visualisation of migrants. Further, I will explore this realm of visibility by engaging with artists' critical interventions in these processes. In short, I want to draw attention not only to what is present, but also to what remains absent in the visual discourse on migration.

THE QUESTION OF IMAGES

As already noted, the recurring images (and imaginations) of migration in mass media discourse have recently been investigated by a number of scholars. Christine Bischoff, Francesca Falk and Sylvia Kafehsy, for example, seek to map out an iconography of 'illegal' migration, analysing 'the actual visual images, figures, symbols, narratives, metaphors – the material forms – in which symbolic meaning is circulated' (2010: 7). These approaches all explicitly refer to W. J. T. Mitchell's (1994) postulation of a 'pictorial turn' in the humanities and social sciences that emphasises the constitutive role images play in the creation of social meaning. Departing from Richard Rorty's linguistic turn (proclaimed in the 1970s), Mitchell and his followers recognise the increasing importance and influence of the visual on the way we perceive, imagine and think of the world. They state that the image has taken over from language as the main structuring agent of social realities. Thus, the 'need for a global critique of visual culture seems inescapable' (1994: 16). Mitchell further sees the question of images as intricately bound to questions of power and hegemony. Highlighting political controversies around images, he describes the visual as a terrain of political struggle and makes ideology itself the subject of his iconological analysis (1986: 164). Many scholars have taken up this suggestion and explore how images constitute, reinforce and influence political processes and how political theory itself relies on the evocation of powerful imagery (for example, see Falk 2011: 15). Mitchell's call for the transdisciplinary study of visual culture has also had an impact on visual anthropology. In their introduction to *Rethinking Visual Anthropology*, Marcus Banks and Howard Morphy argue that the subdiscipline should not only be concerned with the practice and theory of employing visual media for research but also with the anthropological study of (Western and non-Western) visual systems and images as social objects (1997: 21).

Most studies that engage analytically with the visual representation of migrants in mass media discourse have criticised the heavy use of distortions and clichés. Terence Wright (2002), for example, reveals how many press photographs depicting migrants refer to Christian iconography in order to construct the image of the helpless and victimised refugee. Francesca Falk (2010) explores the motif of the (overcrowded) boat as a visual and verbal metaphor in the discourse about refugees and asylum. She shows how it is frequently associated with invasion in political anti-migration campaigns. Both Rutvica Andrijasevic (2007) and Sylvia Kafehsy (2010) analyse media campaigns that the International Organization for Migration (IOM) has sponsored in alleged emigration states in order to discourage would-be migrants. These campaigns associate migration with the dangers of criminal activities such as human trafficking and the sex trade. Together, these studies provide an iconology of the visual conventions in which migration is repeatedly stereotyped. They reveal how migrants are either criminalised or depicted as passive victims without agency. Thus, they aim at uncovering the preconceptions, the ideological 'unconscious', of mass media representations.

All of these studies, however, operate on the level of the icon, the single image, and hence they usually deploy methods of picture analysis derived from art history, Mitchell's disciplinary point of departure for the interpretation of images. Antonia Schmid (2011) has therefore proposed a methodology for 'visual discourse analysis' that seeks to make Mitchell's ideas productive for the study of moving images. Schmid's method seeks to decode 'visual statements' in films in order to reveal their 'latent meanings' and implications. Like Mitchell, she draws on a very broad understanding of what an image is. Her concept of 'topos' encompasses pictures, icons, verbal and 'immaterial' images, and even 'accumulated images' such as film characters (2011: 306). These 'mental images' might thus 'be composed of several parts including auditive and pictorial elements' (2011: 312). This, however, reveals one of the serious shortcomings of the visual culture approach: while it claims to offer a comprehensive theory for everything visual, it relies on a concept of the image as a metaphysical construct withdrawn from all material reality. Its notion of the image falls back behind a considerable body of scholarship that has explored the materiality and communicative specificity of different media and the perceptual processes in which they involve the observer. Despite claiming the contrary, Schmid's method of deciphering the meaning of images is thus ultimately based on a linguistic paradigm, on the easy translatability of images into text. It locates the meaning of a film solely in its signification, in its abstract transmission of decodable signs. While Schmid claims to recognise that the meaning of images is produced in the process of their perception, the only conclusion she draws from this is that one would also have to analyse their specific context in order to pinpoint their meaning. By context, however, she only means the discursive context, not the actual physical situation of their reception. This communicative context can then only be 'read' in yet another act of discourse analysis.

In what follows, I propose to depart from such a generalised notion of the image and take a close look at how visual technologies are embedded in the state's politics of surveillance and how this specific mode of visualisation becomes reproduced in the mass media. An analytical approach to images that is solely interested in their signification and not in their materiality also falls short of providing any real understanding of the power relations that are entailed in visual representations. Schmid's visual discourse analysis ultimately avoids the question whether media images influence or reflect society's views. A mere discussion of the iconicity of migration thus cannot reveal the complex ways in which power is constituted by visibility. Thus, I will draw upon Hannah Arendt's political theory to describe the production of visibility as a political process mediated by specific visual technologies and linked to the exertion of power, regulation and control.

THE POLITICS OF VISIBILITY

In her political philosophy, Arendt offers us an understanding of visibility in political terms. For her, visibility is the basic condition for political participation and the prerequisite for the emergence of a public sphere. Visibility, for Arendt, first of all constitutes our 'common world' (1958: 52), the world we intersubjectively share with our fellow human beings. She describes the sphere of politics as a 'space of appearance'. Reality, 'humanly and politically speaking, is the same thing as appearance. To men, the reality of the world is guaranteed by the presence of others, by its appearing to all ... and whatever lacks this appearance comes and passes away like a dream, intimately and exclusively our own, but without reality' (1958: 199). Arendt insists on the situatedness and worldliness of human existence, rejecting any Platonian dualism of being and appearance, materiality and ideas. She approaches political phenomena not in idealised or abstract metaphysical terms but first of all 'through the way they appear to those living through them ... that is, through the way they experience and interpret them' (Borren 2010: 15). Arendt's writings thus examine the individual and shared experiential dimension of politics. The public sphere, the Arendtian space of appearance, is the space where 'individual experiences are selectively refashioned in ways that make them real and recognizable in the eyes of others' (Jackson 2006: 12). For Arendt, any given physical space can potentially be transformed into a political one, ranging from the coffeehouses that Jürgen Habermas (1962) has described as the breeding ground for public debate in eighteenth-century Europe, to street corners and public places, or even the living room. Individuals access this public sphere as citizens through speech and action; that is, civic participation. However, if people stop acting and speaking together, the space of appearance can vanish as fast as it emerged. As mentioned, visibility is the basic requirement for participation in such an intersubjectively shared space, as any (political) action and speech necessarily depends on recognition. These acts gain relevance in that they are visible to everyone. Arendt, however, distinguishes sharply between this public world of visibility and the private sphere. As citizen, one not only has the right to appear (that is to raise one's voice politically) on the stage of the public realm, one also has the right of non-appearance in the private sphere. In private life, one is (and should be) invisible and hence protected from the public eye (see Arendt 1958: 71). Hence, as Marieke Borren notes, *public visibility* and *private invisibility* for Arendt form a complementary right that is bound to citizenship (2010: 175). Arendt's position, however, is by no means a simple liberalism that argues for a resistance of the private against the state. For her, private and social conditions rather have a political relevance as they make possible our visibility in public life. Without private and social identities, we are not 'at home in the world' (1994: 308); we cannot appear in and discuss a common world.

One of Arendt's most recognised descriptions of political experience is concerned with those who cannot enter this common world of visibility. In *The Origins of Totalitarianism* (1951), she acknowledges the condition of non-citizens, the stateless refugees. Arendt describes the production of this group of people as an outcome of European disintegration after World War I. The stateless refugees lack a political status and a legal personhood. This effectively excludes them from the space of appearance. Simultaneously, it also deprives them of all their basic rights because 'the conception of human rights, based on the assumed existence of a human being as such, broke down at the very moment when those who professed to believe in it were for the first time confronted with people who had indeed lost all other qualities and specific relationships – except that they were still human' (1973: 299). Without legal personalities, the refugees are unable to act or speak politically. Their existence in the public sphere is thus contrary to that of regular citizens. They suffer from *public invisibility* because they don't have access to political representation. At the same time, however, they are forced into natural visibility, because as mere 'natural men' they are left without protection against state intrusion into their lives (see Borren 2008: 224f). In his essay 'We refugees' that explicitly refers to Arendt's article from 1943 of the same title, Giorgio Agamben draws a disturbing parallel between the treatment of stateless refugees by Western nation-states in the first half of the twentieth century and their present-day policy towards 'illegal' migrants. These non-citizens of today might have a nationality of origin, yet 'inasmuch as they prefer not to make use of their state's protection they are, like refugees, "stateless *de facto*"' (1995: 117). No autonomous space exists for them in the current political order, for the status of the refugee is 'always considered a temporary condition that should lead either to naturalization or to repatriation' (1995: 116).

In a similar line of argument, Borren states that the pathological political status of the refugee Arendt describes also applies to 'illegal' migrants in a number of ways (2008: 225ff). Their public invisibility is fostered by an ever more restrictive asylum policy that in Europe in the last decade has resulted in a drastic fall in the numbers of accepted asylum claims. This means, de facto, a denial of legal personhood for an increasing number of people.[7] Undocumented migrants who have been apprehended on the streets and rejected asylum seekers who have exhausted all legal procedures are prone to detention and, finally, to forced expulsion. Those non-convicted migrants in Europe's expulsion centres, police cells or in border custody are frequently incarcerated for an indefinite period of time. Thus, they exist outside the law in a status of non-jurisdiction that excludes them from the most basic human rights, a status in which committing a crime would actually improve their legal position: 'As non-natives, they are "only human" due to the convergence of nationality and citizenship; as non-citizens, the human rights regime is unable to change their situation, due to the convergence of civil rights and human rights' (Borren 2008: 231). A *regime of concealment* not only deprives them of the legal personality needed to enter the political space of appearance, it also withdraws them from the view of society at large. Europe's detention centres, operating in a legal grey zone, are usually inaccessible for journalists and political activists and hence remain largely invisible to the ordinary citizen. Ariella Azoulay has shown in graphic detail how the state's regime of concealment thus keeps the abandoned of the global era from making their claims heard in the public media. She describes how the Palestinian non-citizens in the Israeli-Occupied Territories are kept just 'on the verge of catastrophe' by the regime, thus creating 'a paradoxical situation in which the injury to the population of noncitizens is simultaneously visible and invisible' (2008: 65). Due to the humanitarisation of the occupation through the permanent presence of humanitarian organisations and their assimilation into the apparatus of Israeli rule, the catastrophe is always postponed, making it invisible, even though it is manifest to everybody. It is invisible even though numerous visual and textual expressions might depict it, because the postponed catastrophe does not produce an *énoncé*, an urgent claim for emergency that creates the kind of global attention a war or a natural catastrophe does. The everyday horror on the verge of catastrophe, in which the non-citizens must live, instead becomes a routine event that rarely makes it into the news and does not inspire affection or dispute by the regular citizens.

The illegalisation of migration in Europe or the US equally creates living conditions on the verge of catastrophe for the non-citizens of these states. It creates zones of forced invisibility not only within the institutions of the state. It implements spaces of nonexistence throughout society through the very contradiction between the physical and social presence of these migrants and their official negation as 'illegals' (see Coutin 2000: 27ff). Their 'enforced clandestinity' (Coutin 2000: 33) turns everyday activities such as working or driving a car into illicit acts, resulting in restricted physical and social mobility. As Nicholas De Genova notes, this denial of legal personhood produces 'real effects ranging from hunger to unemployment (or more typically, severe exploitation) to violence to death' (2002: 427). Making themselves visible, attempting public visibility, for example, in demonstrations and other forms of social protest, for 'illegal' migrants thus eminently becomes an insubordinate and very dangerous act as they risk being photographed, arrested, and even deported (see De Genova 2009: 450).

Paradoxically, at the same time a *regime of exposure* enhances the migrants' natural visibility as it exposes them to measures of control, identification and surveillance by the state. Since the earliest days of the nation-state the visibility of migrants posed a haunting problem to government agencies that soon started to utilise technologies of visualisation in order to politically regulate migration. The development of new visual technologies has since gone hand in hand with the need for the visual identification of migrants and the surveillance of migratory movements. In 1892, the Geary Act demanded an obligatory registration of all Chinese immigrants in the US. This law was the first to consider 'illegal' migration a crime, to be punished with 'hard labor' for up to one year (see Falk 2011: 122). It required all members of the growing Chinese community to carry a 'certificate of residence' that included a photograph. As the Chinese were publicly considered individually indistinguishable (see Gordon 2006: 57) this should secure their proper identification. Many Chinese protested against this discriminatory act that applied only to their particular community. It furthermore posed a practical problem, for in the rural areas where many Chinese lived photography was still unavailable. The US demanded identification via photography first from the Chinese, then from Mexicans, and ultimately also from Europeans. The same applied to fingerprinting, another technology of visual identification that was introduced immediately after Isaiah West Taber had produced enlarged photographs of individual thumb marks that were suitable for comparison in 1885 (see Cole 2001: 126). Migrants also were subject to one of the very first police operations that systematically made use of the medium of photography.[8] In 1852, Carl Durheim was assigned by the Swiss federal public prosecutor to produce a photographic survey of foreign 'vagrants' (among them basket makers, mouse hunters, knife grinders and other travelling workers) encountered on Swiss territory. These photographs were distributed among regional police stations in order to secure their fast identification in case of illegal border crossings. Durheim's 220 portraits formed the basis of what would later become a central database for the registration of so-called 'gypsies' (see Falk 2011: 124).

Today, the border is the site where the latest technologies of visualisation are implemented to monitor unauthorised migration. The border fences around the Spanish exclaves of Melilla and Ceuta and the US/Mexican border are equipped with high-end imaging technology like thermal or night-vision cameras, which are able to expose nocturnal attempts to cross. To control their extensive coastline, the Spanish authorities have developed the so-called Integrated System of External Vigilance (SIVE). This system of fixed and mobile sensors (radars, infrared cameras) is able to detect vessels five to fifteen miles from the shore. At a distance of approximately three miles from the coast, it is possible to estimate the course and time of arrival and even the number of people on board. Hence, border police operations can begin long before a boat even reaches the maritime border. The creation of the Schengen Area that eliminated border controls between its member states has not only resulted in a fortification of Europe's external borders but also in the implementation of a new system of internal border control. Pan-European databases now coordinate the application process for asylum seekers who, since the Dublin Convention of 1997, are only allowed to apply once in a EU member state. These European networks also allow border control agencies the fast exchange of information and biometric data (fingerprints, X-Ray, iris scans). Natural visibility thus 'increasingly has to be taken more literally than Arendt ever intended: advanced technologies penetrate the body, right into the very cells out of which it is composed, to identify the individual with what he is by nature: someone who is born at this or that time, to such and such parents, furnished with a particular body, shape, etc' (Borren 2008: 229). These visual technologies of course do not identify 'who' but 'what' someone is: a mere 'natural man' who is politically abandoned and hence reduced to a 'naked life', or a proper citizen equipped with a legal personality (Arendt 1958: 179).

EXPOSURE AND CONCEALMENT

Raphael Cuomo and Maria Iorio's film *Sudeuropa* (2007) offers a lucid analysis of the politics of in/visibility at work in one of Europe's migration hot spots. The small Italian island of Lampedusa, geographically closer to Africa than to the European continent, became a major destination for African migrants since the Spanish authorities had started rigorously to enforce their control over the Gibraltar Strait. From around 2003, the passage to Lampedusa via Tunisia or Libya increasingly constituted one of the most important routes into Europe.

While the Ben Ali and Gaddafi regimes for some years managed to improve their relations with the EU by inhibiting 'illegal' embarkations from the North African coast, their fall in the 2011 Arab Spring upheavals and the subsequent political chaos has currently resulted in a reopening of the route. Since the outbreak of the war in Syria, the number of people trying to reach Europe via the island has reached staggering levels. Although the arrival of migrants on Lampedusa has become a veritable media spectacle that still seems to feed European anxieties of invasion, Cuomo and Iorio instead found themselves confronted with a regime of concealment. Nowadays, the migrants' boats are intercepted far off at sea, miles before they even reach European territory. The passengers are then brought to the island's detention centre that is inaccessibly located in a hidden valley within a military zone from which eventually they are transferred from the island by plane or ferry. To the innumerable tourists who constitute Lampedusa's main source of income, these visitors remain invisible. The southward movement of European tourism and the northward movement of African migration that converge here thus remain distinctly segregated. *Sudeuropa* begins with images of a perfectly blue sea and white beaches where everything seems quiet and normal. Soon, however, the film slowly unfolds the migrants' absent presence on the island as it explores the little traces that have escaped the public invisibility enforced on them: the places of their arrival, incarceration and deportation that are shielded from sight and hence attain a ghostly quality. Abstract green dots on a border control radar might indicate arriving boats, while the ship cemetery is where the migrants' vessels are dumped and shredded into dust. A disturbing

Fig. 4. Traces of migrant presence on Lampedusa in *Sudeuropa*.

graffiti by one of the coast guard crews shows a Guardia Costeria officer dressed up as a Roman centurion. Below him, a boat full of migrants is apparently in distress. The migrants are desperately trying to grab hold of a stream of urine emanating from his exposed penis, as if it were an escape rope. Besides this disquieting evidence, Cuomo and Iorio do find particular moments when the migrants themselves become visible, yet only as they are exposed to the cameras of reporters. In several irritating scenes, Cuomo and Iorio film journalists filming and thereby show us how the images of 'illegal' migrants are produced for a European audience. We see policemen with white latex gloves herding the bodies of the newly arrived together like sheep, lining them up, staging them for the reporters who are waiting to take their pictures.

Those conventional media images, the film suggests, produce a harmful natural visibility as they only convey the migrants' superfluousness to the social order, their potential dangerousness that justifies their treatment as criminals. Thus, these representations inevitably become part of the regime of exposure. The spectacle of their arrival and disembarkation exists only in and for the media. Migrant visibility on Lampedusa hence is entirely under the state's control and the regimes of exposure and concealment mutually reinforce each other. In another layer of their complex work, Coumo and Iorio contrast the political treatment of 'illegals' with a different group of migrants living on the island. Its members, consisting primarily of North Africans who arrived before the creation of the Schengen Area, have established themselves as a cheap work force for the big hotels and restaurants. As cooks, maids or cleaners they keep the tourist industry running while they also exist in the shadows of public invisibility, just out of the tourists' sights. By taking on their perspective, *Sudeuropa* reveals the schizophrenia of a European border regime that spends billions of Euros on fighting migration while important sectors of the European economy depend on a steady supply of cheap, unskilled labour.

BECOMING INVISIBLE

As they are simultaneously subject to regimes of exposure and concealment, many migrants have developed various strategies for evading the state's control. They literally have learned how to make themselves invisible. On 29 October 2010, a strange incident occurred on an Air Canada flight from Hong Kong to Vancouver. After some hours in the air, an elderly Caucasian man went to the restroom and apparently disappeared. After some time, however, a young Asian occupied his seat. Later, the alerted security force at the Canadian airport found a silicon mask, gloves, a cardigan and old-fashioned glasses in an abandoned suitcase, of which the Asian denied being the owner. Upon further questioning,

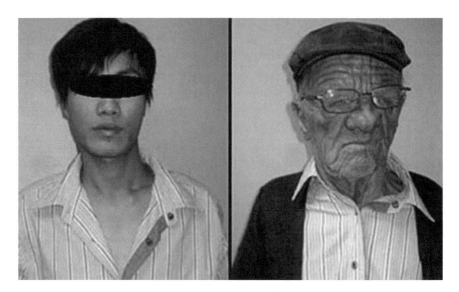

Fig. 5. A Chinese migrant disguising as an elderly Caucasian during an Air Canada flight.

the man claimed asylum. In 2001, Enrique Aguilar Canchola, a 42-year-old Mexican, tried a very unusual way of crossing the US/Mexico border. Inspectors found him sewn into a car seat. He had been covered in a seated position cloaked with leather and stuffing that made him virtually undetectable.

Fig. 6. Enrique Aguilar Canchola, disguised as a car seat.

While these rather spectacular occurrences were widely reported in the media, becoming invisible is an everyday necessity for many 'illegal' migrants. The Moroccan anthropologist Mehdi Aloua, who has conducted research among sub-Saharan transit migrants, describes some of their tactics to avoid police controls as follows: '1. Traveling to Rabat by night with another's identity documents, hoping that the darkness will hide the subterfuge; 2. Renting passports for the day from fellow sub-Saharan students; 3. Dressing hip in order to escape the tarnished image of illegal migrants and thus go undetected' (quoted in Heller 2006: 125).

'Illegal' migrants thus often have to obfuscate their personal identity or adopt a new one. In many cases, however, they are also forced to strip themselves of their legal (national) identity. This is the case because many African countries have signed repatriation agreements with the EU. The revelation of one's national identity hence may result in direct expulsion. In Morocco, this has led to the notion of the 'brûleur' for an individual who pursues the project of an illicit crossing to Europe. This rich term refers not only to a 'burning desire' for a better life but also to the physical act of burning one's passport before the start of the journey. In Moroccan parlance, the 'brûleur' also 'burns' (transgresses) international frontiers (see Pandolfo 2007: 345). These strategies of self-concealment might be beneficial for individual migrants who manage to live a life in invisibility in the country that illegalises them. For 'illegal' migrants as a group, however, this enforces their public invisibility even further (see Borren 2008: 233). In an Arendtian sense, it deprives them even more from any possibility of political participation.

THE DISCURSIVE PRODUCTION OF ILLEGALITY

For anthropologists, this invisibility poses epistemological as well as ethical problems. Besides the difficulties involved in winning the trust of 'illegal' people and in comprehensively studying their lifeworlds, the 'illegal migrant' forms a problematic object of research. In everyday life, most 'illegal' migrants are engaged in social relations with 'legal' migrants as well as citizens and commonly live in close proximity to them. Their illegal status might thus be irrelevant to a lot of their activities and becomes a problem only at certain moments: 'To conduct research on undocumented migrants as such – conceptualized in isolation – is therefore to perpetuate a rather egregious kind of epistemic violence on the social reality of everyday life for those migrants' (De Genova 2002: 422). Hence, anthropologists might unwittingly take part in the naturalisation of illegality as a condition. What is ultimately at stake here is the anthropologist's positionality. De Genova states that studies on 'illegal' migration might easily become part of the regime of exposure and a form of surveillance themselves, taking on the perspective or even working in the service of the state. Therefore, the 'ethnographic documentation and exhibition of such practices can have quite practical consequences and entail certain ethical quandaries and strategic risks at the levels of both research practice and representation' (2002: 422). De Genova emphatically seeks to denaturalise the notion of migrant illegality in order to theorise it as what it is: a political entity, a juridical classification that entails a specific social relation to the nation-state. He thus calls for distinguishing the study of undocumented people from the *study of illegality as a sociopolitical status.* While he deems that too many scholars have been concerned with 'policy-relevance' and thus have taken on the standpoint of the state, the particular socio-historical configurations that have produced migrant illegality (and continue to do so) remain understudied. I therefore take up De Genova's suggestion and expand his analysis of the construction of illegality to the field of the visual. I investigate how media and image-making technologies are actively taking part in the production of this discursive formation. As I have shown, the concurring regimes of exposure and concealment deprive migrants from every right and possibility of self-representation in the space of appearance. Instead, they are *made* visible by the state for the sake of identification and control, or they are exposed as stereotypical clichés in the mass media. In both instances, a public visibility in Arendt's sense is not achieved. On the contrary, both forms of visualisation do not acknowledge them as individuals with an agency (Arendtian 'citizens') but instead produce the powerful label of the 'illegal immigrant'. Hence, in the remainder of this chapter I shall explore how the media actively construct 'illegal bodies' as an object of representation and how technologies of visual surveillance themselves contribute to the production of illegality as a quasi-natural category.

'ILLEGAL' BODIES

Analysing the figure of the 'clandestin' as an object of representation in French television, Mireille Rosello found that 'illegal' migration is never defined, yet always

> *associated* with other concepts or elements, for example clandestinity *and* invisibility, clandestinity *and* papers, or clandestinity *and* the police, and clandestinity *and* race. Images do not try to provide a definition of illegality that one could put into words. Rather, it is assumed that the viewer will be satisfied with a paratactic concatenation of related concepts that dispenses with causal links and articulations. (1998: 139; emphasis in original)

Media representations of the 'illegal immigrant' (a relatively new figure in European discourse that replaced the 'guest worker' of the 1960s and 1970s and the 'second generation immigrant' of the 1980s) are thus based on the construction of a binary logic. Like Durheim's early police photographs of 'gypsies', they entail assumptions about their physical appearance, skin colour, economic status, origin, age or gender. This is but one example for how 'a myriad of practices, usually carried out by people who have no connection to the government (in this case journalists and filmmakers), produce knowledge that constitutes individuals as citizens, illegal aliens, legal residents, asylees, and so forth' (Coutin 1993: 88). Hannah Arendt has commented on the destructive impact engendered by the discursive construction of these kinds of group identities. For her, a person subsumed under a such a generalising label becomes both a 'human being in general – without a profession, without a citizenship, without an opinion, without a deed by which to identify and specify himself – *and* different in general, representing nothing but his own absolutely unique individuality which, deprived of expression within and action upon a common world, loses all significance' (1973: 302). They are, ultimately, destined to 'become some specimen of an animal species, called man' (ibid.).

Hence, filmmakers representing 'illegal' migration regardless of their initial intentions inevitably take part in the construction of what an 'illegal immigrant' might be and look like. Let me demonstrate this dilemma with a discussion of the documentary film *Tarifa Traffic – Death in the Straits of Gibraltar* (2003) by Joakim Demmer. The film is set in Europe's southernmost city, where on clear nights small motorboats jam-packed with African migrants try to cross the dangerous Gibraltar Strait. The film was shot at a time when the Strait was not as systematically controlled as it is today and these crossings still were possible.[9] It has been screened and awarded prizes at numerous documentary and human rights film festivals. Demmer chooses to present this issue from the point of view of the local Spanish inhabitants. A journalist, a border police official, a Red Cross employee and a camping-site owner describe their feelings of mournfulness, anger and helplessness in view of the corpses that are washed up on the beaches of Tarifa. This perspective, however, reduces the constant 'flow' of migrants to a 'humanitarian catastrophe' that seems to occur with the irreversibility of a natural disaster. The reasons behind this high-risk form of migration (the global inequality of wealth and power) and its deadliness (the fortification of the European borders) thus remain obscure. Rather, the film takes on the perspective of the state in that it implies that the surveillance of the maritime frontier is a humanitarian obligation, ultimately in the migrants' own best interest. The actual protagonists, the migrants themselves, enter the film only once and by accident. In the course of an interview Demmer conducts with a Guardia

Civil Officer near the shore, his camera suddenly zooms in on a rubber boat that is just about to arrive on the coastline. It is hopelessly overcrowded with migrants from sub-Saharan Africa. As soon as they reach the first rocks near the coast, they jump into the ice-cold water, swimming against the waves. As soon as the first men put their feet on steady ground the police are already awaiting them. The film then gives us a series of close-ups of drenched, exhausted and shivering bodies. Even though these images have clearly been taken from afar with a tele-photo lens, the sound of their heavy breathing has been made extremely present in the film's sound design. This intervention in post-production fosters the re-duction of these migrants to a state of pure creature-likeness, to a mode of being that Agamben (1998), drawing on Arendt, has called 'bare life'. It is a naked biological existence deprived of political meaning, a non-person in terms of the law. These bodies, unconscious or awkwardly trembling, then receive charitable treatment and are eventually taken into custody by the police. At this point, they are no longer the focus of the filmmaker's attention. Hence, the supposedly critical film only reaffirms existing media images. As Brigitta Kuster writes, the generic migrant body that is made visible at the European border is male, black, passive and at the mercy of his own fatal undertaking. His image thus suggests his 'openness' to political regulation and control (2007: 188).

Although much less prominent, there is also a female image of 'illegal' migra-tion in media discourse, one that is associated with trafficking, domestic work and (forced) prostitution. Anja Salomonowitz's film *It Happened Just Before* (2006) critically engages with these representations. In collaboration with an NGO run by and for migrant women in Austria she has conducted extensive

Fig. 7. The 'arrival scene' in *Tarifa Traffic*.

interviews on the living and working situations of undocumented female migrants. In a Brechtian twist, however, her interviewees do not appear on screen. Instead, their accounts are recited by people who could stand in a (sometimes uncomfortably close) relationship with the events and places of the particular stories: a customs officer, a barkeeper in a bordello, a neighbour, a consul, a taxi driver. Initially, we see and hear these protagonists of the film immersed in their everyday work. At one point, however, the surface of the images cracks open. While still following their daily routines, they suddenly become possessed by the migrants' narratives, at which point sound and image productively begin to work against each other. For example, while she is getting pedicured, the consul narrates the story of an exploited housekeeper in the household of a well-respected diplomat. The barkeeper recounts a woman's unsuccessful attempts to find work outside the sex business while we see him preparing his club for the night. As she refrains from presenting them visually, Salomonowitz does not identify particular bodies as 'illegal'. Rather, she brings into view the structural effects of the regime of concealment. Her film develops an aesthetic form that makes the migrants' public invisibility discernible as such and shows how this eventually leads to their exploitation and abuse. The abusive criminals, however, are not the traffickers, but ordinary citizens from next door.

THE VISUAL ECONOMY OF SURVEILLANCE

The practices of surveillance so far discussed as a constitutive part of the border regime (and hence of the regime of exposure) do not only serve the purpose of control. They also inherit a discursive power that is easily overseen. Images taken by surveillance cameras and other systems of control have become a visual trope that has entered the mass media sphere. CCTV material like the iconic images of the 9/11 terrorists at the airport in New York nowadays feature prominently in newscasts. The particular aesthetics of surveillance cameras, their fixed frame and perspective, evokes authenticity and suggests a neutral and objective point of view, as if reality was recording itself. In 2007, the State of Texas launched the website www.texasborderwatch.com that allowed users to watch real-time streams of videos from a network of surveillance cameras and sensors positioned along the Texas/Mexico border. By signing in to the website, one could become a 'Virtual Texas Deputy' and directly monitor and anonymously report 'irregular' activities. After receiving reports via email, local county sheriffs responded to these reports, conducted investigations and took action. While this border surveillance crowdsourcing programme is currently on hold due to federal budget cuts, the cameras are still in place and various Texas politicians have demanded to continue it. In this virtual border watch setup, every movement on the Mexican side of the border rendered visible by the electronic eye of the surveillance camera is potentially suspicious. It is associated with criminal activity and thus produces the impression of illegality. The technology thus actively takes part in the construction of illegality as a discursive category.

On the night of 28 September 2005, an incident occurred that immediately made migration from Africa a major issue for the European mass media. The discourse that evolved around this incident and its public interpretation, however, was strongly influenced by the specific aesthetic qualities of surveillance cameras. What had happened during this night? Large groups of Africans who were waiting in the forests near Ceuta for a chance to enter European territory had been put under extreme pressure by the Moroccan police. Thus, they collectively decided to take action. Unlike their normal procedure to try to enter the Spanish exclave only alone or in small groups, they planned to risk a joint attempt. Hundreds of them approached the two barbed-wire, three-metre-high border fences equipped only with self-made ladders. The Spanish police, surprised by such a massive attempt of border crossing, used rubber bullets against the migrants. At the end of the night, most of them were wounded, some of them fatally. A few days later, this 'assault' on the border was also repeated at the Melilla border fence. In the days after the initial attempt, the news agency Reuters published video footage provided by the Spanish authorities. It features images taken by the surveillance cameras in which one sees an anonymous mass

Fig. 8. CCTV footage from the Ceuta border fence on the night of the incident.

of bodies crawling over the fence. Many European media that broadcast this disturbing footage evoked an 'attack on the border', a 'massive storm on Fortress Europe'. Yet the nine-second Reuters sequence is far from providing an unbiased and authentic account of what had happened. What the surveillance cameras filmed throughout the whole night was condensed into a few seconds through time lapse. Time lapse is a cinematic tool used to render visible what the human eye normally cannot perceive. In this case, the short sequence suggests an exposure of all 'illegal' incidents that occurred in the course of the night. Yet what the time lapse effect thereby created was the impression of an uninterrupted mass movement. In fast motion the Africans' individual (and very dangerous) efforts to overcome the barbed-wire fence appeared an uncontrollable invasion of a faceless and amorphous mass. As their movements appear jerky due to the low frame rate of the security cameras, their desperate attempts to cross the border resemble the aggressive attack of a swarm of insects, suggesting an immigration that has gone out of control (see Reichert 2011). The sequence thus constructed the persisting image of a dangerous 'flood' of migrants overrunning Europe, an image often invoked in the political discourse about migration.

The artist Florian Schneider has made this footage the basis for his video installation *Ceuta* (2006) that constitutes an intervention in this visual discourse. He exposes the technological manipulation of the material by visual means and thus articulates a critique on the intrinsic level of the image itself. Schneider reversed the editing process in which the footage was speeded up in order to restore the original time span of events. As he did not have access to the original CCTV material, he had to duplicate all the frames from the accelerated sequence that circulated in the media in order to be able to extend the sequence in time. This two-fold manipulation of the image produces an irritating effect. The migrants' movements become static as if frozen in time. All action comes to a prolonged standstill that is only released with the next frame. Because of its low frame rate, the surveillance camera did not record motion continually. What resulted in staccato movements in the fast-forwarded sequence now produces abrupt jump cuts between the single frames in Schneider's slowed-down version. By endlessly extending these images in time, Schneider invites us into a different mode of perception. He wants to draw attention to the 'hors-champ', the off-screen space that lies outside the static frame of the surveillance camera. He allows his audience to reflect on where these border crossers were coming from and what might have happened to them. What might lie, so to speak, on the left or the right side of the frame. Likewise, gaps of invisibility also open in the discontinuous jumps between the single frames, in the dynamic space between two successive images that Dziga Vertov called the 'interval'. For Florian Schneider, these gaps are inaccessible to the regime of exposure (2011: 144). They resemble uncontrolled zones, potential hideouts that may serve as an allegory for the autonomy of migration, anticipating a freedom of movement that is not yet in place.

The aesthetics of surveillance has also found its way into many documentary films on migration, especially into those of the 'passage' genre (see Kuster 2007: 191). In this type of film, a film crew accompanies an individual or a group of migrants on their long journey in a kind of mimetic appropriation of migratory movement, a 'mimicry of mobility' (Holert 2007). Often on the borderline between drama and documentary, these films usually set out to reveal the hardship and dangers migrants face on their way to Europe. In what often are their most crucial scenes, *In this World* (2002), *La Citadelle Europe – Lost in Transit* (2004), *Border* (2004), *14 Kilometers* (2007) and many other films of this genre deliberately make use of material shot with night-vision cameras. In *Passagères Clandestines – Mother's Crossing* (2004), for example, director Lodet Desmet follows Sima, an Iranian mother and her two daughters who are on the run from their violent husband and father. Because it was too dangerous to escort them across the land border between Turkey and Greece, the filmmaker gave their smuggler (the Iraqi-born 'Djouma, the Arab' who eventually became the film's second protagonist) a small infra-red camera to film the crossing himself. Edited into the final film, the graininess and shakiness of the footage produces the impression of authenticity, and suggests an unmediated access to the reality of this event. Mireille Rosello has called this strategy the 'clandestine filming of clandestinity' (1998: 145). The poor quality of the images emphasises the dangerous context of the filming and thus confirms that what is unmistakably represented here is illegality. In a similar vein, both *In this World* and *Border* explore the surreptitious areas of migrant existence. They follow their protagonists into their nightly hide-outs in the bushes near the Channel Tunnel crossing to the UK near Calais or even inside a container on a cargo ship. To make these clandestine scenes visible, the camera has to operate at its technical limits. In both instances, the shutter of the video camera is wide open to compensate for the lack of light. The prolonged exposure time results in a very particular aesthetics: a large trembling grain, blurred and slowed down motions and substantial image-noise, all technical reactions of the camera normally unwanted by filmmakers. These technological manipulations, however, allow for a penetration into the darkness. They virtually carve the migrants' bodies out of the blackness on screen. These representational strategies cannot escape being seen as dangerously close to the state's technological regime of exposure and its visual discourse of criminalisation, surveillance and control. Filmmakers thus run the risk of merely reaffirming the perspective of the police and the ruling law and thereby participating in the despotism of visual identification (see Kuster 2007: 188). The interest these films take in uncovering what

Fig. 9: A still from the night-vision footage in *Passagères Clandestines*.

takes place in secrecy might thrill their audiences as they advance into social realms that formerly were inaccessible to the public eye. However, it is bound to a destructive form of visibility that seeks to shed light on what is forced to hide in darkness.

THE FORENSIC TURN

Just very recently, however, some artists, scholars and independent organisations have begun to use this visual economy of surveillance literally against the grain and deploy the forensic methods by which the state polices and governs its citizens and non-citizens to investigate issues ranging from contemporary political struggle to violent conflict and human rights cases. The research project 'Forensic Architecture' founded at Goldsmiths College, University of London has assembled a group of architects, artists, filmmakers, activists and theorists who undertake research that gathers, interprets and presents data in the form of new imaging processes, satellite images, geospatial data, 3D-scans, physical and digital models and video footage. Through this, they provide evidence for international prosecution teams, NGOs, activist groups or other civil society organisations. Their individual projects (that were, for example, presented in the international exhibition project 'Forensis: The Architecture of Public Truth' at Berlin's Haus der Kulturen der Welt in 2014) reverse the direction of the forensic gaze by holding the state accountable for human rights violations like covert drone strikes, military or police violence or extrajudicial killings. The term 'forensics' derives from the latin word *forensis*, meaning 'of or before the forum', a multidimensional space of politics, law and economy in Roman times. Project initiator Eyal Weizman therefore wants to free the practice of forensics from the reduction of its meaning to the use of medicine and science before a court of law (see 2014: 9). He proposes to reclaim it as a political practice producing 'public truths' that may open up new spaces for discourse and dispute and articulate new claims for justice. The group's investigations frequently take place in areas like war zones, 'failed states' or places under occupation where no effective legal or juridical structures exist and powerful states can violently intervene and subsequently deny to have done so. These states' regimes of concealment are challenged, however, by new visibilities that have emerged with the widespread accessibility of digital media like smartphones, which allow both victims and activists to produce and disseminate visual data that bear witness to human rights violations.

One such forensic investigation in a space where sovereign jurisdiction is ambiguous is the 'left-to-die-boat' case, documented by the 'Forensic Oceanography' project,[10] in which sixty-three migrants lost their lives while drifting for two weeks in the tightly monitored Mediterranean Sea. The migrants' overcrowded rubber boat left the Libyan coast on the early hours of 27 March 2011 heading for Lampedusa. Having only covered half of the distance and running out fuel at the end of this day, the passengers used a satellite phone to call an Eritrean priest in the Vatican whose number circulated widely across the East African diaspora. The priest immediately contacted the Italian coast guards who determined the migrants' location through the provider of the satellite phone. The vessel however was still outside of the Italian and the Maltese search and rescue areas in which these states are responsible for coordinating rescue. While the Italians did not take action, they informed their Maltese counterparts, sent a distress signal to all ships in the Sicily channel and contacted the NATO headquarters in Naples. As this was the time of NATO's military intervention in response to the Libyan uprising against the Gaddafi regime, the central Mediterranean was being surveilled with unprecedented scrutiny and was full of military vessels. The regime of exposure at work in the area comprised optical and Synthetic Aperture Radar (SAR) satellites, thermal cameras, sea-, air- and land-borne radars and vessel-tracking technologies that turn the surface of the sea into an area of heightened visibility. Yet when the migrants' rubber boat finally ran out of fuel and began to drift aimlessly nobody intervened to help them. They were left to die while being actively observed through a myriad of surveilling eyes. When, after fourteen days, the boat was washed back against the Libyan shores, out of the seventy-two passengers only nine had survived. Taking the location of the satellite phone call as a starting point, the 'Forensic Oceanography' team set out to reconstruct the chain of events. The

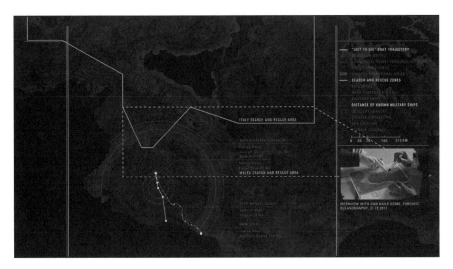

Fig. 10: The screen as interface in *Liquid Traces – The Left-to-Die-Boat Case*.

aesthetic outcome of their research is the video *Liquid Traces – The Left-to-Die-Boat Case* (2014) that presents and analyses the visual material the group has gathered. In the video, we are offered an aerial view of the Mediterranean on to which the collected data is mapped and simultaneously interpreted by a voice-over. In collaboration with oceanographer Richard Limeburner, the group used data on winds and water movements to model a probable drift path that shows that the boat briefly entered the Maltese search and rescue area before slowly drifting through the NATO maritime surveillance zone. With the help of SAR satellite data, they further identified the location of military vessels in proximity of the boat that all did not intervene despite the clear obligation to do so under international maritime law. In *Liquid Traces*, the video screen thus serves as an interface onto which all these different data are projected and put in relation to each other. The routes of the rubber boats and military vessels are modeled in relation to a timeline of events and matched with satellite imagery, while video clips of witness reports, textual information, and other pieces of evidence are embedded in a kind of spatial montage.[11]

This provides the viewer with an omniscient perspective that in this case, however, is strategically used against a regime of concealment. The project members themselves call it a 'disobedient gaze' that turns the knowledge generated though surveillance technology into evidence for juridical claims pertaining the failure to provide assistance to those in distress at sea. Their research has led to a series of legal cases filed by a coalition of NGOs in various European countries. These legal petitions are still ongoing as it is extremely difficult to determine the legal responsibility of the individual NATO member states. Yet what *Liquid*

Traces clearly reveals is how different governmental actors operating in the Central Mediterranean Sea have used the complex overlapping as well as conflicting maritime jurisdictions between the states that border the Mediterranean to evade their responsibility for rescuing migrant boats in distress.

Even though the video also features an interview with one of the survivors, the 'Forensic Oceanography' team did not place emphasis on the subjective dimension of his experience. Instead they used photographs and other memory aids to assist him in recollecting as precisely as possible elements that could help in the reconstruction of the events or lead to further evidence. Yet to overcome the 'natural visibility' described throughout this chapter that is forcefully imposed on 'illegal' migrants and reduces them to their 'bare' biological existence, I believe that we also need to find forms of visualisation that make them appear as distinct individuals instead of ideological categories. To further explore the emancipatory power of visibility, I dedicate the following chapters to cinematic modes of representation that seek to render migrants publicly visible in an Arendtian sense: as individuals with an agenda that subvert the power of the border regime and sound out all their possibilities for political action. I discuss films that carefully avoid taking part in the state's regime of exposure, that refuse to look at migrants from the standpoint of the state. Rather, they take on the perspective of the migrants themselves and try to come as close as possible to their personalities, their practices, their goals and their dreams. Hence, they create spaces of appearance where people's individual stories can be articulated outside of the imposed categories of legality or illegality. In this, they also offer the spectator a different perspective from which to view. A position that does not reproduce the normalising gaze of surveillance and control, but that attends to the lived reality of migration and that is situated in close sensual proximity to the migrant experience.

CHAPTER TWO

Migrant Experience

I n the previous chapter, I suggested that the domain of experience is of great importance to the study of migration, as it allows us to understand global processes from the perspective of the subjects involved in them. Taking on this perspective is crucial if one wants to transcend the hierarchical discourses of those who govern migratory movements and obscure the individuality of migrants, their motifs, their stories and their personalities, by making them invisible. As Maurice Merleau-Ponty proposed, the 'process of joining objective analysis to lived experience is perhaps the most proper task of anthropology, the one which distinguishes it from other social science' (1964: 119). In what follows, I will therefore discuss conceptions of experience offered by phenomenological or existential approaches within anthropology and relate these to the experiential qualities of the cinematic medium itself. As film so obviously both reflects and creates experience, I will argue that the medium has a special expressive capacity to communicate about this subject of anthropological enquiry. The mimetic qualities of film can draw us into sensory participation with the other's lifeworld to an extent that the 'disembodied representation' (Stoller 1997: xiii) of scientific writing cannot. Film, as Vivian Sobchack (1992) notes, expresses experience as experience. It takes experience as its content and as its mode of reception. To argue that this can be a vital way of communicating anthropological knowledge, as I do throughout this book, thus requires a thorough discussion of the involvement of the audience. Unfortunately, most of the recent calls for experiments in representation or an anthropological appropriation of visual arts practice treat experimentation as a value in itself. Seldom do these accounts go further than describing their authors' experimental intentions. The question of what audiences make of these experimental forms, and if and how they may actually produce new insights, is routinely ignored. Hence,

I draw on theories of perception developed in anthropology and film studies to lay the ground for an understanding of film spectatorship that seeks to describe the viewer's active engagement with cinematic evocations of experience. In a phenomenological tradition, I will consider the nature of film viewing as *embodied*. As David MacDougall notes, film sets many bodies in relation to each other: the bodies that were present in front of the camera, the body of the film-maker, the body of the spectator and the body of the film itself (2006: 15). In what follows, this complex web of relations shall be unravelled. In the following chapters, I will, then, further build upon this theory of cinematic perception, which is grounded in the concept of experience. There, I describe how film can facilitate a deeper understanding of the new spatial and temporal formations, the heterotopies and heterochronies that have been brought about by migration as a global process.

ANTHROPOLOGICAL APPROACHES TO EXPERIENCE

I want to begin my discussion with some reflections on the notion of experience in anthropological discourse. Famously dismissed by Claude Lévi-Strauss, who postulated that one would have to reject it in order 'to reach reality' (1973: 58), it still remained a key concept in much anthropological writing before becoming a central construct for the many (though divergent) perspectives that have emerged in the last three decades in reaction to the crisis of representation (see Desjarlais and Throop 2011: 95). Despite its centrality and importance, it has, as Jason Throop (2003) has argued, remained largely elusive and under-theorised. Many authors seem to mean quite different things by the notion or only employ it as a commonsensical, taken-for-granted expression for life as lived through. It was Victor Turner who, in his later writings, engaged in a detailed discussion of the concept. Elaborating on Wilhelm Dilthey's distinction between *Erfahrung* and *Erlebnis*, he suggested a differentiation between 'mere' experience and 'an' experience. While 'mere' experience implies the passive endurance and acceptance of events, 'an' experience 'stands out from the evenness of passing hours and years and forms what Dilthey called a "structure of experience". In other words, it does not have an *arbitrary* beginning and ending, cut out of the stream of chronological temporality, but has what [John] Dewey called an "initiation and a consummation"' (1986: 35). This distinction between two forms of experience also provides an answer to the haunting question of how one can actually research and represent something that seems to be so interior and individual. Edward Brunner, together with Turner co-editor of *The Anthropology of Experience* (1986), notes that 'the former ["mere" experience] is received by consciousness, it is individual experience, the temporal flow; the latter ["an" experience] is the intersubjective articulation of experience, which has a beginning and an ending and thus becomes transformed into an expression' (1986: 6). For Dilthey, experience therefore becomes intersubjectively accessible through the interpretation of its forms of expression: customs, performances, rituals or myths that can be analysed through the methodology of hermeneutics. This thought is, of course, also fundamental to Clifford Geertz's practice of symbolic anthropology. For Geertz, this assorted plurality of expressions of experience is nothing other than 'culture', to be 'read as text'. Geertz, however, strongly dismisses the idea of 'mere' experience as this for him implies 'a mere chaos of pointless acts and exploding emotions' (1973: 46). He deems that anthropologists are mistaken to explore the subjective and inner dimension of experience as it is always mediated and interpreted. For Geertz, experience is not found '"between the ears" or in the "head"' (Throop 2003: 226) but rather in the external, public and material world of cultural symbols. For him, it is only in the exchange of symbols where experiences are loaded with meaning, while the significance of symbolic forms lies precisely in their ability to make sense of experiences. This perspective is echoed in Kirsten Hastrup's well-known critique of ethnographic film (1992: 10). Film's experiential dimension (so obvious that she cannot deny it) she attributes to the 'thin description of the happening' (as chaotic, indeterminate and hence meaningless), while for her, only text allows for a 'thick description of the event' (as loaded with intersubjective significance). Hence, whereas Turner originally was interested in the subject of experience in an attempt to focus on the individual social actor instead of the abstract social system, Geertz and Hastrup have reintroduced a rather totalising perspective through the back door.

We are thus left with utterly contradictory views on the problem of experience. While some anthropologists associate it with the subjective, the interior and the private, others have emphasised its supra-personal and public aspects. In his theoretical exploration of the subject, Jason Throop has suggested that both perspectives are rather limiting. He proposes an all-encompassing understanding of experience that is based on a phenomenological perspective:

> The antimonies, contradictions and conflicts embedded in these various models of experience must, in other words, point to something fundamental about the structure of experience itself. A structure that encompasses the indeterminate, the fluid, the incoherent, the internal, the disjunctive, the fragmentary, the coherent, the intersubjective, the determinate, the rigid, the external, the cohesive, the conjunctive *and* the unitary. (2003: 227)

Throop then draws upon William James', Edmund Husserl's, and Alfred Schütz's thoughts on the temporal structure of consciousness as all these authors recognise the crucial role time plays in the organisation of experience. They describe how our awareness of the present moment is shaped by the persistence of the past and the orientation towards the future. In the stream of consciousness every present moment is structured by a halo of anticipatory and residual movements, by what Husserl has called protention and retention. For Husserl, furthermore, there are more enduring and intentional mental structures that he terms recollections (or secondary remembrances) and expectations (or hopes). Experience is thus shaped in equal terms by the 'immediacy of temporal flux' and the 'mediacy of reflective assessment' (Throop 2003: 233). Throop seeks to develop a complementary model of experience that adheres both to its disjunctive and its conjunctive elements, its pre-reflective and its reflective forms. His mediation between seemingly divergent perspectives on experience thus casts light on how differently the world appears to us when we are actively engaged with it, compared to when we make it the subject of our reflection. Furthermore, it shows how different temporal orientations can lead to broad varieties of experience. As I will suggest in chapter four, a conflicting experience of time forms an important dimension of the lived reality of migration. My protagonists in *Tell Me When...*, for example, had little choice but to endure their immediate immersion in the present while being stuck in Melilla's detention center. They were deliberately left without knowledge about their future and whether they would be brought to Spain and thus could disappear in the country's huge black labour market, or whether they would be sent back to their countries of origin. They didn't even know how long they would have to stay in this liminal situation at the fringes of Europe. Not being allowed to work in the city, they had nothing to do but to wait. Living in a present that is so slowed down it almost stands still, it is hard to keep up the anticipation for the future that once made one start out on this journey. Many migrants thus take refuge in their memories, like Shahbaz in my film, who maintains his relationship to his home in Pakistan through the images, videos and music saved on his mobile phone. Throop encourages us to pay careful attention during fieldwork to our research participants' temporal orientation 'when engaged in, recollecting, or anticipating social action' (2003: 235). Film, as I shall argue later, has a great potential to embody such complex experiences of time. However, before I explore film's relationship to experience in greater detail, I want to outline the foundations, implications and impact of phenomenological approaches such as Throop's within anthropology.

PHENOMENOLOGICAL TRADITIONS WITHIN ANTHROPOLOGY

The epistemological issues that anthropologists have wrestled with in the decades after the crisis of representation included questioning anthropology's status as a science, the anthropologists' position in representing the other, the problematisation of their status as neutral observers, and the ways in which anthropological knowledge should be communicated. Phenomenology as a philosophical discipline has posed similar questions about the authority of science, its claims and its relation to reality. For anthropologists, however, in these issues there is more at stake than mere abstract epistemological reasoning. Their daily business is to translate the lived reality of other peoples into the language, concepts and theories of their own world, the scientific world of Western academia. Despite Bronislaw Malinowski's famous claim to 'grasp the native's point of view', what anthropologists routinely have done is to reduce the dimensions of their research participants' lifeworlds as manifested in beliefs, rituals or customs to factors alien to it, to abstract systems and classifications derived from their own reality. Anthropological accounts often purport to understand the people studied better than they do themselves, claiming to reveal truths that are unconscious to them. These truths, then, are often located in generative forces outside of the immediate, lived reality. Phenomenological anthropologists strongly argue against such a cultural privileging of Western thought over other intellectual traditions. For them, the ethnographic study of other systems of knowledge offers the basis for a critique of Western metaphysics (see Jackson 1996: 35f.). Hence, phenomenology sets out to do justice to the other's perspective, to aspects of human life normally overlooked. It tackles the question of how we can 'understand someone else without sacrificing him to our logic or it to him' (Merleau-Ponty 1964: 115). Michael Jackson (1996) has warned that it is easy to mistake theoretical concepts for the foundations of reality, while they are themselves only abstractions. Kim Knibbe and Peter Versteeg see anthropological concepts as often too metaphorical. Paradigms such as 'culture as text', 'body as text' or 'religion as system of meaning' for them 'privilege and select certain aspects of cultural reality over others and tend to decontextualize them to prove a theoretical point' (2008: 50). Central to the phenomenological approach is hence a refusal to transcend lived experience through theory. Rather, it encourages anthropologists to start out their research without preconceived concepts, to consider the subjectivity of human agents as an objective reality. Phenomenologists try to refrain from making statements of truth in a form of practical relativism. Husserl has called this temporary bracketing of all evaluations *epoché*. In anthropology, this would mean not to judge one's research participant's view on reality as a psychological construct or false consciousness as these perspectives tend to describe culture as an oppressive structure imprisoning the individual.[12] In phenomenological terms the cultural reality, the lifeworld, is much less rigidly conceived of, as experience can always flow into new meanings. Meaning itself is 'lived' intersubjectively. It is something that 'appears to our senses, something that anybody can immediately understand because of our shared human nature, but also learn through becoming an insider' (Knibbe and Versteeg 2008: 52). I believe that these ideas closely correspond to my assessment of film's potential for anthropology, because film can uniquely enable us to see 'things as they are' (Jackson 1996). Jackson mocks anthropologists for always looking in the wrong places, 'beyond' or 'behind' the things to find their meaning, overseeing that it is *revealed* to us, right in front of our eyes' (Knibbe and Versteeg 2008: 51). Phenomenologists hence are engaged in a search for a different kind of knowledge. This knowledge can best be described in the same words David MacDougall (2006: 6) has used to determine the knowledge offered by film: it is not a knowledge of meaning, but a knowledge of being.

Within the study of migration, such a phenomenological approach might help to overcome prevailing reductionism to socio-economic dimensions, to 'push and pull' factors and statistical evidence, but also to 'grand theories' of globalisation. It can also comprise a powerful critique of stereotyping and distorting mass media representations. While a Foucauldian notion of political power has become a major paradigm in anthropology and many other social sciences, Jackson argues for the centrality of what he calls existential power. He criticises a focus on the impersonal forces of history, politics or upbringing as excluding the very site where these forces are played out. By dismissing the subject, these theories would be oblivious to

> where life is lived, meanings are made, will is exercised, reflection takes place, consciousness finds expression, determinations take effect, and habits are formed and broken. Any theory of culture, *habitus* or lifeworld must include some account of those moments in social life when the customary, given, habitual, and normal is disrupted, flouted, suspended and negated. At such moments, crisis transforms the world from an apparently fixed and finished set of rules into a repertoire of possibilities. To borrow Marx's vivid image, the frozen circumstances are forced to dance by us singing to them their own melody. (1996: 22)

For Jackson, a critique of the political conditions that oppress people has to begin with an analysis of how humans actually create their lives in the circumstances given. Much like Hannah Arendt (and often drawing upon her), Jackson's analysis commences from very concrete political-historical experiences and aims at understanding their meaning for the individual. His existential anthropology seeks to describe human 'struggle for being'. It raises 'questions of coping with life or finding meaning in the face of suffering' (1996: 22). Jackson himself has continuously worked with forced migrants and refugees, e.g. among the

Fig. 11: Tactile images evoking the materiality of the environment in *Mirages*: heat, dust, lens flares, and dirt.

Kuranko in post-war Sierra Leone (Jackson 2005, 2006, 2011). Existential anthropology thus seems well suited to describe the ephemeral lifeworlds in which many migrants find themselves, to render visible life on existential borders.

Olivier Dury's film *Mirages* (2008) gives us a particular example of what a phenomenological description of trans-Sahara migration to Europe might look like. In a form of 'phenomenological reduction', the film tells us nothing about the socio-political background of African migration to Europe. It only shows us a small part of the long and perilous overland journey that migrants from sub-Saharan Africa have to endure to reach their goal. The film begins at the outskirts of Agadez in Niger, from where migrants cross the Sahara by paying for a place on an overloaded truck that Tuareg drivers navigate through the vastness of the desert on the eastern route to Libya. It is this part of the journey which turns citizens of African states into undocumented migrants without a legal personhood. Already with the first establishing shots of Agadez we are in constant movement, as the camera is placed on the back of a truck that leaves the city. Though describing an episode of approximately only a week within a much longer journey, the film conveys much of its existential dangers by radically focusing on the passengers' sense perceptions. It never gives the spectator any spatial orientation. Against the blinding sun, one can seldom make out concrete forms in the brown-beige landscape. The horizon disappears behind mirages that mock all attempts to make sense of the distances. The camera is a participant among the passengers on the hopelessly overcrowded loading area of the vehicle. It shows us feet that find no space to rest, legs that disappear in a mass of bodies. It captures the shaking of the truck and the blowing wind in images that attain a tactile quality. The dispersed sand that shrouds the passengers and makes it difficult to breath even leaves its material traces on the camera lens.

Sometimes exhausted bodies just fall off from the car. Despite these existential threats, the passengers try to maintain their dignity. When the drivers make an occasional break, one sees them laughing, chatting or turning cartwheels in the sand. *Mirages* is a 'thick depiction' (Taylor 1996: 86) of the experience of this journey. It is full of images of a rich sensorial quality. Yet whose experience, whose sensory perceptions is it that the film expresses? To answer this question, let us turn to phenomenological conceptions of the film viewing experience.

THE PHENOMENOLOGY OF FILM EXPERIENCE

Phenomenological perspectives see film as depending on experience twice over: 'As form and content, discourse and representation, subject and object – in short, as signifier and signified' (Taylor 1996: 80). All acts of moving, hearing and seeing that constitute a film are 'at once presented and represented as the originary structures of embodied existence and the mediating structures of discourse' (ibid.). Vivian Sobchack, whose groundbreaking volume, *The Address of the Eye* (1992), marks a renewed interest in phenomenology within film studies, developed her approach in distinction to the prevailing theoretical paradigms of the 1970s and 1980s, when film theory was dominated by neo-Marxism and Lacanian psychoanalysis. These branches both depend on the language paradigm of structuralism. Like the structuralist approaches within anthropology, they postulate the inaccessibility of direct experience, focusing instead, with much-proclaimed scientific rigour, on the mediating structure of language. In both anthropology and film studies, phenomenology thus emerged as a reformist project in reaction to the interpretative excesses of (post-)structuralism. Sobchack was particularly dissatisfied with cinema's pathologisation in psychoanalyst and feminist 'gaze theory', that tried to unveil the medium's participation in the production of oppressive ideology, false consciousness and capitalist alienation. For her, seeing film as only abstractly transmitting signs falls short of describing the actual experience one has at the cinema, as film always must express life with life itself (see Mitry 1965: 453) and it offers an utterly embodied experience. Furthermore, structuralism ultimately remains silent about the origin of the cinematic signification it is so obsessed with:

> We can speak of codes and textual systems which are the results of signifying processes, yet we seem unable to discuss that mode of experience we

call signification. More precisely, structuralism and academic film theory in general have been disinclined to deal with the 'other-side' of signification, those realms of pre-formulation where sensory data congeals into 'something that matters' and those realms of post-formulation where that 'something' is experienced as mattering. Structuralism, even in its post-structural reach toward psychoanalysis and intertextuality, concerns itself only with that something and not with the process of its congealing nor with the event of its mattering. (Andrew 1978: 45–6)

For phenomenologists like Sobchack, cinematic signification and significance are based in the reversibility of perception and expression in the film viewing experience. Her concept of experience is thus in accordance with Dilthey's (and later Turner's) idea of the two-fold, private and public structure of experience, seeing cinema as the mediator in-between: 'The cinema thus transposes what would otherwise be the invisible, individual, and intrasubjective privacy of direct experience as it is embodied into the visible, public, and intersubjective sociality of a language of direct embodied experience – a language that not only refers to direct experience but also uses direct experience as its mode of reference' (Sobchack 1992: 11). Perception and expression thus form a dialectical, chiasmic relationship that is inherent within human existence. This is one of the central ideas of Merleau-Ponty's *Phenomenology of Perception* (1962). Applying his existential phenomenology to the cinema, Sobchack refrains from conceiving film as a static viewed object, perceived by a disembodied viewing subject. For her, film is the expressed perception of an 'other'. As we watch the expressive projection of this 'other's' experience, we express our own perceptive experience (1992: 9). Perception is, so to speak, literally turned inside out and towards us as expression. Hence, film is much more than an object of consciousness. It is a *viewing subject* itself, and film perception therefore involves the dialogical engagement of two viewing subjects (who also exist in the world as visible objects). In short, what we have in the cinema is an intersubjective experience. Conferring upon film the status of a subject may seem awkward at first, and Sobchack makes clear that it is not human subjectivity, nor just the subjectivity of the filmmaker she is talking about. Yet film transcends its existence as a mere technological object in its act of recording vision.

[It] manifests a competence of perceptive and expressive performance *equivalent* in structure and function to that same competence performed by filmmaker and spectator. The film actualizes and realizes its ability to localize, unify (or 'center') the 'invisible' intrasubjective exchange or commutation between the perception of the camera and the expression of the projector. As well, it makes this exchange visible and intersubjectively available to others in the expression of its perception. (1992: 22)

For Sobchack, the exchange of perception and expression makes us aware of our own embodiment as the precondition of all sensory and aesthetic experience. Cinema returns us to our senses. Our body responds with 'somatic intelligence' to the film before any cognitive objectification takes place. Sobchack eloquently unfolds these 'carnal thoughts' in the description of her viewing experience of Jane Campion's *The Piano* (1993). The very first shot of the film is a blurry, unidentifiable image of shafts of reddish-pink. In the following reverse-shot, this image is objectified as Ada's, the film's protagonist's, point of view, as we see her holding her fingers in front of her eyes. Sobchack describes how she, before she even knew that there was an Ada, immediately 'grasped' this first image: 'my fingers knew what I was looking at' (2004: 63). This 'pre-reflective but reflexive comprehension' (ibid.), she argues, is hardly an exceptional viewing experience. We see, comprehend and feel films with the entirety of our bodily being, with the full history and knowledge of our senses. Hence, it is no coincidence that Sobchack opens her argumentation with the description of a shot in which there is not much to actually see. She stresses the synaesthetic dimension of the cinematic experience, as the dominant senses of vision and hearing speak to the other senses: 'Our embodied experience of the movies, then, is an experience of seeing, hearing, touching, moving, tasting, smelling in which our sense of the literal and the figural may sometimes oscillate, may sometimes be perceived in uncanny discontinuity, but most usually configure to make sense together – albeit in a quite specific way' (2004: 76).

Now what does all this mean for anthropological representation? Can this 'other' whose experience is expressed in a film be our ethnographic other? Does film offer us the immediate access to other peoples' sensory experiences that phenomenological anthropology seems to long for? Does it perhaps offer a bodily, more direct access than the referential representation that is achieved by writing? In the remainder of this chapter, I want to explore how this phenomenological theory of cinematic signification relates to current anthropological interests.

PHENOMENOLOGICAL KNOTS: EMBODIMENT AND INTERSUBJECTIVITY

Phenomenological film theory stresses the centrality of the body in the film viewing experience. It understands the body not only as a mere object of representation, but as a source of meaning itself. In its 'post-crisis' reorientation, anthropology has likewise discovered the body as the subject of culture, as its existential ground. Thomas Csordas (1990, 1994) has proposed embodiment as a new theoretical paradigm for the discipline. He witnesses a 'move towards the body', as it has become a key issue of interest for interdisciplinary cultural studies. In much political theory and philosophy, the contemporary body is central to the discussion of the recent proliferation of political violence of all sorts: from ethnic conflicts to state-approved torture. Yet Csordas denies many of these studies 'much sense of bodiliness' (1994: 4), as they treat the body only as object, theme or symbol. For him, Foucauldian examinations of the body under power and domination tend to lose the body as subject, deprive it of intentionality and intersubjectivity, identity and agency. Csordas argues that one cannot study the body and take embodiment for granted. Thus, he suggests a phenomenological recognition of the pre-objective character of corporeal being-in-the-world.

Let me discuss this theoretical re-examination of the body with reference to another film that makes the 'illegal' migrant's body its central focus: *Qu'ils Reposent en Révolte* (2010) by Sylvain George. The film is shot in Calais, a coastal town in northern France. Overlooking the Dover Strait, the narrowest point in the English Channel, Calais is only twenty miles away from the UK. In the vicinity of the city, the Channel Tunnel connects the European continent with Great Britain. For many years now, Calais has attracted migrants from Afghanistan, Iraq, Pakistan or Anglophone African countries who desperately try to enter the UK while avoiding the strict immigration controls. Many of these migrants either have family in the UK or simply hope for a future in a country whose language they can speak fluently. The French authorities have tried to fight this movement with increasing violence to further discourage migrants. A Red Cross camp in nearby Sangatte was closed in 2002, and a camping area among the dunes near the port which was known as 'The Jungle' was destroyed in September 2009. The migrants are thus left on the streets of Calais, where they frequently become the victims of raids and harassment by the French police. The two-and-a-half-hour-long film renders these living conditions visible in the form of short vignettes. It abstains from all unifying elements: each scene is a new encounter, each scene has its own protagonists. There is no continuous dramatic structure, no narration, no plot development. We see migrants fleeing from police, desperately trying to hide under trucks that are heading for the Channel Tunnel, sleeping rough under bridges or in parks, washing themselves in the river. Like Olivier Dury's *Mirages,* the film is driven by an urge to bear witness to these circumstances and encounters, and to provide testimony of a reality largely excluded from mass media representation. In both films, close-ups of faces figure prominently and the people filmed return the gaze. Sylvain George seems to want to bridge the gap between him and his protagonists by coming ever more closer with his camera. Likewise, in the last scene of *Mirages,*

Fig. 12: The last markers of the passengers' existence in *Mirages*.

we finally get to see the passengers in the trucks in single or group portraits. Some smile, some look seriously into the camera. They look exhausted, their faces covered with dust. Then, we see the trucks leaving as the filmmaker stays behind. Dury's voice off-screen tells us that they are about 190 miles away from the Algerian border, and that he will probably never see them again. The last images show Dury's address book containing names, phone numbers, email addresses, intercut with the faces of their owners. They are the last markers of their existence before they disappear into an uncertain future.

In films, David MacDougall writes, 'the close-up creates a proximity to the faces and bodies of others that we experience much less commonly in daily life' (2006: 21), as social conventions normally restrict such an intimate approach.

He describes the exaggerated proximity of the close-up as a 'quasi tactility absent in ordinary human relations' (2006: 22) and as one of the means by which filmmakers create corporeal responses in their audience. Yet it is not only the bodies in front of the camera that affect the body of the spectator, it is also the body of the filmmaker that is imprinted in the images as a residue. Sylvain George's and Olivier Dury's films are prime examples for this as both filmmakers hold the camera themselves and consciously use it as a device to establish contact with the people they film. In both films, the physical act of filming, the movement of the filmmaker, is deeply inscribed in the images; for example, when George is running with his protagonists as they are followed by police, or when he is hiding in the bushes, filming their attempts to secretly enter the Calais port area. The filmmaker's body thus has to be seen as an experiencing body itself, further complicating the question of whose experience is expressed by the film.

One of the scenes that is most likely to produce such a 'touching' response as MacDougall describes is in *Qu'ils Reposent en Révolte*, in which we see a group of migrants sitting around a fire. Soon, they pick up an iron screw from the flames with a wire and begin to pass it around. Each of the men then puts the hot screw against all his fingers, burning the surface of the skin. With this self-mutilation, they want to erase their fingerprints so that they can no longer be identified by the police. Many critics have interpreted this haunting scene in

Fig. 13: Sylvain George filming while running with one of his protagonists from the police.

Foucauldian terms as hegemonic power literally inscribing itself in the bodies of these 'nouveaux damnés'.[13] Following Thomas Csordas, however, one could also stress the process of subjectivation that takes place as these men actively challenge the workings of the European border regime by manipulating their very bodies. Rather than subjugating the bodily under the semantic (see Jackson 1989: 122), we could thus ask what this scene reveals about their bodily being-in-the-world. Yet as phenomenological film theory has taught us, we do not (first and foremost) perceive bodies in films in terms of representation. Before we can intellectually interpret this scene in respect of the exertion of power, our fingers know what they see (to use Sobchack's words). This is why this scene is so unbearable to watch. The close-up of the mutilation, the fizzling sound of the burning flesh, all this creates an immediate bodily viewing experience in us. But is our experience when watching this scene in any way equivalent to the experience of the migrants expressed in the film? In Sobchack's argument, there is not simply some sort of experiential transmission going on in the cinema. Rather, film makes us turn our intention inwards, to our own subjectively lived bodies. A scene evoking the sense of pain might thus recall a sensation of pain stored in the corporeal memory of our body. For Sobchack, meaning is neither born in the viewer's body nor in the cinematic representation, but rather in their chiasmic relationship. In this reversible relationship, the spectator and the film are inseparable. Sobchack's model thus does not really allow for questions about the

Fig. 14: The self-mutilation scene in *Qu'ils Reposent en Révolte*.

experiences of the filmed, as the experience she describes is produced only at the moment of the intersubjective encounter between the film's and the spectator's body. From Sobchack's perspective, this is not a blind spot in her theory, because her analytical engagement is with fiction film and her intention is to explain how the viewer's body is affected in the cinema in the first place. For phenomenologically oriented anthropologists, however, the question of intersubjectivity with their research participants is crucial. How is the other's experience accessible to the researcher? Can we achieve any validity in our representations of other peoples' experiences? Are experiences interculturally translatable? I now want to discuss these epistemological problems with reference to some prominent advocates of a phenomenological approach.

Michael Jackson's ethnographic writings constantly deal with the intense experiences of violence and suffering, as he seems to be fascinated by those moments of crisis where human 'struggle for being' manifests itself. Jackson often engages with the traumatic experience of displaced persons or refugees in postwar situations. His phenomenological approach is an insistence on concrete, individual, lived situations that he attempts to recreate and explain as they are perceived and experienced by the other. While in his theoretical contributions he often stresses the active role of the anthropologist 'drawn into the lifeworld as a participant' (1996: 29), his own approach to the other's experience is mainly based on the generation of biographical interviews. His ethnographies unfold and interpret these 'life stories' then at length (for example, Jackson 2005, 2006). He has given his method a theoretical framework by meditating on the role of narration and storytelling as a means of self-empowerment. For Jackson, in telling a story, narrators make themselves the masters of their own fate and restore their agency in the face of circumstances they can neither control nor intervene in. At no point, however, does Jackson question the mediating role of language that is so constitutive for his procedure. 'Life as lived' and 'life as talked about' are unproblematically equated, the immediacy of lived experience is subordinated to the mediacy of reflective assessment. Further, his research participants' narratives are never scrutinised for their rootedness in their specific cultural setting. How violence and other transgressive situations are actually experienced thus seems to be transculturally identical. Jackson seems to deliberately ignore this issue as his project of existential anthropology aims at uncovering universal truths of what it means to be human (while this humanity seems to shine through only in liminal moments of severe crisis).

Other phenomenologically inspired anthropologists take the aspect of participation much further than Jackson. For them, participation in the other's lifeworld, first as an apprentice, but ultimately as a capable actor, is at the centre of the phenomenological method (Knibbe and Versteeg 2008: 52). Some anthropologists even take this participation to lengths that seem irritating for the mainstream of the discipline. One might think of Paul Stoller, who literally became the apprentice of a Songhay sorcerer and learned to work magic yet also was affected by it (see Stoller and Olkes 1987); or Thomas Ots (1994), who became intimately involved in Chinese ecstatic *qi gong* groups. Ots even rejects the idea of observation as a basic ethnographic method, arguing for what he calls 'experiencing participation'. What is central to these approaches is the recognition of the person of the researcher as deeply involved in the process and outcome of the research. This, of course, is one of the prime insights of post-crisis anthropology: that there is no Archimedean point from which to observe the world, that anthropologists always are 'in the picture' and have to reflect on their position. Yet phenomenological approaches take this reflexive stance much further. They see anthropological knowledge as originating in the interaction between the researchers and the participants of the research. The scientific aim of their research hence is not objectivity, but intersubjectivity. For phenomenologists, it is not only the personalities of the fieldworkers that is central to the creation of knowledge (as in more conventional notions of reflexivity), but their very bodies. It is again Csordas who proposes to see (and employ) the researchers' bodies as ethnographic instruments in their own right. By learning to feel and act according to the lifeworld they study, the fieldworkers' own experiences become their data, for they might understand seemingly untranslatable personal experiences of cultural concepts through their own embodied experiences and feelings (see Csordas 1994: 13). Kathryn L. Geurts, for example, could only understand how Anlo-Ewe identity was felt rather than conceived of, when she participated in their practice of curling up their bodies after telling their migration tale. For her, merely observing the gesture was not enough, it was the actual bodily experience that mattered (2003: 369).

For phenomenologists, embodiment thus offers the 'common ground for recognition of the other's humanity and immediacy of intersubjectivity' (Katz and Csordas 2003: 278). For Csordas and Jackson it is the basis for an intersubjective ethics. For Sobchack, the experience of one's own embodiment is the precondition for the empathetic engagement with the other. Phenomenology's humanist orientation thus postulates the return to a 'pre-reflective experience' in which all humans are the same.[14] Many phenomenology-inspired ethnographies are quite optimistic about the accessibility and representability of the experiences of the research participants across cultural borders. Yet some researchers have noted that their bodily engagement in the field also produced feelings of difference and alienation. Can anthropologists simply 'feel' the others' experiences when their habitus is already formed by their own culture? Robert Desjarlais (1992), comparing his own trance experiences to those of the Nepali shamans he worked with, explicitly states that he was not able to experience the same way his research participants did. Knibbe and Versteeg, who both participated in charismatic religious movements, likewise felt that 'the radical phenomeno-logical method told us something about what we shared and did not share with other people in the religious contexts we participated in: our similar experiences as well as the things that we, as cultural producers of meaning, were not able to experience' (2008: 53). The concept of 'pre-reflective experience' that Lévi-Strauss, Geertz and others wanted to see erased from anthropological thinking, however, undoubtedly forms an initial point of attraction for many anthropol-ogists interested in phenomenology while still remaining a contested idea. In recent years, it has come under new attack by an anthropological sub-discipline that is itself concerned with the workings of sensory perception. Yet the 'an-thropology of the senses' disputes the existence of a universal 'pre-reflective' way of knowing and perceiving things as it rather seeks to investigate the vari-ability of sensory experience within and across cultural groups. It sees sensory perception as a 'cultural as well as physical act' (Classen 1997: 401) and thus as an important precondition for the way people interact with others and their surroundings. I find this debate extremely important for reframing the question of how film might express other sensory experiences and invoke them in its audi-ence (for a condensed summary and entertaining exchange of blows, see Howes and Pink 2010; Howes 2011a, 2011b; Ingold 2011b, 2011c).

ANTHROPOLOGICAL THEORIES OF SENSORY PERCEPTION

The practitioners of an 'anthropology of the senses' are interested in how sense experience is differently patterned across cultures and how these cultures at-tach different meaning and emphasis to different modalities of perception (see Howes 1991a, 2003, 2005; Classen 1993, 1997; Seremetakis 1994). David Howes phrases his opening question as follows: 'What is the world like to a culture that takes actuality in less visual, more auditory or olfactory, gustatory or tactile terms than those to which we are accustomed?' (1991b: 6). Scholars of the senses have worked on the cultural history of smell (see Classen *et al.* 1994), or taste (see Korsmeyer 2005), their research participants' aural access to the world (see Feld 1982) or a critical re-evaluation of the dominance of vision in Western societies. Howes proposes a cross-cultural comparison be-tween different cultural configurations of the senses. His aim is to 'trace the influence such variations have on forms of social organization, conceptions of self and cosmos, the regulation of the emotions, and other domains of cultural expression' (1991b: 3). Howes and Constance Classen (1991) provide anthro-pologists with a methodology with which to determine the sensory profile of a culture during fieldwork. Like Michael Herzfeld (2001: 240), they see a sensory approach not as a specialist concern but rather as an important addition that should be incorporated in all studies of religion, gender, identity, art or material culture. Anthropologists of the senses see sensory configurations as learned and cultivated. This differentiates their perspective from the conceptions of sense experience as pre-discursive, which explains the calls for a return to the senses put forth by many phenomenological thinkers. Howes, however, is not so much interested in the individual dimensions of sensory experience, in what Turner called 'mere' experience and Throop later described as immediate, fluid and internal experience. He wants to go beyond the preliminary sensations and into the meaning conveyed and formed by such experiences (see Howes 2003: 49). Sense experience for him is thus only applicable to analysis at the moment in which the embodied sensations of individuals are defined (or 'made sense' of) through the sensory categories that are constructed by their culture (when they become 'an experience' in Dilthey's words). Tim Ingold has argued strongly against such a privileging of the 'determinate, cohesive and unitary' aspects of experience (to use Throop's terms). For Ingold, this shifts the attention away from the lived immediacy of sensory experience and from the act of perception as such. He criticises Howes for seeing the senses as solely expressive of the superordinate values and beliefs of holistic cultural systems.

> Far from helping us to understand how the whole body perceives, and how meaning is generated within the contexts of its activities of looking, listening and so on, this approach reduces the body to a locus of objectified and enumerable senses whose one and only role is to carry the semantic load projected onto them by a collective, supersensory subject – namely society – and whose balance or ratio may be calculated according to the proportion of the load borne by each. (2000: 284)

Howes deliberately ignores all individual variations of sense experience, mapping out sensory difference only between whole cultures or societies (see Howes 1991c: 168). This culturalist stance is, as Laura Marks has argued, a highly problematic presupposition for our context of migration, as in today's multicultural societies 'people's individual sensoria overlap only unevenly with their cultural sensoria' (2000: 208). Howes' insistence on cultures as collective representations of knowledge further involves the problem of separating the physical from the cultural dimensions of perception, the registration of sensations by the body from the construction of representations in the mind (see Ingold 2000: 283). He thus remains locked in the Cartesian dualism of body and mind that Csordas's concept of embodiment, of the body as a site of knowledge, tried to overcome.

What is important in the debate between Howes and Ingold for my re-evaluation of film's potential for anthropology is their different conceptualisations of the sense of vision. Ingold (2000: 284; 2011b: 316) dismisses Howes' critique of vision as an inherently objectifying sense in modern Western culture that is implicit in his cross-cultural comparisons.[15] In Howes' and Classen's accounts, other cultures constantly appear as 'closer' to the senses, whereas Western post-industrial societies over-valorise the visual and hence suffer from an atrophy and alienation of sensuous knowledge. Marks sees such an ascribing of sensory fullness only to non-Westerners as a 'primitivist and exoticizing mistake' (2000: 208). For Ingold, the critique of visuality Howes and others put forth finally avoids any in-depth examination of how visual perception actually works:

> For them, the answer is already presupposed: to see is to reduce the environment to objects that are to be grasped and appropriated as representations in the mind. The irony is that this answer, which critics of visualism are inclined to take for granted, has its source in the very Cartesian epistemology that they seek to dethrone. What they offer, then, is not an account of visual practice, but a critique of modernity dressed up as a critique of the hegemony of vision. (2000: 286)

For Ingold, this alleged hegemony of vision in Western culture lacks any biological basis. He strongly dismisses Howes' and Classen's ideas of a cultural hierarchy of the particular senses. Like C. Nadia Seremetakis (1994), he argues instead that all senses are inseparably interconnected. He shows, for example, how seeing and hearing are so closely conjoined that they are 'better regarded as aspects of one activity' (2000: 243). In a similar vein, MacDougall has described the interrelatedness of seeing and touching, referring to Oliver Sacks' (1995) example of blind people who, after regaining sight in their adulthood, are unable to recognise objects visually before they touch them (1998: 50). Both Ingold and MacDougall thus follow Merleau-Ponty in seeing the senses not as distinct registers, whose impressions are only combined on a higher cognitive level, but rather as part of an entire perceptive field which is the body.[16] The Western discursive distinction between vision and the other senses is therefore not natural, but 'the outcome of a specific historical development' (Ingold 2000: 269). The separation of the senses doesn't happen at the point of perception, but is culturally defined. Therefore Howes' and Classen's project of determining sensual hierarchies among different cultures doesn't give the explanation for cultural differences in sensory experience, but is the very thing that has to be explained. For Ingold, these cultural differences are differences in classification, as individual sense experiences are defined discursively by referring to culturally constructed categories of vision, touch, hearing, smell or taste. For Howes and Classen, people perceive the world differently because their cultures vary in the valorisation of particular senses. For Ingold, people express their individual sensory experiences in discourse and these discursive constructions *then* affect their perceptions of the world around them.

Now what does such a perspective of vision as interrelated with the other senses (which also grounds Vivian Sobchack's later publications on film spectatorship) imply for visual anthropology and the possibilities of visual representation? If all senses are inevitably linked, then visual anthropology does not impose a Western sensory order to other cultures while it reifies its own, as Howes argues (1991: 172). Rather, it might offer us pathways to the other senses, a second route to sense experiences different from the ones cultivated in the West. The visual and auditory dimensions of film might thus be able to express (at least to a certain degree) the non-visual and non-auditory aspects of sensory experience. Before I, however, discuss film's unique synaesthetic qualities and how anthropologists can actually make use of them, let me briefly comment on the understanding of the different representational modalities of visual and written anthropology we now have arrived at.

FILM BEYOND REPRESENTATION

David MacDougall has argued that the new anthropological domains of knowledge that encompass the body and the senses are 'particularly appropriate to visual anthropology' while writing has approached them 'only with some difficulty' (2006: 271). Others, like Anna Grimshaw and Amanda Ravetz (2005) and Arnd Schneider and Christopher Wright (2006), have similarly pointed to the limits of textual representation. As Csordas notes, many critics of phenomenology assume that experience is ultimately inaccessible, because it is always mediated by language and 'therefore one can only study language or discourse, i.e. representation' (1994: 11). He disputes this assumption by concluding that representation itself as an epistemological modality is trapped in its semiotic paradigm. For Csordas, representations of culture only produce objectified abstractions. While the crisis of representation in anthropology questioned existing practices of scientific writing, it did not try to overcome the centrality of the discipline's text metaphor. Even in postmodernist and deconstructivist approaches, Jacques Derrida's (1976) catchphrase that there is nothing outside the text still prevails. Csordas thus understands his notion of 'being-in-the-world' as a more immediate term: while representation is fundamentally nominal, 'being-in-the-world' is fundamentally conditional as it refers to lived experience (1994: 10). I propose that film is the medium that perfectly embodies the immediacy and closeness to experience Csordas is longing for, as it constitutes a form of communication that is not bound to the abstract level of signs or language to convey meaning. As Sobchack has shown, it communicates through establishing a form of direct contact. To describe how film relates to lived experience, one could follow Stephen Tyler and speak of evocation, a term he uses to avoid representation: 'since evocation is nonrepresentational, it is not to be understood as a sign function, for it is not a "symbol of", nor does it "symbolize" what it evokes' (1987: 206). Tyler seeks to 'atone for the original sin of LANGUAGE, that separation of speech and world we know as the disjunction of words and things' (1987: 172). Yet unfortunately he remains silent about this immediate access to the world that is offered by film. He rather hopes to render scientific writing 'occult' through the literary evocation of the inexpressible and inchoate. Such evocative experiments in ethnographic writing, however, have largely remained unsatisfactory (if undertaken at all). The more 'occult' the writing was, the less accessible the cultural reality to be evoked appeared to the reader. Evocative writing in anthropology thus could even be said to set the authoritative power of the author absolute, as it can only be taken on trust and denies a reader unfamiliar with the cultural background any possibility to question its ethnographic validity. Further, when any statement about truth is fragmented in the mirror hall of multiple meanings, the authors eventually make themselves intangible. In a written ethnography, the world is necessarily created by the author and a multiplicity of meaning has to be crafted through literary means. In a film, in contrast, the same polysemy is achieved naturally through the richness of the world in front of the camera that exists independently from the intentions of the filmmaker (see Strecker 2013). Film thus has to be described as evocative in a double sense: in respect to the reality it captures and depicts, but also (as I have shown throughout this chapter) in activating sensory and embodied participation in its audience. This engaging participation is, I will argue, fundamental to the process of cultural translation that film can facilitate.

CINEMATIC SYNAESTHESIA: FILM AS A MULTISENSORY MEDIUM

Laura Marks (2000) has offered a theory of intercultural cinema that seeks to describe how different cultural sensoria can be translated into (and hence translate) cinematic modes of expression. She explores how film can convey sensory experiences that can technically not be represented in an audiovisual medium. Marks explicitly discusses this issue against the background of the experience of migration. She engages with experimental and essayistic films and videos that try to articulate the experience of living in diaspora. Many of the filmmakers whose works she analyses share a 'hyphenated identity', living and working in-between cultures. Marks shows how these intercultural video artists try to express their inexpressible sense memories that connect them to their homelands. They all use cinema to relate to memories of the fabric of everyday experience in their cultures of origin. Marks interprets memories as necessarily involving all senses as they store bodily sensations like touch, smell or taste. She draws upon Henri Bergson (1911) to describe memory not as an inner mental process but as located in the body. This concept of memory as directly linked to the physical awareness of sensory perception is graphically expressed in the oeuvre of Marcel Proust (who was an admirer of Bergson). In Proust's writings any sense perception (like the taste of a madeleine cake plunged into tea, or the scent of a public lavatory on the Champs-Élysées) can conjure up expanding circles of (often involuntary) memory. Proust stresses the force with which these (sometimes repressed) memories manifest themselves. Marks, therefore, urges us to see the often traumatic memories involved in migration not as 'an infinite return to the buffet table of lived experiences but a walk through the minefield of embodied memory' (2000: 152). For her, cinematic images have a similar capacity for triggering physical memories that are embedded in the senses. These images can become tactile, or evoke gustatory or olfactory experiences. Marks describes a haptic form of visuality in which images address the eye like an organ of touch. This allows for a perception of the image that resembles a palpation. Haptic images, as Marks describes them, often lack optical information, as they are blurred or highlight textures or surfaces, often in extreme close-up. The foreground and background of the image thus cannot be separated, the classical composition according to the Western invention of the central perspective is negated. As the viewers may not distinguish objects within the image, they engage in a relationship to the screen as a whole.

An artist who employs haptic visuality to express the experience of displacement is Mona Hatoum. Hatoum was born in Lebanon to Palestinian parents and is now based in London, where she was first stranded in 1975 when, during what was meant to be a brief visit, the Lebanse civil war (1975–1990) broke out. Her video *Measures of Distance* (1988) is one of the first emblematic artistic works emerging from a context of migration, in which the personal, the cultural and the political are inextricably interwoven. The video begins with still images so close as to be unrecognisable, overlaid with meshes of Arabic script. Behind this 'curtain' of text, warm reds and purples pulsate in grainy footage. Only very slowly does one begin to make out the shape of a voluminous female body, that is veiled by the layers of hand-writing. As we hear Hatoum reading them in voice-over, we understand that these texts are letters from her mother. From the letters, we learn that the artist's parents are living in Lebanon, while their children are dispersed all over the world. The letters Hatoum reads with a quiet voice testify the mother's deep longing for her daughter with whom she is unable to communicate, due to the country's increased isolation during the civil war.

Fig. 15: A blurred photograph of the artist's mother in *Measures of Distance*. Courtesy Mona Hatoum and White Cube.

The letters also reveal the images to be photographs Hatoum took of her naked mother under the shower during during a visit to Beirut in 1981. They originate from a very intimate moment shared by mother and daughter, much to the dislike (as we also learn) of Hatoum's jealous father. Hatoum's camera tenderly glides over these photos in close-up, only gradually resolving them into figuration. This relieves these images from their status as objective visual representations. Rather, they convey a tactile, a physical relationship with the mother's body. This mode of haptic visuality brings the viewer close to the mother's skin. It caressingly protects and gently touches her at the same time, evoking both a sense of her presence as well as the painful reality of her absence. It thus triggers a tactile memory that expresses the artist's feeling of longing for her family, a feeling that is first of all a corporeal one (see Marks 2000: 187). The video, made by the daughter in her British exile, is thus not only a powerful meditation on absence and yearning and on the personal and cultural dimensions of touch, it also has the potential to touch its audience and be touched by it.

This concept of haptic visuality requires an understanding of cinematic spectatorship that involves all senses in the audiovisual act of film viewing and a participatory mode of perception, in which the viewers actively produce meaning themselves in the virtual lack of things to see. For Marks this establishes a physical contact between viewer and film. The 'Skin of the Film' (as her book is entitled) thus not only refers to haptic close-up images of human bodies but also to the body of the film itself in its materiality as a migrating artifact. Marks alludes to the physical circulation of the marginalised experimental films she discusses that travel (in only a small number of copies) from galleries to festivals to universities to museums (2000: 6). In this process, different audiences are inscribed in the film, as all these public screenings leave their material traces on the copy, on its celluloid 'skin'. The process of contact and transmission between film and spectator hence is an utterly reciprocal one. Marks thus builds upon Sobchack's phenomenological notion of the intersubjectivity of film perception yet seeks to expand it to an intercultural context:

> The cinematic encounter takes place not only between my body and the film's body, but my sensorium and the film's sensorium. We bring our own personal and cultural organization of the senses to cinema, and cinema brings a particular organization of the senses to us, the filmmaker's own, refracted through the cinematic apparatus. One could say that intercultural spectatorship is the meeting of two different sensoria that may or may not intersect. (2000: 153)

But does this mean that cinema can easily transmit sensory experiences across cultural borders? Can it make the viewer experience what the ethnographic other experiences? Sense experiences of course cannot be represented directly through film, as film obviously cannot record touch, taste, smell or emotions the same way it can record images and sounds. Yet film can approach these senses through evocation. What is interesting about Marks is that she does not start out her analysis with films that are commonly endowed with sensory richness, such as intercultural mainstream cinema with excessive multisensory allusions (for example, to the smell and taste of food or the texture of bodies making love) such as Mira Nair's *Kama Sutra* (1996), Tranh Anh Hung's *The Scent of the Green Papaya* (1993), Ang Lee's *Eat, Drink, Man, Woman* (1994) or popular Bollywood films. For her, diasporan artists do not approach their subjects from such a position of wealth. Rather, they struggle to recreate sensory memories and find their place within their own sensory traditions (2000: 231). Far from being overwhelmed by sensual excess, the viewers of these works have to respond to the multisensory qualities of their images by completing them: by investing their own resources of experience and embodied memories. In the act of sensory translation from one cultural context to the other, many viewers might thus not be able to reconstruct these multisensory images to their fullest and hence might miss many sensory allusions.

With Marks we have arrived at an understanding of cinema as a multisensory embodiment of culture, not just a visual representation of experience. While (following Ingold and others) all images have multisensory qualities (as their perception inevitably involves all the senses) Marks's study explores modes of visuality that intensify the sensual investment of the audience. I believe that these experimental modes of evocation offer a rich potential for anthropologists who explore the lifeworlds and sensory modalities of their research participants through participatory research. Of course, this procedure inevitably is full of gaps. One gap opens between the experiences of the subjects and the experiences of the researcher. As the work of Desjarlais and others has clearly shown, even the most intense forms of experiencing participation will not enable anthropologists to feel the same way the people they study do. The other gap lies between the anthropologist's cinematic evocation and the audience, as film will not make all sensory experience available to the viewer. Yet I propose to consider these gaps as productive for the anthropological endeavor. As Stoller notes, a more sensual gaze will not enable us to see what the other sees, but it can bring us 'more closely to the experience and perception of the ethnographic other' (1989: 68). Likewise, the multisensory images viewers cannot 'fill in for' may at least lead them to a sensibility for what they are missing, to an incisive awareness of their own sensory configuration and its limits. Thus, it might be exactly in those gaps, in the liminal regions between two cultural systems where 'some anthropological insights emerge' (Desjarlais 1992: 19). Furthermore, both Marks and Ingold see sensory formations not as fixed and static but as learned and in flux. Large-scale processes like the global movement of people thus constantly create new subject positions in-between cultures, which increasingly will also produce changes in the organisation of our sensoria (see Marks 2000: 241). Hence, one could optimistically argue (as Marks does) that film can play a vital part in cultivating new sensory epistemologies in a globalised world and thus foster intercultural understanding.

FROM EMBODIMENT TO EMPLACEMENT

Not only with respect to the theme of migration, there remains the question of whether the study of experience really is the most important thing that anthropologists should direct their attention to. Even the best evocation of the sensuous experiences of migrants' often ephemeral lifeworlds does not necessarily communicate any anthropological understanding. Knibbe and Versteeg thus doubt that the ultimate goal for an anthropologist should be the complete immersion in the other's reality. They insist that the knowledge an anthropologist acquires should not simply equate with that of the other participants of the lifeworld. It

77

should rather encompass 'an understanding of history, politics and economics that are important but invisible to most of the other participants' (2008: 58). Hence, they propose a search for knowledge of a different epistemological quality. 'Rather than berating anthropologists for "transcending the lived context", this quality could be seen as an added value, especially for enabling a critique of power, inequality and oppression' (ibid.). Such a critique of the political and socio-economic circumstances is, as I argue throughout this book, undoubtedly of paramount importance when engaging with the lived reality of migration. But does a focus on embodiment and experience allow for the formulation of such a critique? In the approaches discussed so far, a critical stance is manifest only implicitly as an attempt to 'do justice' to the other's experience by overcoming distorting media representations or objectifying scientific accounts. Jackson's and Csordas's works incorporate a political dimension insofar as they stress the importance of existential power and individual agency that often is suppressed in political macro-analyses. Knibbe and Versteeg argue that 'the strength of anthropology, after all, is to show the connections between aspects of social and cultural reality that are normally divided by discipline' (2008: 59). I do believe that a focus on experience can indeed be helpful to put these various dimensions of cultural reality in correlation to each other.

Sarah Pink has proposed such a relational concept that 'attends to the question of experience by accounting for the relationships between bodies, minds and the materiality and sensoriality of the environment' (2009: 25). She advocates a rethinking of the ethnographic process by attending not only to the research participants' embodiment, but also to their *emplacement*. Pink follows Edward Casey's phenomenological understanding of place as arising from human perception: any experience of space and time begins with (and is secondary to) the embodied experience of place. Lived bodies both constitute and belong to places. As Casey puts it, 'we are not only *in* places but *of* them. Human beings – along with other entities on earth – are ineluctably place-bound. More even than earthlings, we are placelings, and our very perceptual apparatus, our sensing body, reflects the kinds of places we inhabit' (1996: 19). Thus, for anthropologists, place is necessarily 'our primary context for any piece of research' (Pink 2009: 30). Yet for Pink and Casey, place is not static, it is an event. Places 'gather experiences and histories' and even 'such unbodylike entities as thoughts and memories' (Casey 1996: 24). Pink's notion of emplacement is thus grounded in a fluid conception of place. This allows her to also take into account the history, politics and power relations that are inscribed into places. Her theory of emplacement seeks to understand the lived immediacy of the local as inevitably interwoven, or entangled, with the global. She wants to describe people's everyday lived experience in relation to and as co-implicated with the complexity of large-scale processes. Her focus on place provides a useful tool with which to conceptualise how 'participants in ethnographic research are emplaced in social, sensory and material contexts, characterized by, and productive of, particular power configurations that they experience through their whole bodies and that are constantly changing (even if in very minor ways)' (2009: 33).

To conclude this chapter, I want to discuss my film *Tell Me When…* as an example of an anthropological work that explores the phenomenological reality of illegalised migrants' lifeworlds in relation to those larger political processes that create places of exclusion and oppression. I find Pink's notion of emplacement helpful to describe how the protagonists of my film experienced these liminal places they had to ensconce themselves in, as well as their own marginalised practices of place-making. Understanding migration through the concept of emplacement is not as oxymoronic as it may seem. As Murat Aydemir and Alex Rotas note, 'migration not only takes place between places, but also has its effects on place, in place' (2008: 7). They argue that migration 'installs movement *within* place', making place the 'setting of the variegated memories, imaginations, dreams, fantasies, nightmares, anticipations, and idealizations that experiences of migration, of both migrants and native inhabitants, bring into contact with each other' (ibid.). In *Tell Me When…*, I have focused on the Spanish exclave of Melilla as a place that is 'thickened' by particular experiences of migration. Two of my protagonists, Opara and Shahbaz, were trans-Sahara migrants. For them, Melilla was merely a transit space, a gateway to Europe, a place where the European border regime stopped their movement and literally condemned them to what Sudeep Dasgupta has called 'waiting-in-the-border' (2008: 192). While being stuck in the CETI (Centro de Estancia Temporal de Inmigrantes) detention centre, their only hope was to leave the city, to continue their journey to the European continent. In contrast, Ilham, the third protagonist of my film, desperately tried to build up a livelihood in Melilla. As she was fairly well integrated into the exclave's Moroccan community, she fought for a work permit that would provide her with a legal status within the city. Through the specificity of each protagonist's experience, I wanted to explore how Melilla is profoundly shaped by the emplacement of multiple experiences of migration. Further, I was interested in how the structuring absent presence of the border regime pervaded every space, every situation in which my protagonists found themselves in. By focusing on their lived experience, I wanted to render visible the workings of the European migration regime through the subjective perspective of those migrants whose lifeworlds are shaped by it. Depicting their little acts of resistance and their attempts to gain public visibility, the film further attempts to show them not only as distinct individuals, but also as political subjects.

TELL ME WHEN…: EMPLACED EXPERIENCES AT EUROPE'S MARGINS

As Casey notes, place is not one kind of thing: 'it can be psychical as well as physical, and doubtless also cultural and historical and social' (1996: 31). Without doubt, Melilla is such a place that crystallises a complex web of meanings and relations. It is charged not only with political and historical, but also with symbolical significance. Melilla is a contested place. As a remnant of colonialism, it is a persisting bone of contention between Morocco and Spain. For trans-Sahara migrants from Africa and Asia, Melilla and its sister-exclave Ceuta are the only places where it is possible to reach EU territory without having to cross the Mediterranean Sea. Since the violent incidents of 2005 and the subsequent reinforcement of the infamous border fence, it is also the prime symbol for the EU's aggressive 'Fortress Europe' policy. Hence, Melilla embodies the complex political and social relations between Europe and Africa like no other place. For my film, this allowed me to concentrate on the phenomenological present of my three protagonists. I chose to make their everyday experiences my main focus, but I understood these at a sensory, emotional and intellectual level not only as embodied, but also as emplaced. Thus, I wanted to explore the macro-level of a larger political situation not through abstract analytical categories but through the concreteness of emplaced experience. This experience is above all marked by exclusion. The CETI detention centre, where Shahbaz and Opara have lived since they first entered Melilla, is located at the very margins of the city. The 700 migrants who stay in the centre thus live right next to the border fence they risked their lives to get across. Their leave is limited to the daytime hours and can be withdrawn as a penalty measure. It is not only because of the distance to the city centre that any contact with the city's Spanish inhabitants is limited. The residents of the camp thus remain largely invisible for Melilla's citizens. They spend their time mainly in close proximity to the detention centre, even though there is very little infrastructure (and not much to do) in the area. Most migrants engage in practices of place-making. To create some privacy and space of their own (inside the CETI, eight people share a small room) almost all inhabitants build their own little huts from wood and cardboard in the coppice around the centre. These so-called 'tranquilo places' or 'chabolas' are furnished with mattresses and, as the migrants are not allowed to find work in the city, they constitute the favoured place in which to kill time. As men and women are strictly separated in the detention centre, these huts are also the only places where relationships (and in some cases even family life) can be lived. Another important pastime is cooking, an activity that is very much divided by nationality as cooking (and, of course, eating) food from their countries of origin constitutes a vital sensual link to the migrants' homes. Communal cooking also offers an alternative to the much-disliked very basic European food offered in the CETI mess hall. Because cooking is not allowed inside the detention centre, this is also done outdoors, under (or beside) a small bridge close to the entrance of the camp. Hence, much of our initial filmmaking was dedicated to the every-day activities our protagonists performed in these provisional places around the camp. Our focus was on concrete, lived situations that were expressive of their emplaced experiences and we tried to let things unfold in front of the camera. Consider, for example, a small scene with Shahbaz we filmed under the bridge while taking shelter from the rain. We spent the afternoon chatting and listening to music from his mobile phone. When it turned 5pm, it was too late for him to go to the mosque, so he decided to perform his prayers just where we were, with only some pieces of cardboard beneath him to protect his clothes from the dirt. We filmed him in front view, facing the camera, in a long take. His praying is concentrated and he ignores the rising background noise of cars crossing the bridge above us. Yet finally he is disturbed by a group of Africans who want to cook beneath the bridge and raucously break up wood for the fire. What is un-folding for me in this scene is a deep sense of exclusion and non-affiliation: there is no place for the CETI inhabitants in the city, and even the little spaces they retreat to are contested by rivaling groups, divided by the migrants' nationali-ties. We experienced this placelessness ourselves whilst filmmaking, because the options of places for meeting our protagonists, for setting up for a conversation or interview, were always limited. This also becomes apparent in the sound we recorded in the places where we filmed. The car- and street-noises always dic-tated the rhythm our protagonists had to adapt to when speaking in order to make themselves understood.

When we met Ilham through a small NGO whose founder José Palazón is very active in the political struggle for migrants' rights, our filmmaking activi-ties shifted more and more from the city's spatial boundaries to its centre. As Ilham is from Morocco, she didn't live in the detention centre but stayed in the

Fig. 16: Shahbaz praying under the bridge in *Tell Me When...*

streets, or occasionally at friends' places, relying on a large social network consisting mostly of fellow Moroccans (almost half of the exclave's population is of Moroccan origin). Ilham lived the life of a drifter and when filming her we were in constant movement. Thus, following her with the camera, filming her from behind or only the shadow she cast on the streets, became a visual strategy by which to approach her daily routine. We mainly focused on her survival strategies and her ongoing fight for a work permit that would give her access to a legal personhood and hence allow her to find a livelihood in the city. While her applications routinely were turned down, she had to survive on the streets. A lot of our footage was thus shot after dark when she hangs out with friends or roams the streets in search of a place to spend the night. After a while, when we had gained her trust, she led us to those hide-outs in the port area from where Moroccan would-be migrants try to sneak on a ferry to Spain. It was after these encounters (and after her application for a work permit again was neglected), that she confronted us with her risky plan of leaving Melilla as a blind passenger.

After a few weeks of shooting, an incident occurred that allowed us to further explore the relationship between the residents of the detention centre and the Spanish inhabitants of Melilla. Shortly before Easter week, the 'Semana Santa', one of the city's Christian brotherhoods was not able to find enough participants for the traditional procession marches, in which a huge statue of Mary is carried through the city. Hence, the idea came up to approach the Christian inhabitants of the CETI. Opara, who played a very active role in Melilla's small Pentecostal church and had somewhat gained the status of a spokesperson for the large group of Nigerians in the centre, took the responsibility for organising the group's participation. While they definitely were happy to take part in such a prestigious religious ceremony, I sensed that they also hoped that this would have positive effects on the outcome of their deportation process. For the organisers of the procession, it was difficult to dispel these hopes, as the migrants' Semana Santa participation was covered by the national media and Opara even gave some interviews to newspapers. They even intensified when the whole group was invited to the official closing ceremony. When Opara was told that he would be allowed to give a short allocution in the presence of the governor of Melilla, he was electrified. He immediately sensed a chance to actively do something to improve his situation and achieve some public recognition. He wanted to use this opportunity to call attention to the despair of the CETI inhabitants, thus making a civic address and gaining access to public visibility in Arendtian terms. For days he worked on his speech, which he wanted to deliver in Spanish. In it, he conjured up a common bond between the migrants and the inhabitants of the city through their mutual faith in Christianity and strongly expressed their dream of being allowed to find work in mainland Spain. The governor,

Fig. 17: Opara delivering his speech in front of Melilla's dignitaries in *Tell Me When...*

however, showed no reaction to this in his own speech. For Opara, it was hard to accept that the amenities of the party should remain only a temporary inclusion into the Arendtian space of appearance and that he was about to return into invisibility. Inside the bus that brought the group back to the detention centre, he tried to interpret the medal he was given as a gift from the brotherhood as a sign that he would soon receive his papers. Unlike Shahbaz, whose thoughts more and more wandered back to his family in Pakistan, Opara clearly was not willing to give up his hope for a future in Europe.

In *Tell Me When...*, I explored the social and sensory experiences of these three strong individuals stuck in a liminal situation (and in a liminal place) between Africa and Europe. Throughout this chapter, I have discussed how film can evoke the phenomenological reality of the lifeworld, the embodied and emplaced experiences of our ethnographic subjects. I have shown how this understanding of the medium's capacities has informed my own filmmaking practice. In the next chapters, I want to expand these notions of experience to fully take into account the more abstract spatial and temporal coordinates of migration. Therefore, I want to reconcile my phenomenological theory of the sensory participation that film facilitates with Gilles Deleuze's (1986, 1989) ideas of cinema as a new image of thought. I consider film as a 'way of thinking with the forms of sensibilia' (Rajchmann 2008: 313), as a mode of communication that allows space, movement and time to be rendered in hitherto unexplored ways. I seek to understand how film as an aesthetic form can analytically relate the lived reality of the subjective lifeworld to the complexity of global processes, and how it can fuse the micro- with the macro-level of analysis.

CHAPTER THREE

Migratory Spaces

I n this chapter I propose to explore how the current acceleration of global mobility has to be reflected in anthropological thought; how migration as a social movement 'moves' anthropological theory. My aim is to rethink and readjust the discipline's spatial concepts with regard to the transnationalisation of subjects and cultural processes. I will show how anthropological notions of space are deeply inscribed within the construction of cinematic space in ethnographic films. I argue that innovative cinematic practices can profoundly influence the spatial perspectives of contemporary theorising. They may give conceptual form to some of the discipline's current concerns, namely how to employ multiperspectivity and multivocality to approach the increasing complexity of a globalised world. In my discussion, I will put specific emphasis on montage, a cinematic principle *par excellence* and a methodological tool that remains underestimated. As my examples will suggest, montage as a mapping strategy can not only render visible the connections between different locations, it can also fill the gaps and absences produced by large-scale processes of deterritorialisation. Hence, montage may introduce a systemic perspective that is able to give us the bigger picture and transcend the limitations of some bounded concepts of the ethnographic field. Transnational processes, however, also induce transformations 'on the ground'; in the concrete materiality of place. Accordingly, we need an analytical perspective that takes into account both a macro-perspective on global interconnectedness and a micro-perspective on the concrete emplacement of local actors.[17] Therefore, I will discuss how this need for a bifocal approach has informed the making of my own cinematographic installation, *A Tale of Two Islands*. This work charts the Comoros Islands as a contested postcolonial space by focusing on the particular places that form the nodes of the islands' migratory system. In transferring observational cinematic techniques into the 'activated space' of an exhibition set-up (see Mondloch 2010), the work provokes a productive tension between the illusionistic on-screen representation of space and the actual material environment of the exhibition space. As the spectators physically have to engage with the multiplicity of perspectives offered to them, I argue that this form of presentation disrupts habitual viewing conventions and allows for 'kinesthetic insights' (Morse 1998: 156). In producing a bodily experience of space, it encourages a mobile way of thinking and also conveys something of the contradictory aspects of the contemporary experience of mobility.

VIEWS OF THE FIELD

In much classical anthropological research and writing, space and place have not been treated with much conceptual rigour. In traditional notions of fieldwork and 'realist' modes of representation it was assumed that anthropology's 'objects of study' exist in non-Western, non-industrialised locales and, thus, in intact and coherent spatial and temporal relations. In this view, space and place are simply locations; unproblematic frames for the things people do. Arjun Appadurai (1988) has noted that anthropologists have often exemplified anthropological concepts through the use of specific places to position particular groups of people. India, for example, has come to represent hierarchy and the caste system. Liisa Malkki has raised a similar critique against such an abstract conception of space as mere setting for culture. She has challenged readily assumed equations of identity with territory, culture with place. For her, the territorialisation of cultures is tantamount to their spatial incarceration. 'Terms like "native", "indigenous", and "autochthonous" have all served to root cultures in soils' (1992: 29) and thereby made them appear as cut off from all global influences and connections. Thus the 'field' in which anthropological practice takes place often was imagined as a remote, confined and consistent place the ethnographer enters in a form of 'intensive dwelling' (Clifford 1997: 58) and leaves after a time of deep, extended research. As James Clifford notes, this conception of the field was modelled after the natural sciences and played an important part in the discipline's self-definition and subsequent demarcation from other sciences and cross-cultural practices. Effectively, it stipulated the segregation of the anthropologists' world from the static, fixed and timeless cultural world they describe.

Ethnographic filmmakers equally have taken part in such 'sedentarist metaphysics' (Malkki 1992: 31). Films of the observational cinema tradition construct ethnographic locales in a fixed spatial-temporal unity. The observational method, for example, as Paul Henley still promotes it, seeks to 'capture the rhythms and spatial configurations of the social world represented' (2004: 115). To achieve this, Henley favours long sequence shots that reproduce a quasi-natural relation of space and time over marked interventions into the filmic material. The characteristic mode of representation in observational cinema is based on an insistence on the integrity of the pro-filmic world. As Anna Grimshaw notes, the truth of such a representation has to be embodied by observational filmmakers (2001: 131). They are the witnesses; the ones who have genuinely 'been there'. The effect this style of filmmaking produces in the audience parallels the paradigm of realist ethnographic representation: 'you are there, because I was there'.[18] We, the spectators, are made to share the observational standpoint of the anthropologist with the camera. Hence, cinematic space in conventional ethnographic film is constructed around the illusion of being present at the field site. In *To Live with Herds* (1972), for example, David MacDougall wanted to give his audience the feeling of actually being situated directly among the people and cattle within a Jie compound in northeastern Uganda (see MacDougall 1998: 200). This impression is achieved through an unobtrusive, conjunctive style of editing and a 'humanized, situated camera with its flawed, partial view' (Grimshaw and Ravetz 2009: 83). It allows for continuity of perception, from the perspective of an individual observer that is tied 'to the specific historical act of filming' (MacDougall 1998: 205). A particular example of this is a long uninterrupted shot in which MacDougall's camera slowly moves around his protagonist, Logoth, as he maps the topography of the Jie territory. Logoth points to the different cardinal directions and explains the surrounding landscape; he describes the neighbours of the Jie and locates the feeding grounds of the cattle. Logoth, and with him the camera in this shot, is the static point from where the territory is observed. For the audience, orientation within the diegetic space of the film is thus achieved through the eyes of the human observer whose perspective the camera adopts. Jie lifeworld in *To Live with Herds* is thus explored by Logoth's firm emplacement in it.

In an age of transnational movement however, such representations of rooted, immobile, coherent and unaffected cultural worlds have come to be questioned; the same goes for the stable standpoint from which they could be observed. For anthropology, the increasing global mobility and interconnectedness of people, places, things, stories or conflicts thus poses new epistemological problems. It demands new methods of research and representation that also go beyond the rather constricted subject matters encountered in most observational films. Today, as Michael Peter Smith notes, the 'challenge is to develop an optic and a language capable of representing the complexity of transnational connections, the dynamics of cross-border networks, and the shifting spatial scales at which agency takes place' (2001: 174).

REPRESENTING TRANSNATIONALISM

In two widely read articles, George Marcus (1994, 1995) has argued that in order to come to terms with the increased dissemination of actors, goods, knowledge, ideas and economic entities on a global scale, anthropologists would have to leave the *mise-en-scène* of their traditional field sites and take on a systemic perspective. For Marcus, anthropology's focus on single site investigation and bounded concepts severely limit perception and analysis. Therefore, he calls for a mobile ethnography based on multi-sited fieldwork in which the anthropologist follows the 'circulation of cultural meanings, objects and identities in diffuse time-space' (1995: 96). This methodological revolution, however, for him has to go hand in hand with new modes of representation, as problems of representation have to be understood as anthropology's 'distinctive medium of theoretical and methodological discourse' (1994: 51). For Marcus, traditional 'realist' forms of representation cannot account for the complexity of a globalised present. He therefore proposes that anthropologists should embrace the artistic principle of montage as an excellent inspirational form for contemporary ethnography. Marcus cites avant-garde constructivism, especially the work of Russian director Dziga Vertov, as an aesthetic practice that permits the relation, comparison and juxtaposition of different cultural spaces. The concept of montage as an analytical tool has since gained increasing anthropological attention (see Taussig 2004; Willerslev and Ulturgashewa 2007; Kiener 2008; Suhr and Willerslev 2012, 2013). What is striking, however, is that Marcus evokes the 'cinematic metaphor of montage' only for innovation in ethnographic text production. His ideas have not yet had a broad impact on ethnographic filmmakers who still show a great deal of suspiciousness towards more expressive forms of montage; rather restricting themselves to single-site, single-observer concepts (see Schneider 2011: 183). Thus, there lies an unfulfilled potential in an 'ethnographic cinema of montage' that consciously addresses the transnational condition.

Wilma Kiener proposes an alternative cinematic poetics that is 'capable of understanding and conveying the experience of living in worlds of (dis)location and of (a)synchronism' (2008: 393). She argues that transnational subjects (migrants, refugees, travellers) experience global processes foremost in the form of absences: the homeland, the family and friends that are left behind, the political protest that is only possible in a foreign state. She explores how montage can address these absences by adding an additional reality to the actual observational scene, thereby expanding and enhancing it (see 2008: 395). What is absent can thus be expressed as a necessary part of the whole. Kiener's own film, *Ixok-Woman* (1990), is an early attempt to achieve such a 'transcultural montage'. It portrays the Guatemalan actress and dancer Carmen Samayoa in her European exile. As critical intellectuals, Carmen and her partner Edgar Flores were threatened by a paramilitary organisation during the Guatemalan Civil War and had to flee their country. The film follows them touring Germany and Austria with a performance in which Carmen takes on the stage persona of a Guatemalan peasant woman who becomes a victim of the violence inflicted on the indigenous population by the military regime. Whilst filming, Kiener was confronted with the challenge to deal with the multiple absences in Carmen's life. Accompanying her in Europe, she found it difficult to find scenes that conveyed Carmen's experience of exile as her personal background and the political context that made her flee lay elsewhere. Furthermore, Carmen's pantomime performance also played with absences, evoking a multiplicity of people and situations on a stage almost devoid of props and stage design. To fill these voids, Kiener decided that she had to film in Guatemala. As it was too dangerous for Carmen to return, Kiener sought to document scenes that expressed the situation there, that would tie into the film's overarching narrative. She then connected both realities in a style of editing Gilles Deleuze describes as 'false continuity' (1986: 28). For Deleuze, classical (traditional or mainstream) cinema is determined by the continuity of movement. In what he calls 'movement image cinema', editing serves to establish an uninterrupted progression of actions and reactions in a plausible cinematic space. In *Ixok-Woman*, however, Kiener frequently joints two different geographical spaces, thereby creating an abstract transnational space. In one scene, for example, we see Carmen on the passenger seat of the ramshackle bus in which she and Edgar tour Germany. She is looking out of the window onto the rain-soaked highway. With the next shot, however, we are suddenly transported to a Guatemalan country lane where a blue truck passes from the right of frame. The following shot, then, in a similar graphic composition, brings us back to the rainy German expressway. This works seamlessly as these shots are sutured according to the editing convention of the so-called eye-line match. As we have seen Carmen look out of the window, we accept the following shot as her point of view.[19] False continuity editing is used here to hint at the important presence of another reality, in this case the homeland longingly remembered by a person in exile. Thus, Kiener is able to include what Deleuze calls the 'virtual' aspects of a given reality: the memories and imaginations of her protagonist, as well as her feeling of deterritorialisation.[20] This style of editing culminates in a harrowing montage sequence that expresses the political reality of Guatemala's Civil War, a situation that produced a multitude of exiles and absentees (all those who have been kidnapped, killed or disappeared). It unfolds by interweaving Carmen's stage performance with authentic documentary material. Alone on an empty stage, dimly lit in red, Carmen performs how a village raid by the military forces turns into a massacre, intercut with footage Kiener filmed in a training camp of the Guatemalan army. Thus, following Carmen's fearful gaze towards the approaching soldiers on stage, we actually see them leaving their concealed position and storming into a clearing. With the next shot, we are back on Carmen as she acts out the rape of the village women by the soldiers. Then, in a fast-cut alternation of images, we see the Guatemalan troops practicing shooting and a disquieting dance by Carmen, in which her body trembles as if shattered by the impact of their bullets. This cinematic representation of action and reaction, cause and effect is entirely constructed; yet it works. In both actions the counterpart is absent: the enemies in the soldiers' training operation are only imagined, as is the military presence in Carmen's performance. It is the combination of these images that creates the truth of the sequence; a 'poetic truth' of a different epistemological order that transcends actual time and exact place (Kiener 2008: 407). It strongly evokes the context of the political violence that forced Carmen into exile without recourse to conventional realist means of representation, such as interviews or eyewitness accounts. Kiener's creative use of montage duly provides a powerful means to convey the spatial and temporal disruptions, the gaps that are so constitutive of the experience of exile.

However, the experience of absences for which Kiener sensitises us is not the only difficulty ethnographic filmmakers face when they seek to represent transnationalism. The complex interrelations of people and places and the simultaneity of global cultural processes constitute a vast field of invisibilities that can equally be addressed through the use of montage. As Christian Suhr and Rane Willerslev note, montage allows for viewing experiences that are multi-spatial and multitemporal. It offers a multiplication of perspectives on the filmic subject matter and, consequently, a mode of perception in which 'we find ourselves decentered in an infinite totality of views that no longer affords us the illusion of ourselves as the unique center of the world' (2012: 291). In this way, montage is a means for transcending the limitations of the micro perspective of situated observers and their subject-centered vision. Using this device can enable an enhanced perception of connections and causalities on the macro level of global structures. I will now focus on Ursula Biemann's piece *Sahara Chronicle* (2006–07) to illustrate this point. This work brilliantly orchestrates such a plurality of complementary or contrasting viewpoints to approach the complexity of a transnational migration system spanning from sub-Saharan Africa to the Maghreb countries. Biemann's cinematographic installation achieves such multi-perspectivity through a montage of multiple screens and projections in space. As a work of 'expanded cinema' (Rees *et al.* 2011), it not only poses a challenge to the linearity of conventional film, it also spatialises the viewing experience itself.

Fig. 19: The massacre sequence in *Ixok-Woman*.

THE CINEMATOGRAPHIC INSTALLATION AS NETWORK:
SAHARA CHRONICLE

Biemann's multi-screen installation was produced as a part of her artistic research project, *Maghreb Connection: Movements of Life Across North Africa*. The installation consists of twelve short videos that document the different nodes and pathways of a network that transports African trans-Sahara migrants towards Europe. Depending on the exhibition space, these videos are arranged on a variable number of wall-sized projections and monitors with accompanying headphones. The videos were shot during three fieldtrips to the major hubs and transit points along the main migration routes from West Africa to the Mediterranean. All of these documents describe states of transit and forms of movement. One video is set at a bus terminal in Agadez, Niger, where former Tuareg rebels now organise transportation through the desert on overcrowded four-wheel-drive trucks. Another video follows the iron ore train from the mines of Zouerate to Nouadhibou. For the migrants, its tracks also mark the route to the coast of Mauritania where vessels depart to the Spanish Canary Islands. We watch reconstructions of surveillance imagery taken by Moroccan desert drones, encounter military patrols in the no-man's-land between Algeria and Morocco, witness haunting scenes from a deportation prison in Laayoune, Western Sahara. We encounter Sid'Ahmed Ould Abeid, the president of Nouadhibou's Fisheries Federation, who describes how the unregulated over-fishing practiced by European companies near the West African coast has had devastating effects on the local economies. Politically backed by EU pressure to increase fishing contracts, this constitutes one of the reasons for the mass emigration of young Africans. Abeid's interview relates to another video showing visceral images of the working conditions in an octopus processing plant. Each video takes up a different angle on the complexly interwoven modalities of the migration system, both from within the human observer perspective (as in the material shot by Biemann with her handheld camera) and outside of it (as, for example, in the desert drone footage). The individual films not only centre on the subjects involved in this form of mobility but also describe the politics of containment opposing it. Thus, the installation charts a fragmentary diagram of interrelations. For the spectator in the exhibition space, there is no preconceived route through the material. Rather, the possible narrative paths are constantly shifting as the videos that are played simultaneously differ in length and thus loop at different points in time. One video, for example, is shot in a uranium mine in Arlit, Niger. This mine brought a short-lived prosperity and international influx to the town before the prices of uranium collapsed after the end of the Cold War. This description of the rise and downfall of a local economy connects to a video interview with a Tuareg ex-rebel leader that reveals that the Niger state systematically excluded the Tuareg from the jobs created around the mine. Consequently the Tuareg began to take up the business of migrant trafficking through the Sahara. Yet by association it also connects to the footage of the iron ore railway line that is operated by the Mauritanian Mining Company. This route has now also become a new fugitive passage for migrants heading towards the Canary Islands. This cluster of videos thus exposes the intimate relation between the infrastructure of local economies and the establishment of new migration routes.

Sahara Chronicle maps a vast geopolitical space and allows its audience the perception of an extensive transnational system. It makes clear that contemporary migration can no longer be thought of in the simple bipolarity of 'sending' and 'receiving' countries but rather has to be understood in terms of 'multi-layered, multi-sited transnational social fields' (Levitt and Glick Schiller 2004: 1003). In many ways, the work's complex spatial structure mirrors the multi-nodal migration network itself. In their physical arrangement in space, the multiple screens all resonate with or against each other, thereby suggesting connectivity and entanglement. Hence, Biemann's installation gives aesthetic form to anthropological research designs that are constructed around 'chains, paths, threads, conjunctions, or juxtapositions of locations' (Marcus 1995: 105). In this way it can be seen as a representational analogue for the 'flow', 'scape', and 'network' concepts of contemporary cultural theory (for example, see Appadurai 1996; Hannerz 1996; Clifford 1997; Castells 2000a, 2000b, 2004; Urry 2003), notions that are part and parcel of a 'new mobilities paradigm' (Sheller and Urry 2006) in social science that seeks to rethink culture through the prism of movements and interconnections. To achieve this, however, Biemann goes beyond the forms of sequential montage I have discussed so far as she presents a form of 'spatial montage' (Manovich 2001: 322ff) instead. This practice transcends the possibilities of linear media like film or text that can only arrange their material in temporal succession. Her work, in contrast, allows the viewers to explore

Fig. 20: *Sahara Chronicle* installation view. Kunstmuseum Bern 2011.

connections between multiple locales, viewpoints and points in time as they are presented to them *simultaneously* on different screens. Accordingly, as Marcus has called for, her installation is able to render visible transcultural processes that occur 'in parallel, separate but simultaneous worlds' (1994: 40).

In Biemann's installation, it is ultimately upon the spectator to link local practices to political processes, economic conditions to legal frameworks, historical legacy to individual decisions, sensuous detail to abstract analysis. Large-scale political processes are thus made understandable in their effects on the individuals and their lifeworld. Relating these disparate pieces becomes an actual bodily activity that is, as I will discuss at the end of this chapter, deeply meaningful with regards to its ethnographic content. However, before I thoroughly explore the viewer's physical and perceptive engagement with such forms of ethnographic exhibition practice, I will return to the changing concept of space and place that grounds present-day studies of mobility and transnationalism.

RE-EVALUATING PLACE

The current orientation towards mobility and transnational processes has effectively overturned some all-too static conceptions of cultures as coherent 'wholes' within anthropology and also widespread 'methodological nationalism' within the social sciences (see Amelina *et al.* 2012). Yet the 'nomadic metaphysics' of contemporary theorising (see Cresswell 2002) that values the routes of the migrant or traveller over the roots of located identities also has its analytical shortcomings. The emphatic focus on movements, paths, nodes and networks and the obsession with relationality and connectivity only allows for a cursory understanding of space and, moreover, underestimates the significance of place. If places are only examined for their interconnectedness, this profoundly marginalises the theorisation of their particularity, depth and history as lifeworld and thereby the actual strength and primary context of committed anthropological research. Therefore, we have to develop a timely understanding of space and place; one that goes beyond both the sedentarist concept of place as a mere 'container for culture' or exclusive focus on flows and networks that bring solely the global dimension into view. The abstraction of such a systemic perspective neglects individual actors and their practices and is thus unable to describe how global mobility is emplaced, how it thoroughly affects concrete places. As Peter Jackson, Phillip Crang and Claire Dwyer (2004) argue, space and place have to be seen as constitutive of transnationality. Alex Rivera's video *The Sixth Section* (2003), for example, explores the intimate links between the post-industrial suburb of Newburgh, New York and the tiny Mexican desert village of Boquerón, Puebla state, two marginal places that, however, are connected by a long-standing migration circuit. Rivera portrays a community of Mexican migrants, almost all of them undocumented, who work in upstate New York yet also try to support their hometown over three thousand miles to the south. The men have formed an organisation called 'Grupo Unión' that raises money in the form of small but weekly donations from each of its members in New York as well as from their wider network. With this money, they seek to rebuild the place that they have left behind and aspire to create positive change. Over the years, the group's donations have brought a kitchen for the kindergarten, a basketball court, an ambulance car and even a new-built baseball stadium to Boquerón. The inhabitants of the village in return send videos to the group that document the progress of their building projects or show the ritual blessing of their gifts. Rivera's formally inventive film is a wild montage of such home video footage, archival material and digital animations that reveals how the group members utilise the Internet, video letters and mobile phones to maintain active roles in their place of origin. The migrants thus are absent yet present at the same time. Like quantum particles, they exist in two places at once (see Davis 2001: 93f). Rivera finds compelling images for the simultaneity of their transnational existence, for example, when he uses digital animation to smoothly morph the image background to seamlessly transfer his protagonists from Newburgh's winter streets to the dusty roads of Boquerón, or from their workplace in a restaurant kitchen to their hometown's corn fields without a single cut. Grupo Unión is one of at least a thousand of such 'hometown associations' formed by Mexican migrants in the US. *The Sixth Section* also documents how these

Fig. 21: The use of digital morphing to convey the experience of transnational existence in *The Sixth Section*.

groups start to become a major influence on Mexico's politics and economics as their remittances often create local infrastructures that the state is unable to provide. The film concludes with a visit by the governor of Puebla state to the group, during which he promises a paved highway to Boquerón that would link the village also physically closer to the country and the rest of the world, a connection the group has long since already established. The title of the film also confirms this. It refers to the five districts or 'sections' of which Boquerón consists. The villagers now consider Newburgh to be the 'sixth section' of the town. Thus, these faraway places are now connected by a transnational circuit of solidarity, and they mutually affect each other.[21]

The evolution of such transnational social forms creates spaces that are 'complex, multidimensional, and multiply inhabited' (Jackson *et al.* 2004: 3). Yet global mobility has not yet transcended space, and its flows are not as smooth and frictionless as some of the more celebratory studies within the 'new mobilities paradigm' might infer. Contemporary reality is not as borderless and deterritorialised as the frequently elite ideology of transnationalism would make us believe. Distance and borders still matter; to be connected without problem across the globe is therefore a privilege of the few. As Rivera's video also reveals, some members of the Grupo Unión risked their economical existence in the US when they decided to visit their hometown for the inauguration of the baseball stadium they donated without having papers to legally cross the border. Accordingly, Nina Glick Schiller and Noel Salazar distinguish different 'regimes of mobility' in order to explore 'the relationships between the privileged movements of some and the co-dependent but stigmatized and forbidden movement, migration and interconnection of the poor, powerless and exploited' (2013: 188). They shed light on the entrapments that constitute the flipside of global mobility. Asylum seekers are often subject to settlement restrictions (as they are stipulated, for example, in the German asylum laws). 'Illegals' who live and work undocumented may have to spend all their free time confined to their living spaces to avoid deportation; and the furtive journeys of those who attempt to cross borders most often involve multiple stopovers and detours. Hence, the current mobility regime creates new spatial configurations and transforms actual places. One might think, for example, of transitory spaces like the provisional camps that trans-Sahara migrants have set up in the mountains outside of Melilla and Ceuta, of spaces of exclusion like detention centres, or of those very particular places that have become major transportation hubs along the different migration routes towards or within Europe, like Agadez in Niger, Nouadhibou in Mauretania or Calais in France.

The new significance of place for the understanding of contemporary migration becomes particularly obvious when we consider the changing role of borders. European borders have ceased to be mere border*lines*, abstract demarcations that separate clearly marked nation-states. Rather, these borders have become spatialised. They extend to the outside as well as to the inside. The European border control agency, FRONTEX, frequently stops migrant vessels in the Mediterranean long before they come even close to European territorial waters. Bilateral agreements between Italy and Tunisia and Libya have allowed a European nation-state to carry out surveillance on the North African coast and to train local coast guards. In Gaddafi's Libya, Italy even funded detention and repatriation programmes for irregular migrants. Likewise, inside the EU, border controls are increasingly exercised deep within the territory; at airports, checkpoints or in random passport controls within major cities. As Eyal Weizman notes:

> The linear border, a cartographic imaginary inherited from the military and political spatiality of the nation-state , has splintered into a multitude of temporary, transportable, deployable and removable border synonyms – separation walls, barriers, blockades closures, road blocks, check points, sterile areas, special security zones, closed military areas and killing zones – that shrink and expand the territory at will. [...] The dynamic morphology of these spaces resembles an incessant sea dotted with multiplying archipelagos of externally alienated and internally homogenous ethnonational enclaves under a blanket of aerial surveillance. In this unique territorial ecosystem, various other zones – those of political piracy, of 'humanitarian' crisis, of barbaric violence, of full citizenship, 'weak citizenship', or no citizenship at all – exist adjacent to, within or over each other. (Quoted in Godfrey *et al.* 2010)

Thus, the European mobility regime creates border*lands*, large transitory spaces in which particular places are transformed into provisionary waiting zones, excluding and confining migrants at the same time. These transient places, however, do not appear by chance; they are not devoid of history. As my film fieldwork in Melilla and the Comoros Islands made clear, their specific status often dates back to colonial times and their social spaces are shaped by centuries of transnational relationships. We therefore need a theoretical perspective that is sensitive to both the traces of the past and the movements of the present in order to explore how both affect each other.

PLACES IN TRANSITION

Places are, as Tim Cresswell points out, 'never complete, finished or bounded but are always becoming – in process' (2002: 20). This dynamic, however, is difficult to explore with the methodological toolkit of multi-sited ethnography. Marcus's imperative of 'tracking' a particular object of study (be it an actor, a symbol or an idea) will certainly reveal its dynamism, yet it produces only static snapshots of the multiple sites that are involved. What changes occur in the migrants' home villages after they have left? How does their emigration affect those who are left behind? And don't we have to understand these changes as an important part of the phenomenon of 'migration' even though no further movement is involved? To arrive at a theoretical perspective that is attentive to the transformative qualities of places, it is useful to take a look at the recent rethinking of place in contemporary geography. In what has inaugurated a 'spatial turn' in the wider fields of social science, cultural geographer Edward Soja (1996) has applied theories of social practice to describe space and place as lived and inhabited. For Soja, space has no meaning by itself and therefore cannot be understood as distinct from the social sphere. Drawing upon the work of Henri Lefebvre (1991), who analysed space as a product of complex social construction, he seeks to overcome the binary opposition between objective (measurable, or cartographic) and subjective (perceived, or imagined) space. Rather, his notion of 'thirdspace' understands space as practiced and performed. For this reason, Soja's work provides the theoretical groundwork for a much-needed exploration of the politics of space and place, for as Margaret Rodman notes, we cannot understand place without emphasising 'the agency of individuals and of forces beyond individual control' (2003: 205). In this vein, Doreen Massey has offered a groundbreaking work that is essential for an understanding of the spatial in political terms. Like Soja and Lefebvre, she seeks to overcome the 'taming' conceptualisations of space as static, permanent and closed. Instead, her work is based on three intertwined premises:

> Space is always the product of interrelations and interactions.
> Space provides a sphere of possible multiplicity and of coexisting heterogeneity.
> Space is always under construction, always in the process of being (re-)made (2005: 9).

Massey understands places as 'integrations of space and time, as *spatio-temporal events*' (2005: 130). They are constituted by both what happens inside of them *and* by their relations to the outside, to other locations, actors or things. Hers is a progressive, radically open sense of place; one that challenges not only essentialist concepts of place as circumscribed and settled but equally those overly abstract notions of global flows and movements that are devoid of social content and thus make place all but disappear. She sees places as constellations of trajectories, as intersections in the meshwork of global relations, as 'articulations of the wider power-geometries of space' (ibid.); therefore their 'thrown-together-ness', their multiplicity and changing nature demand negotiation. As we cannot assume any pre-given coherence, community or collective identity that can be ascribed to them, they pose a political challenge (2005: 141). A politics of place accordingly has to consider internal and external relations, processes of inclusion and exclusion, the local context and the global dimension. Hence, space and place constitute the very ground of the political because it is in place where we engage with the question of coexistence.

Massey's complex understanding of place as relational and processual has informed all three cinematic works that constitute the practical part of this project. As discussed in chapter two, *Tell Me When…* explores how the Spanish exclave of Melilla is transformed not only by the individual trajectories of migrants for whom the city constitutes a transit space on their way to the EU, but also by the politics of confinement supposed to decelerate their unregulated mobility. In the remainder of the present chapter, I will describe how my video installation *A Tale of Two Islands* charts the postcolonial space encompassing the French island of Mayotte and its African sister island Anjouan and how it relates the particularity of these local lifeworlds to a larger transnational scale.

For centuries, both Melilla and the Comoros lay at the crossroads of transnational flows: Melilla at the intersection between Africa and Europe, the Comoros at the centre of a large transcultural network spanning the Indian Ocean and the French métropole. *Intimate Distance*, the trilogy's conclusion, then extends the perspective to the virtual space of Skype and explores how social media constitute transnational spaces. While it explicitly focuses on new technologies of instantaneous communication, it refutes the annihilation of space, the 'time-space compression' that often is celebrated in economic and technological narratives of globalisation. Instead, my protagonists are painfully aware of the distance that separates them from their beloved. As I will discuss in the next chapter, the film, as much as it shows the potentialities of virtual co-presence over spatial distance, also reveals the limits of such mediated proximity. It is a reflection on what the medium does and does not convey. Far from transcending space, webcam-based communication seems to give particular importance to the domestic spaces in front of the camera. In the social interactions of all my protagonists, the spatial environment captured by the webcam feed became a kind of stage that was frequently played with, asked about and commented on.

THE MATERIALITY OF PLACE

At the end of the previous chapter, I discussed how phenomenology might offer a useful approach to the study of place and the particular emplacement of individuals. Following the work of Sarah Pink (2009), I explored how a deep, phenomenological understanding of place can reveal how the local, in its lived immediacy, is both inscribed with history and influenced by global processes. In the description of my film fieldwork in Melilla, I have discussed how film provides access to the concrete materiality of places as well as to actors' individual strategies of place-making and performing place. There I described how an *in situ* and insistent style of filmmaking that is attentive to the slow unfolding of events in front of the camera might offer the spectator a phenomenological engagement with the particularities of a given lifeworld. Therefore, we should not readily discard the cinematic techniques that invite this kind of viewing experience. Such a sense of the lived experience of place is, for example, not provided by Kiener's disruptive montage spaces that demand a reflexive mode of spectatorship and are not 'inhabitable' in a phenomenological sense.[22] Her dismissal of the techniques of observational filmmaking, such as long takes and extended sequences, might consequently deprive us of a cinematic methodology that is suitable for the investigation of the (often subtle) transformations that occur in place.

An exemplary work that explores such a complex metamorphosis of space, materiality and identities is Aryo Danusiri's *The Fold* (2011). It proves that the aesthetic of the long take does not necessarily produce the impression of coherence and stasis, as Kiener's critique implies. Filmed in the Masjid Manhattan, a basement mosque in downtown New York that is frequented by migrants from Asia, Africa and the Middle East, *The Fold* observes the fluid transitions between sacred and secular space. Consisting only of one uninterrupted long shot, the video begins with a religious service. Throughout the whole event, the camera remains in a fixed position at a high angle covering almost everything of the room. After the prayer, however, we witness how the space slowly begins to transform. The blue mats that meticulously covered the floor on which the men were praying (and which they only dared to enter with their bare feet) are folded together one after the other then stored away. At the end of the 12-minute-long sequence shot, a ping-pong table is set up on the red vinyl flooring of

Fig. 22: The smooth transition from sacred to secular space in *The Fold*.

the basement and the mosque has then changed back into a community centre. Danusiri thus shows how space is a product of performance. There is nothing in-trinsically sacred or profane about this place. Such qualities are only constituted by collective acts of worship or leisure.

For the members of the Masjid Manhattan, however, the mobility of their mosque is an unwelcome necessity. Following the termination of the lease for their original space (after almost four decades) by the new owner of that build-ing, it proved to be almost impossible to find a new location. In the aftermath of the 9/11 attacks, the mosque's committee was confronted with doubt and suspicion everywhere. Eventually, the community was drawn into the heated discussions around the 'Ground Zero Mosque' in which the appropriateness of building an Islamic centre near the World Trade Center site was publicly disputed. Since then, the mosque has been located in the multi-functional base-ment owned by the Asian-American Cultural Center of Tribeca that rents out the space in time units of two-hours. Thus, the spatial transformation Danusiri's video investigates points to wider political processes such as the exclusion of minority groups and the negotiation of coexistence in the multicultural and multi-religious city.

SHIFTING PERSPECTIVES: MAKING *A TALE OF TWO ISLANDS*

To transfer the theoretical considerations of this chapter into cinematic practice, I will discuss how the analytical perspectives on space and place I have presented here have informed my own approach to conceiving my two-screen video instal-lation *A Tale of Two Islands*. What I wanted to achieve with this work was a bifocal perspective, equally 'zooming in' on the grounded reality of places in their particularity and 'zooming out' to bring their interrelatedness on a transnational scale into focus. Aesthetically, this approach combines the long take aesthetics of observational film with the reflexive techniques of constructive montage. Hence, it offers a vantage point that 'cross-cut(s) dichotomies such as the "local" or the "global", the "lifeworld" and the "system"' (Marcus 1995: 95).

As already mentioned, *A Tale of Two Islands* investigates a border zone quite far removed from geographical Europe; the border separating two of the Comoros Islands in the Indian Ocean. On 31 March 2011 the small island of Mayotte officially received the status as the 101st department of France; on 1 January 2014 it also became a full part of the European Union as one of its 'outermost regions' (the political term for a grouping of territories located at a great distance from the continent). Thus, Mayotte is politically separate from Anjouan, its African sister island belonging to the Union of the Comoros. For a long time both islands were part of the French colonial empire. In the wake of the African decolonisation movements of the 1970s, referendums were organised on the Comoros. While Anjouan declared its independence, the overwhelming majority in Mayotte voted to remain a part of France. This spectacular decision of the Mahorais (the inhabitants of Mayotte) can only be understood with regard to the fact that Mayotte, as the 'oldest daughter of France' (the first of the islands to be colonised), had always profited most from the presence of the Colonial administration that employed many islanders and stimulated economical activity (see Boisadam 2009: 45). Since the referendum, Mayotte benefits to an even greater degree from French investments into its infrastructure, education and health system. A prospering middle class exists who work in administrative jobs; the supermarkets are full of imported goods from metropolitan France. Meanwhile, Anjouan looks back onto a history full of *coups d'états*, political turmoil and economic depression. Because of these severe economic imbalances, many Anjouanais try to reach their neighbouring island in night crossings with small motorboats; so called *kwassas*. France has reacted to these migratory movements with a fortification of the border that separates both islands. The citizens of the Union of the Comoros now require a visa to enter Mayotte and all border control activities have been greatly expanded both in terms of the manpower and technical equipment available to the French border police. The illegalisation of an inter-insular circulation that was lived for generations in the form of familial ties, trading and seasonal labour migration has also made these crossings much more dangerous. The small (and often hazardously overcrowded) boats that try to make the forty-mile clandestine journey at night consequently often become the victims of rough seas or the sharp coral reefs that surround Mayotte (see Muenger 2011: 46). Despite these dangers, a large group of people is on the move between both islands. According to official statistics, forty per cent of Mayotte's population does not posses French citizenship (see INSEE 2010: 34). The French border police react to the steady influx of migrants not only with the enforcement of border controls, but also with an uncompromising deportation practice. In 2010 alone, more than 24,000 people were arrested and deported from Mayotte, almost ten per cent of the island's total population (see World Policy Institute 2011). The motivation behind these absurd numbers, however, transcends the level of local politics. They are a cheap and convenient way for the Metropolitan government to polish their statistics and demonstrate a hard take on 'illegal' migration from Africa that is very popular within the EU (see Muenger 2011: 54f). The postcolonial space encompassing both islands is, hence, marked by a complex historical situation and ties into larger political processes, such as the formation of the European border regime (see Tsianos and Karakayali 2010). While my aim was to map the islands' migratory system, I wanted to do so by focusing on its nodes and filling them with social content, history and lived practice. I was interested in how the islands' migratory culture transformed actual places; how it was acted out within them.

THE NODES OF THE SYSTEM

At an early stage of fieldwork, Paola Calvo, my camerawoman, and I encountered two particular places that very concretely 'told the whole story'. They not only revealed the postcolonial inequalities between the islands, but also the daily reality of illegalised migration and the French politics of deportation. It is these places we chose as settings for the two synchronous films that make up the installation. Both places are located within major port areas: in Dzaoudzi, the old colonial capital of Mayotte, and in Anjouan's capital Mutsamudu. Both sites are connected by the only means of public transport operating between the islands, the ferry Maria Galanta, which provides a twice-weekly service. The first of these two places is actually nothing more than a metal-grilled window that we discovered in Mayotte's Dzaoudzi harbour. Almost every afternoon we saw large crowds of people gathering at this place, chatting and seemingly waiting for something. Talking to some of the bystanders, we learned that they were the friends and relatives of Comorians who were about to be deported to Anjouan and that they came to see them off and, if possible, give them some money. Through the window bars, they pointed to a ferry waiting at the landing stage, the Princesse Caroline, apparently the vessel the French use for the deportations. Shortly after these conversations, an old French city bus, accompanied by police cars, arrived at the place. We were told that this bus brought the deportees from the detention centre in Pamandzi to the ferry. As soon as the deportees departed from the bus, the waiting group came to life. Some waved and shouted to get the attention of their kin, while others bargained through the grills with local members of the boat crew so they would hand over letters or some notes to the involuntary passengers. Through their relatives, we heard some of the deportees' stories. Many of them had lived for quite some time on the island and found work as day labourers in farms or as craftspeople, all jobs the members of Mayotte's middle-class now refuse to take on.[23] They all became the victims of the infamous raids the French police conduct at work places, or openly in the streets and public spaces in order to hunt down the *sans papiers*. Others had been caught at sea before even arriving on the island. For many of them, it was the second or even third deportation from Mayotte.

When we came back the next morning, the scene had somehow changed. This time, the window was open and served as the ticket counter and baggage drop-off for the Maria Galanta, the regular ferry to Anjouan. The place was jam-packed with local tourists, mostly Mahorais visiting their families on the neighbouring island. All passengers carried absurd amounts of luggage. We spotted TV sets, piles of clothing and huge cans of milk powder. We were told that these items were all meant for relatives living on Anjouan, where these kinds of goods were not so readily available. With 150 pounds of baggage allowance allocated to each ticket, many Mahorais came to the counter just to find a passenger willing take their parcels along, in the hope it would reach their kin. The place had thus transformed into a giant post office, channeling the support for the economically weak sister island. When we returned a few hours later, the Maria Galanta had still not embarked, yet, again, we saw a crowd of people waiting in front of the now barred window. At this very moment, the familiar city bus appeared on the scene and we learned that the government buys all the unoccupied seats on the tourist boat to fill them with deportees. Intrigued by the close proximity between tourism and deportation, support and separation, we decided to make this place the focus of the work.

When we came back with a camera on the next day, we decided that an observational approach would be most suitable for establishing these complex transformations on film. We chatted with the people waiting for the next deportation and asked for the permission to film some wide shots. As we returned the following days, many people soon heard about us and told us about their experiences with the local police. We also gained the confidence of some of the members of the boat crew and the port security, who were in a conflicted position. On the one hand, they had to oversee the deportations, while on the other they also had relatives in Anjouan and, like most Mahorais, knew many illegal immigrants on the island. In this way, they were the gatekeepers acting between the deportees and their relatives. Whenever people allowed us, we filmed these interactions and their conversations in front of the window. After observing the ever-repeating spectacle of deportation for a couple of days, we also began to film what happened behind the window bars: the boarding of the regular travellers, the arrival of the bus from the detention centre, the embarking of the migrants, the departure of the ferry. We documented this recurring course of events with a telephoto lens in order to use these shots in editing as POVs, conveying the perspective of the waiting people. On one occasion we witnessed a border police operation. As we were filming, a police boat returned with the exhausted passengers of a *kwassa* who, in plain view of the audience behind the window, were arrested on the spot. This rather unspectacular metal-grilled window thus became the site of fascinating transformations and practices. For us, it not only symbolised the political separation between the islands, it also became an aesthetic means that helped us link the screening situation in the exhibition space to the actual place we portrayed. Alternating between the wider shots of the waiting relatives and the subjective long lens shots of the deportations, we

Fig. 23: A glance through the window bars in Mayotte's Dzaoudzi port.

could establish the window as a frame within the frame – a kind of screen or canvas that displayed the political drama.

When we continued our fieldwork on Anjouan, we looked out for a place that would mirror the experiences we found on Mayotte and that would lend itself to a 'thick depiction' of everyday life on the other side of the border. We came across such a place in a littered strip of beach right next to the harbour of Mutsamudu. From this spot, one can observe the ferries departing and arriving. Here there was a tree that offered protection from the burning sun and some

Fig. 24: The fishers' settlement near the harbour of Mutsamudu.

of the neighbours keep their livestock nearby. As in the rest of Mutsamudu, it constituted a stark contrast to the glossy colonial architecture around the port of Dzaoudzi. Here it seemed that nature has long since covered all the remains of the colonial era. Originally, we had heard rumours that some of the local fishermen would offer the night-time journey across the border from this part of the coast, but we soon found that people were too scared to give us more information, let alone film on such an occasion. We could, however, film the fishermen embark in the morning and return just before sunset and the conversations of the unemployed men who took a rest under the tree. They all had their opinions on local politics and the dangers and rewards of an illegal migration to Mayotte.

THE EXHIBITION SET-UP

Each film creates for itself a coherent cinematic space in the phenomenological tradition of observational ethnographic cinema and its aesthetics of long-take, deep-focus photography and extended shot lengths. They both situate the spectators within their respective settings by implicating them in the perspective of the subjects through the frequent use of POV shots and subjective framing. The constant viewing direction in both films is towards the maritime border: through the window grills in Dzaoudzi, onto the open sea in Mutsamudu. As an installation, both films are projected onto two opposing walls. The audience is thus virtually placed 'in-between' both lifeworlds, a viewing position that evokes the very border separating both islands. Corresponding to the demands of an exhibition, the films are structured as a loop, narrating the course of a single day, from sunrise to sunset to sunrise again. While the films do not present a progressing narration, they still follow a comprehensible temporal sequence. The spectators, therefore, are free to enter and leave the exhibition space at will and the work has no definitive beginning or end. The cycle of events unfolds simultaneously on both sides of the border. This circular narrative form corresponds not only very closely to the slow and ever-repeating rhythm of the daily activities in the port of Mutsamudu but, of course, also to the everyday drama caused by the French deportation policy on Mayotte. The simultaneity of the two projections makes it impossible to see both films at the same time. This inhibits the viewers' immersion in the work to some degree, but it also allows them to actively create their own editing by diverting their attention between the films. As in Biemann's *Sahara Chronicle*, the operation of montage as a means of 'saying "both … and", "neither … nor": North and South, here and there' (Kiener 2008: 397f) is installed into space. It is transferred into the mind of the spectators who physically perform the cross-cutting between both places by turning their heads. The exhibition set-up can therefore be described

Fig. 25: *A Tale of Two Islands* exhibition view. Courtesy: Kassel Documentary Film and Video Festival/Sven Heine.

as a 'contrapuntal system of montage' (a concept Demos [2013: xvi] borrows from Said's [1993] method of 'contrapuntal analysis'). It insists on the cultural and geographic proximity of both lifeworlds, not only exploring it in aesthetic terms, but also making it physically manifest in the exhibition space. Thus, it does not only invite the spectators to discover the invisible bonds that connect both islands, it also defies the politics of separation that divides the Comoros along the militarised borders between a Global North and a Global South. *A Tale of Two Islands* further presents such a bifocality of perspective in terms of scale: a micro perspective on the grounded reality of specific, lived situations and a macro perspective on a larger postcolonial space that is marked by political and economic inequality. Hence, it also allows the seamless shift between two differing modes of reception: an immersion into the situated viewpoints of the filmed subjects and a reflexive turn to the spectator, who has to put together the perceived fragments.

MOBILE SPECTATORS, MOBILE THOUGHTS

To conclude, I briefly want to discuss in what sense the bodily and spatial experiences offered by cinematographic installations such as Biemann's or my own are meaningful with regards to the social phenomena they portray. In *Sahara Chronicles*, the viewers become wanderers choosing between different trajectories. They follow the routes of a network, divert their attention between the different screens, and at times even get lost in a virtual form of displacement. In *A Tale of Two Islands*, they can compare two different yet interrelated lifeworlds by physically performing a kind of parallel editing. Thus, these installations demand a form of spectatorship that requires physical movement, the will to take up different viewpoints and the acceptance of the fact that they cannot be perceived from an Archimedean standpoint. Whenever I focus on one of the perspectives offered to me, I simultaneously miss out on the others. As the works leave me uninformed about their exact length and do not provide a clear beginning or end, they deliberately overstrain my perception. At times, however, they allow me to draw surprising connections between people, stories or places, associations, that might be exclusively my own. In this way, such installation art ultimately puts the spectator in-between two conflicting modes of viewing experience. On the one hand, it demands our first-hand presence in the exhibition space as a crucial component of the work. The particular screens still engage us in the situated form of spectatorship Sobchack and other phenomenologists describe, in which the projected film turns us to our senses; to our own subjectively lived bodies. On the other, the installation of multiple screens in space profoundly decentres our subjectivity. The multiplicity of simultaneous perspectives fragments our perception and induces a strong sense of disorientation. Therefore, as Claire Bishop notes, such work 'insists on our centred presence in order then to subject us to an experience of decentring' (2005: 130). One could draw a parallel here between this destabilising, fractured, physical form of reception and the contemporary experience of mobility. The migrant, as the Greek-German video artist, Angela Melitopoulos, and the Italian philosopher, Maurizio Lazzarato, state

lives simultaneously in many worlds but cannot reduce them to one. Each world has to be allowed to exist alongside the other. If worlds are placed against each other, or if their differences are transformed into oppositions, there is the risk of destruction. To avoid this destruction, it is worth observing the singular closely, to see how, at each moment, one detail can be linked to the next detail, one singularity to other singularities. One has to be able to transform an opposition into an adaptation, that is to say, through creation and innovation. Instead of simultaneously placing differences against each other, they can be alternated through the possibilities of mobility and then understood as consequences or rhythms. In this sense, there is a constant tendency to maintain mobility relations in migration, which means practising non-linear thinking, such as exists in the non-linear montage. (2006: 74)

In his famous essay, 'The Work of Art in the Age of Mechanical Reproduction' (1936), Walter Benjamin interpreted the tactile, shocking effects of cinematic montage as an exercise in perception that was utterly necessary for mastering life in the big cities, an initiation into mass-culture, opening up the viewer's mind to the modern world. In the same way, one could argue that the cinematographic installations I have presented here reproduce in the spectator the duality, contradictions and simultaneity of a deterritorialised existence (see Naficy 2012: 479). Accordingly, they require a mobility of thought that might provide the perfect state of mind to approach our globalised present in all its complexity, its transformations, disruptions and uncertainties. Not only do these works produce aesthetic effects that convey something of the contradictory aspects of the contemporary experience of mobility, they also allocate the recipient an active role in the work itself. Unlike written ethnographies, their geopolitical issues are not only represented but *presented*. As these works 'hinge upon connection, expressed in an almost intangible, emphatic moment' (Grimshaw and Ravetz 2009: 136), they make us present; that is, they insist on our physical, intellectual and empathetic presence as engaged observers.

CHAPTER FOUR

Migratory Times

I n this chapter, I will develop a notion of migration not only as a movement in space, but equally as a movement in time. I offer a phenomenological understanding of migration as an (often disturbing) experience of time; 'of time as multiple, heterogeneous – the time of haste and waiting; the time of movement and stagnation; the time of memory and of an unsettling, provisional present, with its pleasures and its violence' (Bal 2012: 211). Migrants often live simultaneously in many temporal worlds but cannot reduce them to one: the past of the motherland left behind, a present that is often precarious, and an uncertain future. Building upon phenomenological approaches within anthropology, I discuss how research into our research participants' temporal orientations can provide us with a rich account of the broad varieties of migrant experience. I further argue that these experiences also have a political significance: migration nowadays is increasingly also governed through time, for example by making enforced waiting time an instrument for the regulation of migratory movements. In a Deleuzian sense, images often crystallise such complex experiences of asynchronicity and temporal displacement. The migratory experience is further exemplary of the persistent presence of the past within the present. Drawing upon a number of recent film and video works by diasporic artists offering a performative approach to memory, I will discuss the role of images as objects of recollection. I contend that it is the concrete material presence of these works that evokes the remembrance of a homeland (that in some cases, is only an imagined entity). Yet as Gilles Deleuze (1989) argues, film cannot only represent (or relate to) time; it is the quintessential medium of time itself. For Deleuze, the advent of modern time-image cinema effectively reconstructs Kant's so-called Copernican Revolution in philosophy that freed time from its subordination to movement. His classification of different time-images thus forms the background for my exploration into the ways in which ethnographic film can present the temporal complexity that shapes our present age of migration.

TOWARDS AN ANTHROPOLOGY OF TIME EXPERIENCE

Time is an inescapable dimension of all facets of social experience and, therefore, has attracted much anthropological attention. However, as a theoretical problem, time has, as Nancy Munn notes, 'often been handmaiden to other anthropological frames and issues (political structures, descent, ritual, work, narrative, history, cosmology, etc., as well as, at another level, general theories of anthropological discourse) with which it is inextricably bound up' (1992: 93). Hence, many scholars have explored the local conception and measurement of time while paying little theoretical attention to its actual experience. In an era in which philosophers like William James, Edmund Husserl or Henri Bergson rigorously began to describe the inner, subjective dimensions of time (its 'motion' or 'flux', the temporal stream of consciousness and the workings of memory), Emile Durkheim and other founding figures of academic anthropology positioned time in the public realm of 'collective representations': as a product of culture, manifesting itself in words and actions in society. Durkheim aimed at an emic understanding of time; one that could be achieved by an analysis of the terms used to measure and describe it. Durkheim's advantage of 'social time' over the 'personal time of subjective consciousness' (Munn 1992: 95) has proven to be extremely influential within anthropology and has since inspired numerous ethnographic studies that describe (often outlandish) indigenous conceptions of time. By contrast, Alfred Gell, in his groundbreaking theoretical contribution to the subject, strongly argues against what he perceives as a prevailing temporal cultural relativism that asserts the existence of fundamentally different notions of time. He accuses authors like E. E. Evans-Pritchard, Claude Lévi-Strauss or Edmund Leach of engaging in unjustifiable metaphysical speculation when interpreting their research participants' temporal concepts. Gell sets out to demystify anthropological accounts of temporality stating that 'there is no fairyland where people experience time in a way that is markedly unlike the way in which we do ourselves, where there is no past, present and future, where time stands still or chases its own tail, or swings back and forth like a pendulum' (1992: 315). Gell's critique thus sheds light on what many anthropologists, in their obsession with different time worlds, routinely have failed to recognise: namely how much the meticulous study of our research participants' temporal orientations can tell us about their lived reality; their emplacement in particular lifeworlds.

As already noted in chapter two, Jason Throop and other phenomenologically-inspired anthropologists have developed intriguing concepts that recognise how much the modalities of human existence are embedded within ever-shifting horizons of temporality: 'Our existence as humans is temporally structured in such a way that our past experience is always retained in a present moment that is feeding forward to anticipate future horizons of experience. This includes the dynamic ways that individual actors shift between differing attitudes in the context of their engagements with their social and physical worlds' (Desjarlais and Throop 2011: 88). This anthropological research into the variable structures of temporal experience is deeply indebted to Husserl's phenomenology of time-consciousness with its understanding of time as dynamic and becoming. Husserl states that we experience time as a constant stream or flow, as a successive 'series of now points' (1991: 29) that arise and then immediately sink into pastness (a process he captured in the famous image of the 'comet's tail'). These faded moments, however, remain present in the scene of consciousness: as residues of the recent past (retentions), or as intentional acts of memory (recollections). Likewise, our perception also extends forward, either immediately in anticipation of the next arising moments of awareness (expectations, protentions) or, in a more reflective form, as imaginations, dreams or hopes. Our consciousness continually mediates between different tracks of awareness: the present moment of perception (containing immediate sensory impressions, retentions and protentions) as well as the actively recollected past and the imagined future. For this reason, there are different kinds of past and future time, and the subject relates to them in different ways. Husserl distinguishes them by their phenomenological status: retentions and protentions are not representations (images, or mental pictures) that stand in for something absent. Rather, they are a constitutive part of the perceptual process at any given moment: they are present in the now. As Merleau-Ponty puts it: 'I belong to my past and, through the constant interlocking of retentions, I preserve my oldest experiences, which means not some duplicate or image of them, but the experiences themselves, exactly as they were' (1962: 376). Only what once was present (as sense impression, retention or protention) can later become re-presented (*vergegenwärtigt*) through an act of recollection; that is, a memory. Our consciousness thus comprises a 'mazelike configuration of flows given inside each other: perception, empathy, memory, anticipation and fantasy creating a nested arrangement. We all inhabit many time zones simultaneously' (Birnbaum 2007: 135). We all know these forms of temporal synchronicity that phenomenology describes from our daily lives: when we watch a passing landscape out of the car window on our way to work and suddenly remember last night's dream, or when we imaginatively plan our next holiday while being trapped in a boring meeting. As these simple examples hopefully suggest (and as I will further argue in this chapter), this account of temporal experience is deeply cinematic.

What is of particular anthropological interest here is how a social actor's experience of self and world is profoundly influenced by their temporal orientation. Throop proposes to differentiate at least four different forms of temporal orientation:

> (1) an orientation to the present moment that consists of unfulfilled protentions as open anticipations toward an indeterminate future; (2) an explicit future orientation that consists of imaginal anticipations of a determinate future that are predicated upon residues of past experience that emerge, as [Cheryl] Mattingly points out (1998: 155), 'even in the midst of action'; (3) a retrospective glance that entails the plotting of beginnings, middles and ends over the already elapsed span of a delimited field of experience; and (4) the subjunctive casting of possible futures and even possible pasts, across the 'fluid space between a past and a future'. (2003: 234)

In what follows, I want to discuss how these temporal orientations shape the experiences of migration. Interestingly, Throop also notes that the particular methodologies that anthropologists make use of might have a severe influence on the data regarding the varieties of experience they attribute to participants in ethnographic fieldwork. He deems that a number of methods tend to privilege a certain temporal orientation, and therefore also tend to privilege a certain aspect of experience. Many anthropological methods focus explicitly on retrospective assessment and so might not be able to account for the entire range of the various articulations of experience. Interviews, questionnaires and other forms of enquiry privilege a recollective production of meaning and, for this reason, 'depend upon those explicit reflective processes that *tend* to give coherence and definite form to experience' (2003: 235). Recall here my critique (put forth in chapter two) of Michael Jackson's biographical approach that strongly depends on the mediation of language and the coherence of narration. Throop therefore advocates filming as a method for the systematic observation of everyday interaction that allows focus upon 'capturing the often pre-reflective, real-time unfolding of social action' (ibid.). My point here, however, is that film gives access to pre-reflective and immediate sensations or experiences (the lived momentum of cinema Sobchack describes) yet also importantly embodies the complex workings of time: the operation of memory and the persistence of the past within the present.

MIGRATION AS A TEMPORAL EXPERIENCE

In what ways is the migrant experience structured by a particular attention to the future, an immersion into the past, or the contingencies of the present? What aspects of migration, which circumstances, influence these temporal orientations?

Some recent phenomenological accounts of 'illegal' high-risk migration from Africa to Europe have highlighted these issues with regard to the different stages of the migration process. Henrik Vigh's (2009) study among would-be migrants in Guinea Bissau, and Hans Lucht's (2011) chronicle of the lives of a group of fishermen from Ghana who took the long and dangerous journey to Southern Italy, both point to the ways in which 'migration becomes a technology of the imagination, as an act through which people come to imagine better lives in other times or places as well as the tragic consequences of this imaginary bridging of severed points' (Vigh 2009: 94). Both studies are based on multi-sited fieldwork, and hence are able to take into account the changing temporal orientations of their migrating research participants: Vigh's exploration of imagined migration and migrant imaginaries further traces the realisation of these hopes in the streets of Lisbon, while Lucht moves in a reverse chronology of events from Naples to Senya Beraku in the Volta region, where he immerses himself in the lifeworlds of those left behind. Both Lucht and Vigh show how the social imaginary of their research participants is strongly influenced by the global spread of media imagery. New technologies of communication serve as constant 'reminders of the existence of better places and times' (2009: 103) for the young Bissauians and trigger their imagination. These mediated images shed light on the miseries of their home and the possibilities that can be found abroad. In a similar vein, Lucht explains his research participants' obsession with the latest mobile phones with their power as a 'quintessential symbol of having connections to the world' (2011: 88), while the everyday experience of their users is that of a 'global disconnect' (see Ferguson 2002).[24] The would-be migrants Vigh encountered thus project all their hopes and put all their energies into an imagined future elsewhere that in turn shapes the experience of their present lives in Bissau. Like the North African 'bruleurs',[25] they are filled with a burning desire so strong that they disregard their existence in the present. Unfortunately however, even for those who make it to Europe, a worthy existence often remains in continuous distance. Being confronted with the hardship of an 'illegal' existence, badly paid jobs in Europe's black labour market and often blatant racism, the struggle to get into Europe for many migrants does not pay off. As one of Vigh's research participants phrased it: 'same shit, different continent' (2009: 104). While having moved spatially, they remain stuck socially. Their dreams and imaginations thus begin to move again: quite often this time into a different direction, towards an orientation to the past.

In a brief but unsettling essay, Ranajit Guha (2011) reflects upon the 'temporal maladjustment' that even the 'successful' migrant experiences. Guha painfully describes the existential crises that arise from the migrants' attempts to find a foothold in the present of their host societies, while at the same time they rapidly lose all communitarian links to the former home. Belonging, for Guha, is foremost a temporal problem: it is 'nothing other than temporality acted upon and thought – and generally speaking, lived as being with others in shared time' (2011: 4). The migrants' dilemma is that they do not yet have a mutual past to relate to with their new neighbours, and neither can they share a common present with the communities from where they originate. In this way they have lost the living present, what amounts 'to a loss of the world in which the migrant has had his own identity forged' (ibid.). Guha's deeply personal account of a 'shared yet unequal heterogeneous present' (Mathur 2011: ix) explains why so many migrants, alienated and excluded from the host community, now choose to install themselves in the past. As Michael Samers notes, many migrants live with a 'permanent sense of the temporary' and a 'temporary sense of the permanent' (2009: 10) as they keep alive the 'myth of return'. As I now want to discuss further, images (be it old photographs, films or home-movies) often play a crucial role in this production of nostalgia and memory, in the ways people immerse themselves in a recollected past.

MEDIATED MEMORIES

A video that strongly expresses migration as an 'out-of-synch'-experience (see Hernández-Navarro 2012) is Mona Hatoum's *Measures of Distance*, a work discussed in chapter two. To recall, Hatoum composes her video from the main source material of several still photographs she took of her naked mother during a visit to Beirut in the midst of the Lebanese civil war. Like many other migrants, Hatoum treasures these photos as 'recollection objects' (Marks 2000: 81) that call up memories of her absent relatives, embodying a common past that is lost. Upon these still photographs, Hatoum stacks other layers: the Arabic script of her mother's letters, her own voice slowly reading these letters in English translation, conversations between mother and daughter recorded at the parents' house. As a result, her work does not follow a logic of linear narrative but one of superimposition and temporal polyphony, as each of these different layers conveys a different temporality, its own temporal flow. The voices and images of the past are contemplated in the present. The photographs of Hatoum's mother thus become the fetish objects of a longed-for past. Commenting on its ontological status, Vivian Sobchack describes how the photograph

> in its conquest of temporality and its conversion of time's dynamism into a static and essential moment ... constructs a space one can hold and look at, but in its conversion to an object to behold that space becomes paradoxically thin, insubstantial, and opaque. It keeps the lived body out even as it

> may imaginatively catalyze – in the parallel but dynamically temporalized
> space of memory or desire – an animated drama. (2004: 144)

While a photograph refers to, and in fact represents, an experience that once was real, it cannot incorporate its present, it cannot be inhabited. It may fix, objectify and thus preserve a moment, yet it is irrevocably filled 'with loss, with pastness, and with death, its meanings and value intimately bound within the structure and aesthetic and ethical investments of nostalgia' (2004: 146). In *Measures of Distance*, however, the photographs of Hatoum's mother are constantly blurred into one another, and in this way become animated in the form of what Sobchack in her phenomenology of the cinematic experience calls an 'intentional stream of moving images' (2004: 147). They slowly bring her naked body into figuration while other streams of moving layers of script form shifting levels of protection. Hence, these images are brought up from the photographic realm of eternal past to the lived momentum of cinema. They are made present, or, as Sobchack puts it, 'coming-into-being' (ibid.). In embodying different layers of time within a single screen, Hatoum's work can be viewed as a phenomenological description of the functioning of memory. It quite accurately conveys the intentional act of recollection as the representation of a fixed impression that is past onto the 'screen' of consciousness within a temporal flow. Like the video-screen, this consciousness comprises different layers or tracks of temporality that all coexist at any given moment. The heterogeneity of time is further conveyed by the epistolary structure of the video. The epistolary contact is marked by a temporal delay; a gap that opens between the sending and the receiving of a message. It is precisely this gap that makes the letter a 'metonymic and a metaphoric displacement of desire' (Kauffman 1986: 38), of absence, loss and separation. Yet its production and reception, as Hamid Naficy observes, are always already embedded in each other, for the 'very fact of addressing someone in an epistle creates an illusion of presence that transforms the addressee from an absent figure into a presence, which hovers in the text's interstices' (2001: 103). In her last letter, Hatoum's mother informs her exiled daughter that the local post office was destroyed in a car bombing, and that mother and daughter from now on can only rely on the unstable telephone connection. It is in the face of such an unbridgeable distance that still pictures, home videos, letters or family albums are 'turned into ethnic objects and nostalgic fetishes' (2001: 120) that carry the remembrance of the past. These media thus play an important role in the lifeworlds of many migrants, in the construction of their identities and their affiliation to different times and places.

This constitutive power of media for remembrance is strongly addressed in a work by Lebanese-born filmmaker Rania Stephan. In *The Three Disappearances of Soad Hosni* (2011), she focuses on the mythology of the famous Egyptian actress (the 'Cinderella' of Arab entertainment), frantically beloved through-out the Arab countries and the Arab diaspora.[26] Stephan's film is composed solely from the footage of more than sixty feature films in which Hosni starred throughout her career. Structured like a classical three-act tragedy, the film ex-plores the legendary actress as a star-persona in the form of an experimental biopic that is artfully constructed from (and thus supersedes) Hosni's singular roles. As the footage used spans a time from 1959 to 1991, we see Hosni ageing on screen, sometimes even within a single scene. In this way, Stephan's poetic reinvention also examines how the representation of the Arab woman in popu-lar culture was subject to change over time. With her early films, Hosni became the icon of Abdel Nasser's Egyptian Revolution of 1952 and, consequently, of its enthusiastic pan-Arab spirit. Later, as a mature actress, she starred in social dramas that revealed the tensions between conflicting modern and traditional concepts of Arab femininity in the 1970s and 1980s. *The Three Disappearances of Soad Hosni* further alludes to her tragic and untimely death that still nurtures conspiracy theories. In 2001, Hosni was found dead on the pavement in front of her London apartment, apparently having thrown herself from the balcony. The officially proclaimed suicide has subsequently been contested by rumours, citing the prepared publication of her biography as a motive for murder. As this material was said to be capable of hurting important political figures within the Mubarak regime, these theories see the Egyptian intelligence agencies behind her death. Hosni's career mirrored the rise and fall of Egyptian cinema, the old-est in the Arab world. Thus, it also mirrors the rise and fall of pan-Arabism that was a product of the (unfulfilled) promises of the early postcolonial era. These 'disappearances' the film's title refers to are also reflected in the work's material-ity. Stephan edited her work solely from VHS copies of Hosni's films and thus from the medium in which they were foremost consumed throughout the Arab world and diaspora.[27] Stephan's film is hence marked by the worn aesthetics of home video: blurry and scratched images, often close to disintegration, distorted colours stemming from multigenerational copy, noisy sound. From a phenom-enological perspective, it matters in which format we experience a film (as a projection, VHS tape or DVD), for the concrete material conditions of different media technologies have a constitutive effect on our temporal consciousness and our bodily sense of existential presence (see Sobchack 2004: 155). *The Three Disappearances of Soad Hosni* is therefore a film about film spectatorship. Its viewing experience corresponds very closely to the dominant mode in which Hosni's fans in the Egyptian exile or the other Arab countries (and also Stephan herself) were used to seeing her films. Hosni's films are rarely screened in public today. They are not available on DVD, and their sensuality nowadays appears too controversial, too frivolous for most Arab TV stations. What remains are

Fig. 26: The worn-out video aesthetics of *The Three Disappearances of Soad Hosni.*

I don't remember...

the worn-out videotapes that circulated from friends to family-members, often across national borders, degraded over the years or by the process of constant copying. Outside of these private networks, they only live on in private collections where their decaying images call up memories of an Egypt that is past.

Transnationally circulated media like Hosni's films have in recent years become important means for establishing and maintaining diasporic connections. Globally present cultural products, like Bollywood movies, increasingly play a constitutive role in the production of diasporic identity. They offer a sense of belonging, cultural knowledge and, sometimes, even language training for their migrant audience and mobile viewing subjects. By admiring the same stars and being emotionally affected by the same narratives, a diasporic audience makes use of the same archive of images and memories as the respective audience in the homeland, thereby imaginatively reconnecting with it. Indian cinema is a particularly apt example that is seen by members of the diaspora, the so-called NRIs (non-resident Indians) and PIOs (persons of Indian origin), as mediating or even teaching cultural knowledge of 'lost' traditions. Manas Ray (2006) has drawn upon the example of the Fiji-Indian's imagined sense of nationhood to show how Bollywood serves as both the principal provider of motherland culture and as an archive of a collective memory for diasporic Indian communities: 'With time, as memory of "roots" – the *real* India – was fading away, films took over the responsibility of constructing an empty, many-coloured space through its never-ending web of images, songs, "dialogues" and stars' (2006: 149). What these films provide, however, is an idealised image of India, one that constructs the homeland as an entirely 'imagined nodal point of identity' (2006: 140).

A remarkable reflection on the meaning of this phenomenon, which Appadurai, in his celebrated analysis of global cultural flows and social imaginaries, has termed 'nostalgia without memory' (1996: 30), can be found in Gariné Torossian's *Girl from Moush* (1993). In this work the Canadian filmmaker, of

Armenian descent, reflects upon the images that represent the homeland for the members of the Armenian diaspora. These images, however, could not have been re-presented from the past by a Husserlian consciousness. Rather, her film consists of images of images: reproductions of paintings, postcards, photographs and illustrations taken from books or calendars; as well as footage from the films of Atom Egoyan and Sergei Parajanov, both directors of Armenian heritage. They show landscapes, landmarks (like churches or memorials), folk dances or human faces: an archive of images that was meant to keep the culture of the homeland alive; a culture that almost was destroyed by genocide. Torossian copied this found footage onto film stock with the help of an optical printer, or else simply by gluing it directly onto the celluloid. She then arranged these images in layers, resulting in an animated collage that produces strange compositions in terms of scale and perspective. This physical process gives her film an extremely tactile appearance. Scratches, dirt and bubbles of glue serve to make the film's texture, its material surface, become extremely present. The images of landscapes and places thus lose their indexical relationship to reality. They are what Deleuze calls virtual images and, hence, do not correspond to actual perceptions. As mere icons they form a symbolic system that is uninhabitable in a phenomenological sense, not accessible as experience of the past for an individual consciousness. As these markers of an Armenian identity are visible only for a couple of frames and then fade, they appear as ephemeral and elusive,

Fig. 26: The layering of images in *Girl from Moush*.

consumed by the power of collective forgetting. In this way, the homeland *Girl from Moush* refers to consists only of empty signifiers. It is a mythical Armenia, one that cannot be visited in reality. In an account of the experience of exile, that is at once personal narrative and analytical description, Naficy comments on the fetishisation of images representing the homeland and the seductiveness of the past. He cites the Iranian television service in Southern California as an example of an exile culture that has given in to hermeticism and continually restages the longing for a past that has ceased to exist, that can only be embraced in a metaphorical reunion (1993: 151). Naficy warns that such an exilic nostalgia that clings to images, objects, or other signifiers of a real or imagined memory, might make the creation of a new life in the diaspora impossible.

IMMERSED IN THE PRESENT

Between a past left behind and a future not yet achieved, for many migrants lies a precarious present. In what follows, I want to point to the political significance that the study of migrants' temporal experiences may imply. Therefore, I introduce Elias Grootaers' film *Not Waving, But Drowning* (2009), a meticulous exploration of the temporal regulation of migration. As Grootaers so radically seeks to convey the temporal experiences of his protagonists to his audience, I will draw on Gilles Deleuze's (1989) notion of time-image cinema to thoroughly discuss how film can embody the workings of time. *Not Waving, But Drowning* is set in a detention centre in the Belgian harbour town of Zeebrugge and documents the waiting time of a group of young Indian migrants who were arrested here on their way to the UK. Left without a translator, they remain uninformed about the nature and length of their detainment. Their bodies are disassociated from all productive activity in this confined space. Their existence revolves solely around fighting boredom and killing time, they are reduced to an immediate immersion in the present moment. They are drowning in a sea of time. There is nothing to do for them but to lie around: to sleep, to eat, to compulsively wash hands, to stare out of the window, to sing mournful songs. In such a situation, Throop notes, 'protentions remain unfulfilled as what were previously taken-for-granted properties of self, body and world are recurrently challenged' (2003: 234). Refraining from investigating their past and future, or commenting on the political discourse around the detainment of migrants, Grootaers' film tries solely to convey how time becomes a prison. 'Where nothing happens, temporality makes itself felt, viscerally. Time hurts' (Birnbaum 2007: 116). His is an attempt to show time through the body, 'through its tiredness and its waitings' (Deleuze 1989: xi). In their analysis of the European border regime, Vassilis Tsianos, Sabine Hess and Serhat Karakayali (2009) make evident that the unregulated wait-time in the deportation centres, the prolonged waiting periods in the asylum process and the time 'illegal' migrants have to spend in hiding are all politically orchestrated to decelerate migratory movements. By enforcing such temporal experiences, wait-time is used as a political weapon to discourage (would-be) migrants as well as to 'impose a regime of temporal control on the wild and uncontrollable unfolding of the imperceptible and excessive movements of the trans-migrants' (2009: 9). In order to explore how this temporal regime manifests itself in the migrants' minds and bodies, Grootaers frequently takes on the detainees' perspective. His camera stands on their side, follows their views through the glass door to the exterior corridor, and shows us what they can see. Thus, the policemen appear as intruders in the migrants' space and we feel their disconcertment about the incomprehensible explanations and orders they receive. The images he composes feel constricted and often are framed by doors or barred windows. The sound attains a haptic quality, with the locking and opening of doors producing a visceral feeling on the side of the audience.

The experience of indeterminate waiting is further conveyed by the long duration of the shots that are not sutured by the montage conventions of classical cinema; with its succession of perception, action and reaction. Grootaers' images are not linked by continuity, perpetual motion or narrative causality. Deleuze famously argues that such a break with the 'sensory-motor schema' of what he calls movement-image cinema enables the presence of time to appear on the screen. He shows how, in conventional films, time is subordinated to

Fig. 27: Taking on the detainees' perspective in *Not Waving, But Drowning*.

movement in space as action progresses in a linear way. Time is therefore only represented indirectly in movement-image cinema as the editing merely serves to advance in time, to skip moments of dead time. In *Cinema 2: The Time Image* (1989) Deleuze then describes a new type of cinema in which the individual shots do not tie into a proceeding chain of events, do not refer to an action or a movement but only to time itself. Deleuze situates the advent of this time-image cinema within the modernist cinematic movements that emerged after the crisis of World War II with its destruction of spiritual, moral and psychic certainties. In the post-war films of directors like Roberto Rossellini, Yasujiro Ozu or Michelangelo Antonioni, meaningful action has become impossible. Therefore, the act of seeing takes on the greatest importance for a film's protagonist as 'the situation he is in outstrips his motor capacities on all sides, and makes him see and hear what is no longer subject to the rule of a response or an action' (1989: 3). As a mere observer, the protagonist becomes the alter ego of the spectator, whose problem in turn becomes '"What is there to see in the image?" (and not now "What are we going to see in the next image?")' (1989: 272).

Before I explore the impact of Deleuze's cinematic philosophy on questions of time and consciousness, let me discuss how meaningful his observations are for the understanding of Grootaers' film. As with the protagonists in the post-war films Deleuze draws upon, the migrants in *Not Waving, But Drowning* are deprived of the possibility to act. They are mere seers, and their limited perception also strips the viewer of all sense of time and space. According to Deleuze, the breakdown of the sensory-motor schema of action and reaction leads to the genesis of 'pure optical and sound situations'. Such cinematic 'situations' do not retain a given moment or fix it (like photography does); they let it linger. They do not 'narrate' time, they merely persist. They do not represent time but rather present the temporal flow itself. In time-image cinema, the image's representational qualities are weakened as it mixes the real and the imaginary. Dream-images fuse actual perception and virtual aspects. Recollection-images might interrupt the sensory-motor chain in its unfolding presence: while one aspect of the image refers to a future sequence of events, another refers to the past (1989: 47ff). Subjectivity and objectivity thus are not automatically given by the causal relationships implied by the progression of narrative but have yet to emerge.

Not Waving, But Drowning is full of such dense optical and acoustic situations. Consider, for example, the montage sequence in which we see a group of migrants who have fallen asleep on the bunks in their cell. At first we only hear their snoring sounds; then, slowly, a melancholic Indian song fades in. The voice of the singer sounds grating, as if played from a very old record. From the sleeping migrants, Grootaers cuts to a shot showing seagulls gliding over the sea. The next image is some old archival footage of breaking waves. In addition to the song, we now also hear the sound of the water, yet it seems much calmer than the apparent storm we see in the image; the film then cuts back to a wide shot of the two bunks where the migrants lay sleeping. Shortly before the cut, yet another layer of sound fades in: the sound of exploding fireworks. In the following shot we now also see the fireworks as an abstract play of light against a pitch-black sky. We begin to hear cheering and applauding people who seem to be witnesses to the spectacle. At this point, all the other layers of sound have disappeared. After about forty seconds of only synchronous sound, the noise of exploding fireworks is replaced by the Indian song, previously heard in the earlier shots. We then return to some detail shots of the bodies of the sleeping detainees. Now we also hear them snoring again, in addition to the continuing song. In the last shot of the scene, we are back on the fireworks while we hear nothing but the snoring. The whole sequence produces a deep uncertainty about the status of the images. How are we to interpret the shot of the seagulls? As a metaphor? As a subjective dream-image that represents the migrants' desire

Fig. 28: The montage sequence in *Not Waving, But Drowning.*

to cross the North Sea, as it would be in the conventional sensory-motor chain of classical cinema with its clear distribution of subject (dreamer) and object (dream)? What about the image of the fireworks? Is it another metaphor, referring to the migrants' past or future? Or can it be read literally as a concrete marker of time, suggesting the migrants' presence in the detention centre at a specific place in time (during a festival or New Year's Eve, maybe), as the moments of synchronicity between the sound of the exploding fireworks and the images of the sleeping migrants imply? And to whose memory or consciousness do the breaking waves refer?

Obviously, these images defy any clear identification as real or imaginary, subjective or objective, past or present. Rather, this sequence is characterised by a thick temporal complexity. As Deleuze writes, time-image cinema goes 'beyond the purely empirical succession of time – past-present-future. It is, for example, a coexistence of distinct durations, or of levels of duration; a single event can belong to several levels: the sheets of past co-exist in a non-chronological order' (1989: vii). In Grootaers' film, the sound actually supports the localisation of an image in two layers of time at once. As I mentioned, this sometimes suggests the simultaneity of two images in the present, and sometimes situates it in the realm of the virtual. Hence, the sound also adds to the complex temporal structure of the work, and of this scene in particular. The song that underlies this sequence, at first glance, resembles the mournful songs (stemming from Bollywood movies) we have already heard the detainees sing in previous scenes. Yet the constant crackling reveals it to be some record from the past. The song actually was recorded in 1916 at the 'Halfmoon Camp' in Wünsdorf, a war prison in which German scientists studied colonial soldiers of the French and British armies. One project, pursued there by linguists and anthropologists, was the systematic record and archiving of the different languages and music of the prisoners. Grootaers' use of the song as an echo of the past thus points to an uncanny parallel between colonial and postcolonial practices of detention.

INTERLUDE: DELEUZE AND PHENOMENOLOGY

Deleuze's take on cinema is one of radical immanence as it seeks to understand cinema on its own terms. It provides a taxonomy of its images (and their linkage through editing) without depending on any external reflective system (such as, for example, semiotics, linguistics or psychoanalysis). Thus, it is very much in line with a phenomenological approach. Here, I have to discuss the differences and incongruities between Deleuze's cinema philosophy and the phenomenological understanding of film I have put forth so far. Deleuze's philosophical project radically opposes all subjectivist and anthropocentric positions. In this way he

rejects Husserl's transcendental phenomenology as the centrality of the dimensions of space and time in the perception of an individual consciousness. He also
dismisses Husserlian intentionality (the idea that consciousness is always di-
rected towards an object, is always consciousness of something) as presupposing
a stable relationship between subject and object. Deleuze attacks the promise
of transcendental security he deems inherent in the idea of an anchored subject
observing and reflecting upon reality. Consciousness, for him, does not neces-
sitate human intention. It already is in the world, accumulated in the materiality
of existence. In the same way, he says in his second commentary on Bergson,
cinema already is, and its images do not depend on a subject who perceives them
(1986: 59). Consciousness emerges on and from the cinema screen. The world
perceives and thinks itself in the mode of cinema. Film does not represent reality;
it produces it. If cinema does not depend on a perceiving subject as the source
of consciousness, he argues, we cannot and should not understand the perspective it offers in terms of subjectivity. For Deleuze, the eye of the camera is not
to be confused with the all too immobile human eye (1986: 40). Rather, cinema
offers us a radically pure perception, free from the restrictions of a perceiving
human body. As Bruce Kapferer, who develops a new theory of ritual based on
Deleuze's cinematic philosophy, notes, cinema proposes 'an understanding of
human being not only through human being but through a dynamics of going
outside the human and from perspectives that are not necessarily those from the
positionality of the human' (2013: 24). I certainly agree that cinema can offer
us perceptions freed from or exceeding the human perspective. Yet I propose
to separate Deleuze's insightful descriptions of the shifting subject positioning
and multiplicity of perspective that is possible in cinema (for example, through
the use of montage, as we have seen in the last chapter) from his larger (and
practically rather challenging) project of dissolving human subjectivity. There
are films that quite accurately emulate a subjective stream of consciousness and
the operation of personal memory (as seen in Hatoum's *Measures of Distance*),
while in other films (like *Girl from Moush* or *Not Waving, But Drowning*)
the 'past coexists with the present, in a manner irreducible to flashbacks or
conscious recollection, rendering the present uncertain and forcing us to think
while dispossessing us of our ability to say "I" or "We"' (Rajchmann 2008:
314). Sobchack's phenomenological film theory, however, is not as naïve as to
propagate an idea of cinema as the expression of some sort of natural perception
conceived from a fixed position before the world. She draws less on the static
sameness of Husserl's transcendental notion of consciousness than on Merleau-
Ponty's existential consciousness of an embodied self-in-becoming. Sobchack
rejects the idea of a stable primary identification in the cinema (with the protagonist or the camera) and also 'such abstraction as *point of view*' (1992: 61).

Instead, she asks how the constant emergence, shaping and reshaping of perspectives that constitute a film, the peculiar ways cinema has found to 'undercut the divisions between objective and subjective viewpoints or between the sound and image space' (Rajchmann 2008: 320), engage with our bodily presence as spectators; whether in the cinema, a gallery space or in front of a monitor. Deleuze, in contrast, ignores this question of spectatorship, of how a film (even one that thoroughly decentres subjectivity) actually affects our embodied experience. He wants us to 'make ourselves a body without organs' (see Deleuze and Guattari 1987; chapter 6) but 'his interest is not in exploring how cinema relates to the bodies we have already been given' (Marks 2000: 150).

CRYSTALS OF TIME

As Sobchack's approach is foremost concerned with the ways in which cinema creates existential presence and immediacy and devotes little attention to the dimension of time, I propose to take Deleuze's analytical description of time-image cinema as an important complement to a phenomenological film theory. Hence, while Sobchack describes the spectator's embodied relation to film in terms of space – 'the significant space lived as and through the objective body-subject, the historical space of situation' (1992: 31) – Deleuze exposes the operation of time in modern cinema as no longer subordinated to movement, but as appearing in itself (1989: 271). Deleuze's work draws heavily on Bergson and his understanding of *durée*, or pure duration. For Bergson, as for phenomenologists like Husserl or James, time is not an abstract measurement but, in its flux, an indivisible whole (whereas he considers mathematical time, or 'clock time', the immobile, divisible time of science, as a form of space). For Bergson, each present moment we inhabit is characterised by a split, between a present that passes and a past that is preserved. Time splits itself, in every future moment, into the actual (the pure, immediate perception), and the virtual (memory or imagination). This split is the founding moment of time. Without it, time would not be in motion; the present moment would not pass and the new present could not arrive (see Deleuze 1989: 79). Time is a paradoxical unity in which, on the one hand, every moment irrevocably passes and, on the other, nothing passes because everything is preserved as past. Past and present thus emerge at once and exist concurrently. These two aspects of time Deleuze sees embodied in the actual and the virtual image. At the moment of their division, they create two utterly disjunctive representations of the same moment (see Marks 2000: 40). A film like *Girl from Moush*, for example, is composed only of virtual images. Its images of Armenia do not correspond to anybody's actual perceptions (that once were present) and so to any living memory. The present-that-passes, the unique situation in which the landscapes, monuments or faces were photographed, can never be recalled (and neither can the perceptions and feelings of the photographer). In *Measures of Distance*, by contrast, the present-that passes, the moment in which Hatoum took the photos of her mother in the shower, is constantly actualised and reflected upon. Actual image and virtual image, present and past, are in steady interplay. The past exists in these images as the pre-existence of the present. When the actual image connects itself to virtual images, Deleuze says, the crystal image emerges. In the way a beam of light is split up in the reflection of a crystal, the actual and virtual split in the crystal image and then produce strange duplications and reflections:

> In fact the crystal constantly exchanges the two distinct images which constitute it, the actual image of the present which passes and the virtual image of the past which is preserved: distinct and yet indiscernible, and all the more indiscernible because distinct, because we do not know which is one and which is the other. This is unequal exchange, or the point of indiscernibility, the mutual image. The crystal always lives at the limit, it is itself the vanishing limit between the immediate past which is already no longer and the immediate future which is not yet... (1989: 81)

The crystal image is, thus, in one way or the other, doubled (or double-sided), with actual image and virtual image short-circuiting. It can appear as an actual reflection on a window or a water surface (in which interior and exterior spaces are overlaid), a reflection of mirrors (as in the famous hall of mirrors scene in Orson

Fig. 29: A crystal image in *Not Waving, But Drowning*.

Welles' *The Lady from Shanghai* [1947]), or as a view out of a window with depth of field producing a nesting of frames. An exemplary crystal image forms in *Not Waving, But Drowning* in a shot that shows the detained migrants reflected in the eye of a security camera. Folded into each other here, are their actual image and the virtual image produced by the surveillance camera, an image that preserves the past (and makes it accessible for monitoring) while it does not account for an actual (lived) perception. In such an image, the present coexists with its own past. All the temporal complexity cinema is capable to express is crystallised into one single image that, in turn, fully realises time-image cinema. At this point, let me turn to a work that uses the time-image to reveal how contemporary routes of migration are profoundly shaped by the heritage of colonialism.

SAPHIR

Colonial legacy and postcolonial present, historical and contemporary patterns of migration; these temporal layers conflate in the images of Zineb Sedira's two-channel video installation *Saphir* (2006). Set in present-day Algiers, the work engages with the history of migrations and diaspora, passages and displacements between France and Algeria; between former 'motherland' and (post)colony. *Saphir* (English: sapphire) crystallises these different circuits of movement and time towards their indiscernibility. On two adjoining screens, it follows the movements of two solitary figures: a French woman aimlessly wandering through the empty rooms and corridors of a colonial-era seashore hotel, and a local Algerian man rambling around the harbour area and repeatedly staring out to the sea. These two nameless characters come to embody the different diasporas that traverse both countries. The woman appears to be of *pied-noir* (colonial European settler) origin, while the man, who longingly observes the arriving and embarking boats, behaves like a typical *harrag*, a 'bruleur': a young man who dreams the collective dream of finding a life on the other side of the Mediterranean. The two speechless figures constantly revolve around each other. They are caught in a kind of ritualistic dance that never quite brings them together. They are always on the move, yet never do they arrive anywhere. Their complicated choreography spans across the two screens that in turn sometimes compound into one large image. In these moments, both images appear to directly refer to each other. The woman, standing on the balcony, seems to notice the man who passes the stairs that lead to the hotel. At other times, however, the two screens give us disjunctive perspectives.

Time and again, motions and actions repeat on both screens, making circularity the work's central motif. Time seems utterly out of joint. The woman seems to be trapped in a different layer of time, the time of the colonial past embodied

Fig. 30: Compounding images: *Saphir* (2006), Zineb Sedira. 19 min. Two-channel video installation. © Zineb Sedira / DACS, London. © Photo. Charles Duprat. Courtesy the artist and kamel mennour, Paris.

by the ghostly presence of the hotel. As Sedira states in an interview, the history of the hotel Es Safir is actually intimately connected with the French presence in Algeria. Built in the Art Deco style by French architects Bluysen and Richard in 1930, it housed the city's casino and was the central meeting-point for the colonial high-society in Algiers (see Van Assche 2006: 60). The woman moves through the seemingly abandoned hotel like a spectre haunting the place. She repeatedly gazes out to the sea from the balcony or through a window, yet she somehow seems unable to leave. This phantasmal impression is reinforced by a wide shot in which she wanders down a long corridor and then suddenly vanishes into thin air.

Sedira's powerful image of a ghost disturbing the postcolonial present is reminiscent of Avery Gordon's compelling exploration of haunting as a social experience that reveals how past social forces continue to control present life. For Gordon, 'haunting describes how that which appears to be not there is often a seething presence, acting on and often meddling with taken-for-granted realities' (2008: 8). The woman's appearance (or apparition) thus conjures up the French colonial history in North Africa that has not yet sufficiently been dealt with and so still haunts contemporary encounters and political relations. Moreover, the legacy of this colonial past is virtually nonexistent in the debates and mainstream media coverage of 'illegal' migration, which, in this respect, is represented as a social phenomenon without a geopolitical history. On the level of the image, this conflation of past and present is manifested in *Saphir* in time-images of a crystalline quality.

Many shots are composed as views through doors, curtains or windows. Depth of field is used to organise the action and information contained within the image into different zones: into fore- and background. Often, the characters move from one zone of the image to the other; for example, when the woman walks from the hotel room onto the balcony and then gazes out on the harbour, all contained within one shot. For Deleuze, such compositional use of depth of field allows for the simultaneity of several layers of temporality. At one poignant moment the camera looks through the hotel window onto a ferry, then slowly pulls back to reveal the woman having a French breakfast in the dining hall. In this way it moves, in one single shot, from the actual situation of the Algiers port to the virtual realm of the ghostly hotel. In a similar vein, the wide shot of the man leaning on a decaying sea-shore balustrade and staring onto a ferry that, like a Fata Morgana, is shrouded in mist contracts his actual presence with a dream-image of his future. For Deleuze, depth functions 'to constitute the image in crystal, and to absorb the real, which thus passes as much into the virtual as into the actual' (1989: 85). Depth of field, as a result, is 'a figure of temporaliza-tion'; it creates a cinematic space that contains multiple 'virtual zones of past' (1989: 110) and makes them accessible from the present.

This oscillation between actuality and virtuality, present and past, presence and absence, is not only manifest on the level of the single image but rather forms a defining characteristic of the work as an installation. The 'actual image of the characters and the virtual image of their roles' (Deleuze 1989: 85) are further blurred by Sedira's casting decisions that complicate the work's neat classifica-tion as either documentary or fiction. While Samir El Hakim, the Algerian actor, had previously worked in France, he now lives in Algiers and has no desire to return. Likewise, Caroline Olssen is not strictly speaking a *pied-noir*, although her father was. In the process of the filming, she discovered the country she had previously only known from family accounts and photographs (see Van Assche 2006: 61). The frequent separation of these two characters on adjacent screens stresses their apparent invisibility to each other. We now understand that their movements toward the other are in vain, for each of them is trapped in a differ-ent temporal realm. Unable to travel in space, they both only move in time. As the woman is bound to the past and the man is obsessed with the future, Saphir depicts a postcolonial present that is barren and uncertain.

I would like to end the discussion of this piece with some thoughts on how we are to understand the ways in which a multi-channel video installation like *Saphir* affects a spectator's temporal consciousness. As the parallel flows of mov-ing imagery on both screens sometimes converge yet more often conflict, the work conveys a multiplicity of movements, perspectives and perceptions and is thus able to express two distinct temporal flows at the same time. Daniel Birnbaum notes that the temporal complexity conveyed by such a work of post-cinematic experimentation effectively probes the limits of a phenomenological notion of spectatorship. On the one hand it 'allows for the participation of the viewer but also brings the viewer's unity and stability into question' (2007: 174). As the mul-tiple screen installation also departs from the linearity inscribed in the medium

129

Fig. 31: Multiple perspectives in *Saphir* (2006), Zineb Sedira. 19 min. Two-channel video installation. © Zineb Sedira / DACS, London. Courtesy the artist and kamel mennour, Paris.

of film, it 'grants the possibility not only of dense and temporally multi-layered imagery, but also of intricate constellations and juxtapositions' (2007: 122). It is able to spatialise temporal events (see Mondloch 2010) and the immersion it creates in this respect has to be understood in both temporal and spatial terms.

MIGRATION, NEW MEDIA AND TEMPORAL EXPERIENCE

Throughout this chapter, I have described the multiplicity of temporal experiences that transnational migrations inevitably bring about. As my examples hopefully have made clear, audiovisual media are a necessary part of this process. Analysing the works of Grootaers and Sedira, I have discussed how Deleuzian time-image cinema may offer artists and ethnographic filmmakers new possibilities for evoking the temporal polyphony of our research participants' experiences. Yet film and other media also involve us in complex temporal experiences themselves, as I have examined with recourse to the phenomenological film theory of Vivian Sobchack. Drawing on the films of diasporic artists like Hatoum, Stephan or Torossian, the fieldwork experiences of Vigh and Lucht, and the work of cultural theorists like Naficy and Appadurai, one could actually argue that the history of migration and the history of media are in fact deeply entangled. Migrants have always belonged to the very early adopters of new media whenever these promised to satisfy some of their basic needs. One could indeed write a history of migrant media (or a media history of migration) that would, for example, encompass the rise of VHS home video as a means to store (and trigger) personal memories (as evoked in the films of Rania Stephan and Alex Rivera). It could incorporate the success of media technologies that allow migrants to stay connected to their homeland culture (such as the satellite dishes the Turkish diaspora in Germany bulk-purchased in the 1980s in order to watch Turkish domestic TV), and also the new possibilities to stay in touch with relatives and loved ones over spatial distance that are now provided by mobile phones and other information and communication technologies (ICTs). In this line of thought, I will now explore how new technologies of instantaneous communication, that have come to constitute the cheap 'social glue of migrant transnationalism' (Vertovec 2004), are used by transnational families and how these technologies eventually shape their users' temporal consciousness.

I begin my discussion with a short look back into a recent past. In *Mimoune*, a short documentary video released in 2006 that has been screened at almost a hundred film festivals and won several prices, the Spanish artist Gonzalo Ballester seeks to reunite a long-lost family with the help of video. He records a video message with Mimoune, a Moroccan migrant living and working undocumented near Murcia in the south of Spain. Facing Ballester's camera, Mimoune addresses the wife and family he hasn't seen in years and sends them his love. Ballester then takes this video to Mimoune's family in Morocco and films their reaction to this message. After the screening, he records the family's answer to Mimoune. The video ends with a close-up of Mimoune's face in tears while he watches the message that was sent by his relatives. What makes this film particularly interesting however is the temporal complexity it portrays. In an 'epistolary act of mercy' (Bal 2008: 42), Ballester has acted as a kind of postman who physically transports the video letters between the separated relatives. His film was 'born out of the desire to bring together, even if it was only through a camera, a family that since long ago wishes so', as he states in the video's introduction. Despite the passage of several weeks between the two recordings, in which Ballester carried the taped messages from Murcia to Oujda and back, his film is edited to give the impression of witnessing an instantaneous communication. In a kind of Deleuzian false continuity editing, we see the family's reactions to Mimoune's message while he is speaking and vice versa. Ballester has thus constructed a filmic dialogue through shot/countershot editing that produces the effect of action and reaction taking place simultaneously. In *Mimoune*, the temporality of the letter that is marked by the physical transport of the message thus clashes with an instantaneity of communication constructed in editing that seems to abolish all temporal and spatial distance. While at the time of shooting, the telephone and ICTs like texting or email had, of course, already symbolically obliterated this distance, it was still difficult for (live) images to arrive at such speed (using consumer technology at least). Hence Mimoune's emotional reaction to the video images of his family.

In the very same year that Ballester's film was released, however, the Internet telecommunication company Skype allowed its users to make free video calls between two computers equipped with webcams, in this way giving its customers the opportunity of direct real-time communication with image and sound (in some moments, Ballester's edited video in fact almost feels like such a Skype conversation). In 2013, Skype had more than 300 million daily active users (see

Fig. 32: A dialogue constructed in editing in *Mimoune*.

Skype 2013), which, in that year, produced traffic of 214 billion minutes (see Telegeography 2014). These impressive numbers show that despite the 'digital divide' that still exists both within and between the countries of the Global North and the Global South, a very large number of people have access to this new form of communication. Anthropology and the other social sciences are only beginning to understand the importance of Internet-based forms of communication through Skype, Yahoo Messenger, Apple FaceTime or the Chinese service QQ in transnational settings, and how their users appropriate these technologies to maintain or negotiate relationships over geographical distance. Initial studies done in this field (see Madianou and Miller 2012; Longhurst 2013; Hyndman-Rizk 2014; Miller and Sinanan 2014) reveal how new media are transforming the ways separated family members can continue to care for one another, in this respect diminishing one of the biggest social costs of migration that is affecting the Global South. They point to the creative ways in which many migrants have adapted webcam to collapse distance and to build a synchronic social space with their faraway families. Dittz, the overseas domestic worker who is one of the protagonists of my film *Intimate Distance*, for example, can now finally play an active role in the life of her son Hadji, whom she left with her mother when she went to Italy eleven years ago to earn money for her children's education. Hadji just recently moved out of his grandparents' house to live in a dorm provided by the University of the Philippines in Baguio where he now studies communication.

Through Skype, Dittz can now see his friends, be introduced to his girlfriends, and provide maternal advice. Mirca Madaianou and Daniel Miller (2012) have provided a detailed ethnographic survey on how Filipina migrant mothers working in Great Britain use new media technologies (like video and mobile phone calls, social networking sites and email) to conduct the performative work of parenting their left-behind children. Before the advent of these new ICTs, migrant families could only communicate through asynchronous media like occasional letters or through very infrequent and expensive phone calls (if access to landlines was at all given on both sides). Mothers, therefore, often felt they had become disconnected from their children who remained with their grandparents on the Philippines. Yet with the new digital communication technologies being available at (almost) no cost, things have changed. These migrant mothers can now call or text their kids several times a day, befriend or follow them on social networking sites or leave the webcam on for hours to achieve some feeling of synchronicity and co-presence with their loved ones. Madaianou and Miller argue that Skype's video call function, especially, has revolutionised communications between mothers and children, as mothers can now actually see how their children (who might have been no more than toddlers when their mothers left) are growing up in front of the webcam. While most authors who initially analysed the rise of ICTs focused on the pitfalls and possibilities of reconfiguring spaces and identities in the virtual realm, as users were no longer tied to their physical bodies, Robyn Longhurst in her study on Skype mothering finds that video calls actually convey 'something of the materiality of bodies. It is about hearing, and seeing the lived flesh of the "real" person or people on the screen. It is about being able to observe the expressions, comportment, clothing, movements, and surrounds of others on screen' (2013: 665). Hence she argues that the instantaneity of webcam communication 'may have the potential to prompt different feelings of proximity (distance and closeness) between mothers and their children' (2013: 667).

For *Intimate Distance*, I was interested in exactly these user experiences of proximity and synchronicity with others' lives that the video communication, via Skype, seems to make possible. I was, however, unconvinced by the methodology of the studies mentioned above. Madianou and Miller and Longhurst gathered their data only through interviews with mothers and children about their Skype use patterns. Hence, they sought to explore the experiences of their research participants merely through retrospective assessment. However, such a recollective production of meaning might not be the best approach to account for the pre-reflective and immediate experiences involved in such an instantaneous form of communication, as Throop (2003) has noted. For my project, I therefore asked three intensive Skype users who all deploy the medium to stay connected to their loved ones across borders, to actually record their webcam

conversations with the help of simple software. These many hours of recordings then provided not only a much more immediate set of data unbiased by
retrospective assessment, but also the raw material for a film that directly conveys my protagonists' many fascinating webcam rituals to its audience. This
methodology obviously raises the important issue of informed consent, as these
recordings offered me a very intimate view into my research participants' private
lives. Therefore I agreed with all participants that they would only hand me over
recordings they didn't feel were too sensitive with regards to private family matters. They also had the possibility to cut out parts of conversations they didn't
want me to see, using a basic, easy to use editing software I provided. With
regard to the film I edited out of this material, every participant had a say in
how I presented their relationship and also had the right to veto any particular
scenes. For this reason, as my protagonists themselves generated the footage for
the film (and I wasn't even present while recording), this ended up being a very
collaborative process of filmmaking. I tried out different ways of editing and
presenting the resulting material, such as using two screens, a split screen or as
frame within frame (to emulate the Skype user interface during an active video
call). Yet, ultimately, I decided to weave together the webcam feeds of each side
of a conversation by means of shot/countershot editing and present the work
on a single screen. I felt that this established cinematic technique allowed for a
natural rendering of a given communication. Unlike in *Mimoune*, however, the
temporal integrity of every conversation was left intact.

The most fascinating aspect of my research participants' use of Skype is
surely that the mode of communication they engage in often does not have
much to do with mere visual telephony anymore. On the contrary, they all use
the technology predominantly to visually join the domestic spaces in front of
the webcam in order to achieve a feeling of co-habitation. Axel and Serpil, the
German-Turkish couple, for example, leave the webcam on for hours, often
without having any conversation at all. Serpil would read in front of the camera
or go out of its range to have a shower and come back, while Axel positions his
laptop so that the webcam takes in his whole kitchen while he cooks or washes
the dishes.

Very often the couple shares a mutual breakfast before the webcam, even
when Serpil is out, as she has also installed the software on her smartphone. Axel
would even watch Serpil sleep via the webcam when he stays up longer than her.
Miller and Sinanan have called this phenomenon 'always-on' webcamming and
argue that it aims at a kind of intimacy analogous to the taken-for-granted presence of a partner with whom one lives together in the same place (2014: 54f).
Both authors see webcam not as a mere substitute for 'real' unmediated intimacy
but argue that relationships are always mediated, predicting that webcam 'will

Fig. 33: Achieving a feeling of co-residence via webcam in *Intimate Distance*.

lead to quite unprecedented genres of sort-of-co-presence that transcend mere comparison with these prior forms' (2014: 80). For Patricia in Germany and her sister Milena in Colombia, for example, webcamming actually allows for a degree of closeness they might not even have if they would live in the same town. As Milena's second son Juan Pablo is just eight months old, she spends most time of the day at home caring for him. Milena's husband Oscar works long hours, so she spends large spans of time in front of the webcam, making it easy for Patricia to find some time for her sister in between her office work. Their webcam sessions tend to be lively with Milena's other son Alejandro carrying the webcam around the house and Patricia playing new songs to them she down-loaded from the Internet. For Milena, these hour-long webcam sessions counter the feelings of loneliness and boredom that come up during the long days she spends at home solely with her children. Hence, Skype and other webcam-based communication media not only create a contemporaneity between two separate locations that may be geographically and temporarily totally disjunctive.[28] As Daniel Miller (2011) has argued for the case of Facebook, we might further have to understand these media as a kind of third place where people take refuge in, and within which they, in some sense, actually live. Madaianou and Miller (2012) have shown how many of the Filipina migrant mothers they interviewed in London spend virtually all their free time in front of the computer to take part in the lives of their families on the Philippines, making it questionable if these women actually really *live* in the UK.

At this point, I want to come back to the question of the temporal experi-ences the instantaneity of communication via webcam brings about. As from a phenomenological perspective each new medium 'alters our subjectivity while each invites our complicity in formulating space, time, and bodily investment as significant personal and social experience' (Sobchack 2004: 136), we have to understand technological revolutions also as perceptual revolutions and thus how technology transforms us as embodied subjects. Both Vivian Sobchack and

Merleau-Ponty's former student Paul Virilio (2000) argue that the instantaneity of digital communication ultimately obliterates their users' temporal experience. Real time, for Virilio, has now superseded real space, as digital technologies collapse physical distances within an instant. In this way the geographical difference between 'here' and 'there' is eliminated by the speed of light as human history 'crashes headlong into the wall of time' (Armitage 2001: 9). Hence, while Ballester still had to artificially construct the communication between Mimoune and his family in editing, webcam actually allows its users' simultaneous 'presence' at the other's location. For Sobchack, the digital instant, 'in its break from the modernist and cinematic temporal structures of retention and protension, constitutes a form of absolute presence (one abstracted from the objective and subjective discontinuity that gives meaning to the temporal system past/present/ future)' (2004: 158). What she finds so radically new in digital temporality is its 'lack of temporal thickness'.

For Sobchack and Virilio, the seamlessness of digital time, the timelessness of digital communication that makes everything available within an instant, has made the 'here and now' of experience vanish into 'telepresence'. With real-time technologies, time is no longer experienced in terms of Bergsonian duration, as a slow unfolding of events in succession, but is suddenly exposed instantaneously 'with the speed of light'. This allows us to experience events that take place at a distance and immediately react to them. Yet I argue that *Intimate Distance*, while it obviously accounts for the fascinating novel forms of intimacy such instantaneous communication via webcam makes possible, also provides strong ethnographic evidence that the 'friction of distance' (Knox and Marston 2012: 28) is still in place. The time and costs of overcoming distance cannot be abolished so easily by the time-space compression of digital technology that Sobchack and Virilio describe with their very own mix of horror and fascination. One of the main problems with their observations is that they presuppose a smoothly running and stable technological infrastructure. As my film strongly conveys, this is by no means always given. Instead of being provided a crisp image and sound, a typical Skype user experience might also be marked by distortions, low resolution, bad video compression and even the occasional breakdown of connection. When Dittz, for example, webcams with her teenage son in the Philippines, the 'instantaneity of digital communication' more often than not sounds like a bad joke. Her son's image frequently gets stuck and the sound of their conversation turns into distorted noise. In this respect, Dittz's temporal experience is not one of 'real time', but one of waiting, interference and dropouts due to the slow Internet connection. I have deliberately included such moments in the film, as they make apparent very precisely how the 'digital divide' is still very much in place. The particular strength of ethnography (as Brian Larkin [2008] has eloquently pointed out) thus lies in providing a much-needed local corrective to Virilio's and others' claims about the 'annihilation of space by time'; as well as to the celebratory techno-utopianism of the 'Californian Ideology' (see Barbrook 2007), with its promise to connect us immediately across the globe. As my film makes clear, without the appropriate infrastructure, the actual experience of these new ICTs may rather be one of asynchronicity. As *Intimate Distance* is completely composed from the digital images my protagonists transmitted via Skype, the work not only documents my protagonists' individual use patterns but also directly recreates their particular user experiences. Now that new communication media like Skype have become such a ubiquitous part of our daily lives, I am convinced that this must also be reflected in contemporary ethnographic filmmaking. In this way, *Intimate Distance* may be seen as a work of digital visual anthropology that directly engages, in both form and content, with those technologies that shape our global present. As the film is itself a product of the technology it examines, one can further argue that it is no longer set within the cinematic realm of the Deleuzian time-image, with its Bergsonian 'elegiac mysteries of *durée* and memory' (Jameson 1991: 16). Rather, it conveys a new, a third regime of images that is marked by the atemporality of the digital.

Possibilities

n one of his earliest works, the activist-filmmaker Želimir Žilnik (who later produced some of the very first documentaries on the social impact of the German guest worker recruitment programme, the European asylum policy and the fortification of the EU borders) provocatively explores the effectiveness of committed filmmaking. Concerned by the growing poverty in communist Yugoslavia, the young and idealistic director decides to attempt to solve the problem of homelessness himself. At the beginning of his *Black Film* (1971), we see him approaching a group of homeless people in his hometown of Novi Sad. He invites them to stay in his two-room apartment (much to the chagrin of his wife and their small child) and promises to fight for their rights. Armed with a camera and a microphone, he then interviews representatives of institutions as well as passersby to find a solution for his protagonists. Yet his efforts are in vain. The people in the streets answer indifferently and do not feel responsible for the social inequalities in their socialist country. A policeman and other officials abstractly refer to insufficient laws as the barrier to a solution and seem equally blind to the problem. Not even the homeless themselves have an idea of how to change their situation. After a couple of days, Žilnik runs out of film stock and has to bring the project to an end. Stating that he helped them as much as he could, he asks the homeless to leave his apartment. In the end, nothing has changed and his film apparently did not achieve anything. The work ends with the artist's ironic self-questioning: 'What is film – weapon or shit?'

In this last chapter, I want to take up Žilnik's sarcastic question and, in doing so, reframe the relationship between aesthetics, politics and ethics. Accordingly, I will expand on some of my thoughts laid out in the previous chapters of this book. In chapter one I discussed some of the political implications of the aesthetic (broadly understood as the world of images and mass media representations). I have shown how images inevitably carry political assumptions and thus can be (mis-)used for political ends. Drawing on Hannah Arendt, I have explored the regime of in/visibility at work in mass media discourse. In subsequent chapters, I have outlined the ethical imperative of finding modes of expression that come close to the migrant experience; those that consciously use the sensory qualities of film to forge a bond between spectator and subject. Anthropologists have become sensitive toward the politics of representation; toward the hierarchies inscribed in the processes of research and writing and the forms of domination the speaking about others might entail. Besides raising such important concerns regarding the level of representation, some anthropologists have also, quite self-consciously, developed a sense of how their writings might transcend academic discourse and constitute critical interventions in the public sphere. In the inter-war years, scholars such as Ruth Benedict, Margaret Mead and Edward Sapir saw the aim of their work not in the neutral recording of cultural difference but in the pointing out of viable alternatives to the roads taken by Western civilisation. Franz Boas openly challenged the then mainstream convictions of many of his contemporaries in his writings against racism. Likewise, in the 1960s and 1970s there were many anthropologists who felt the need to create a postcolonial relationship to their subjects and thus positioned themselves against neocolonial oppression: Stanley Diamond organised Vietnam 'teach-ins'; Sol Tax developed an 'action anthropology' that sought to achieve social and political goals in (and with) communities that faced serious threats; and Dell Hymes (1972) wanted to 'reinvent' anthropology on an anti-imperialist stance. Such forms of 'engaged Anthropology' (Low and Merry 2010), in their broadest sense, employ anthropological methodology and theorising to arrive at a social critique that unravels structural inequality and power relations. These scholars all reject cultural and moral relativism, a position that anthropologists at times held up to secure their status as 'neutral' scientists (as, for example, in the American Anthropologists Association's 1947 condemnation of the Universal Declaration of Human Rights). In her call for a 'militant anthropology', Nancy Scheper-Hughes declares the position of the 'objective observer' as inappropriate in the contemporary world and grounds the discipline on the primacy of the ethical and moral responsibility; she imagines anthropologists as witnesses, 'accountable for what they see and what they fail to see' (1995: 419) and sees anthropological writing as a potential site of resistance. Yet how can we theorise (or simply understand) the political impact of our representations? Scheper-Hughes addresses this dilemma openly:

> As writers and producers of demanding images and texts, what do we want
> from our readers? To shock? To evoke pity? To create new forms of nar-

rative, an 'aesthetic' of misery, an anthropology of suffering, an anthropological theodicy? And what of the people whose suffering and fearful accommodations to it are transformed into a public spectacle? What is our obligation to them? Those of us who make our living observing and recording the misery of the world have a particular obligation to reflect critically on the impact of the harsh images of human suffering that we foist on the public. [...] To what end are we given and do we represent these images as long as the misery and the suffering continue unabated? (1995: 416)

It is these haunting questions that are at the heart of Renzo Martens' *Episode III: Enjoy Poverty* (2008), a film about the exploitative image economy that mediates the social reality of the war-torn and poverty stricken Democratic Republic of Congo (DRC) to the Western audience. Although his exploration of how we relate to the other in and through representations is dismal, and even appears cynical at times, Martens' radical reflections on the paradoxes of politically engaged art and journalism and the discourse of humanitarianism bear important lessons to be learned.

PLEASE ENJOY POVERTY

The feature-length film chronicles Martens' months-long journey through the DRC. He travels alone and documents his activities with a small non-professional camcorder. Frequently pointing the camera at himself, he takes on a kind of stage persona, that of the archetypal white man as ambassador of Western civilisation. Part abusive spectator ('Experiencing your suffering makes me a better person', he once thanks a group of Congolese men), part journalist, part saviour, he performs the typical roles in which Westerners interact with Africans and takes them to the extreme in order to reveal the degree to which they are embedded in global power structures. Taking up the humanitarian rhetoric of NGOs, his stated mission is to train and empower the Congolese. In an eerie twist on capitalism's logic the message he proclaims is that they must embrace poverty as the country's biggest natural resource that generates more revenue (in the form of international foreign aid and donations) than traditional goods like gold, diamonds, cocoa or coltan put together. Images of poverty, he claims, must therefore be understood as Congo's most lucrative export. As with the country's other resources, however, those that provide the raw material, the poor who are being photographed and filmed, are denied their fair share. While NGOs like Doctors Without Borders and institutions like UNICEF depend on images of suffering to generate charitable donations or media attention that in turn secures the political will to provide development aid, the poor cannot exploit their poverty themselves, they have no ownership over it. As most NGOs spend a large percentage of the donations they receive on their overheads and PR, most international aid effectively flows back to the country that gave it. Martens urges the Congolese people to see themselves as producers; as providers of something the market needs (he frequently refers to poverty as 'a gift that creates deeper understanding'). He goes on to set up an emancipation programme and gives lectures on possible business models that would allow the locals to profit from the 'economical value' of their situation.

In Kanyabayonga, a town in the east of the DRC that suffers from continued violence between militias and the state, Martens learns from Western photojournalists what they earn with images of civil war victims and violated women. Hence, he teaches a group of local wedding photographers how to cater the demands of this market that promises a markedly much bigger profit. In a harrowing scene, he brings these young men to a hospital where he instructs them from which angle to best photograph the malnourished children who await their premature deaths. Through this action, Martens wants to expose to what extent Western media coverage is based on an image economy that requires the victimisation of Africans. His critique, however, not only targets the systems of photojournalism and the PR activities of NGOs but also the sphere of politically engaged art. At one point he visits a gallery exhibition in Kinshasa where stylised black and white photos of Congolese plantation workers are on display. It turns out that the artist is actually the wife of the manager of the plantation where the workers are being exploited like slaves. Martens then meets the plantation owner who buys three photographs of his own underpaid workers for $600 each. This scene succinctly demonstrates what Martens observes: how supposedly critical documentary images become commodities in the art market and might ultimately even be bought (or funded) by the beneficiaries of the exploitation. The art system is thus based on the same exploitative arrangements that shape all the other economic activities between the Global North and the Global South. Yet the empathy these images evoke in the spectators allow them to effectively ignore their own role in the system. The plantation owner can forget that he is the cause of the miserable situation because the suffering has been aesthetically masked in the photograph.

Martens' position here echoes Susan Sontag's (2003) argument that the aesthetics of empathy tends to cover up the structural causes of the represented pain. For Sontag, in most artworks with an ethical appeal the viewers are addressed as the ones to help; the ones who have the power to improve the situation for the suffering other. Yet their own complicity, their privileges, their benefit in these structures of inequality is beautifully obscured. In Martens' film, one can see how the others who offer themselves up to their image have completely accepted

Fig. 34: Renzo Martens presents his message to the Congolese.

this logic of empathy and, consequently, play their assigned role. Martens is frequently asked to deliver reports about the miserable situation in the country, to do something when he is back in Europe. Yet instead of promising this kind of support and giving false hope, he tries to make the mechanisms of the peoples' exploitation clear to them. After a representative of Doctors Without Borders refuses to buy the images the former wedding photographers have taken in the hospital, he declares his emancipation project a failure and modifies his message. He now seeks to convince the Congolese that it is better to accept their suffering, instead of fighting a forlorn fight, and be unhappy. In a remote village that lies outside the reach of UNICEF and Doctors Without Borders and, therefore, also outside the coverage of the journalists that travel in their tow, he puts up a large neon sign that reads 'please enjoy poverty'. He explains to the villagers that they are unable to change their situation and neither can he or his art. Emancipation, he claims, in this situation would mean to not believe in hope from the outside, from Western charity workers, artists, documentarians or institutions.

Towards the end of the film, he confronts a plantation worker and asks him if he owns a TV set, access to water and electricity, a suit or good shoes. As the man negates these questions, Martens tells him that if he wasn't able to obtain these things in the last ten years of working on the plantation he probably never will; that he will always have a job with extremely low wages. As the worker objects that a man needs his salary, Martens answers that 'in Europe we wouldn't want cocoa or coffee or palm oil or coltan to be more expensive'. The radical nature of his work thus lies in enacting its own (and ultimately also the spectator's) complicity in the prevailing system of inequality. In an interview with T. J. Demos (2012b: 92), Martens states that everything his character says or does in the film 'represents the careful reproduction of ruling policies' in order to make them visible to his audience. The strength of his method is that he asks very simple questions that challenge the unquestioned status quo and reveal the inner policies of reality. In an overcrowded camp for war refugees run by the UNHCR, he asks a UN employee why all the plastic sheets that cover the huts carry the logo of the refugee agency and if it would be possible to be sheltered from rain and yet be without a logo. In another kind of Socratic conversation, he interrogates a photojournalist about the ownership of the images he takes. As the photographer is quick to answer that he is the author of his pictures and therefore owns them, Martens counters this by arguing that the people within the images have 'organised' everything that is in his pictures. Hence, Martens' work wants to expose how representations are entangled within a wider set of parameters that normally remain invisible, be it the economic interest of institutions or the career progression of artists, journalists or anthropologists and their place in the market economy. His position on the question of representation is bleak. Images of filmed and photographed poverty for him are not part of the solution. They do not wake up the world, they do not entail a potential for political change. Instead, they are yet another commodity, made in perfect analogy to the exploitation of natural resources and human labour, thus maintaining and actively supporting the status quo.

Martens' radical self-reflexivity thus transcends the questions of voice, position and rapport that are familiar from anthropological discourses on representation. While these debates merely seek to make the 'making' of representations transparent, Martens' analysis also scrutinises their implication in wider economic, social and political structures. He asks for the (literal) cost at which these representations are made; the cost of their inconsequentiality (see Demos 2012b: 98). In this way, he raises fundamental questions about their potential for resistance and criticism, questions that are all-too often avoided by 'radical' scholars or artists. As Scheper-Hughes (1995: 417) has called for, Martens' work is 'politically complicated and morally demanding' and his images are 'capable of sinking through the layers of acceptance, complicity, and bad faith'. Yet his self-questioning and his will to bring to visibility realities that are otherwise obscured from sight do not free him from the ethical demands that his encounters with the other entail. What are we to make of his claim that he wanted to reproduce prevailing power relations in order to expose them? What Martens thereby willingly accepts is that the Congolese people in his film are depicted as destitute victims without agency, dependent on him and his emancipation programme for help from outside. He refuses to portray any aspects of their lives other than those necessary to put forth his thesis. His work thus perpetuates the very images of victimhood it critiques. In some instances he clearly crosses ethical lines to make his point, for example, in the scene where he arranges starving children in an ill-equipped hospital for the lenses of the photographers, to whom he gives entrepreneurial advice. Asking the doctors where to find the 'most severe cases of malnourishment', he performs the cruelty of his character through to the bitter end so that nothing relieves the spectator from the horror of this scene. As the children are undressed for their picture and pushed around like commodities nothing in this scene invites empathy, nothing lulls the viewer into that false proximity with the other's pain that Sontag and others have criticised. All this scene transports is the banality of the toddlers' starvation. Martens here may succeed in displaying the gap between artistic critique and the reality of suffering, in revealing the utter impotence of the aesthetics of empathy. Yet how can he stand by, expose even, the vulnerable bodies of these abandoned children who are reduced to 'bare lives', to their literally naked biological existence? Can his deconstructive aims justify his non-involvement in this situation and the suspension of its ethical demands? For Scheper-Hughes, the position of the detached observer is untenable as it claims to be 'above and outside human events' (1995: 419). Drawing on Emmanuel Levinas, she declares our 'responsibility, accountability, answerability' as the non-negotiable ground for our relationship with the other. Acknowledging his own complicity in the system of inequality thus does not legitimise Martens' non-engagement with its concrete results; his refusal to assist the most vulnerable.

Besides these ethical concerns, Martens' fundamental critique of representation and political engagement bears another problem: if one accepts that the 'system' inescapably determines an image's meaning and that art, or other engaged modes of representation, cannot work against or even escape its terms, then one ultimately surrenders to it. Martens' sermon that the Congolese should opt to submit to an irrevocable reality hence ascribes so much power to the prevailing global arrangements that they appear without alternative. This leads

Fig. 35: Picturing the pain of others in '*Episode III: Please Enjoy Poverty*'.

in the end to a very reactionary position that only helps those who benefit from the status quo. Yet is an image, a text or a work of art really unable to politicise an audience, to inspire protest, to implement the kind of 'civil contract' Ariella Azoulay envisions? How can we define the political dimension of such work? At what point, under which circumstances and in what context might a representation still gain political momentum? To explore these complex questions, I now return to the work of Jacques Rancière. His explorations of the politics of aesthetics focus on the realm of art, yet I believe that they should be productively adapted to the discourses on representation and engagement in anthropology and ethnographic filmmaking.

RETHINKING POLITICS AND AESTHETICS

What Martens' bleak vision ultimately depicts is, to use a Rancièrean term, merely the process of the police. For Rancière, however, art is capable of much more. It may actually subvert the established order by creating experiences that are opposed to the ruling distribution of the sensible. Art can provide a form of dissensus that places what is given in conflict with a different conception of the world. This is exactly what makes an aesthetic articulation potentially political. Politics, Rancière defines as an action of dissent that occurs at the moment when two distinct processes meet: the process of the police and the demand for equality. Hence, 'it places one world in another – for instance, the world where the factory is a public space in that where it is considered private, the world where workers speak, and speak about the community, in that where their voices are mere cries expressing pain' (2010: 38). Politics for him is a clash of two heterogeneous distributions of the sensible; a battle over the image of society: not a conflict of interests or opinions, but a dispute about what appears as given. This is precisely the point where aesthetics come into play. For Rancière, art offers a privileged space for the formulation or imagination of another world, of that what is not (yet). Art does not inhabit a sphere of its own; it is not a separate activity detached from everything else. Rather, it is 'the transformation of thought into the sensory experience of the community' (2006: 44) and it is only through aesthetic articulations that the real can be thought. Aesthetic acts may therefore propose a new access to reality and suggest new forms of communion. They might inspire a new distribution of the sensible: an adjustment, however small, of the ruling division between the visible and the invisible, the audible and the inaudible, the sayable and the unsayable. Political art, therefore, is not necessarily about the communication of a political message but about an intervention in the organisation of communicable form. Art's 'effectivity', that Žilnik and Martens so passionately dispute, for Rancière might thus lie in reorganising

145

visibility in such a way as to reveal the hidden power structures that the consensual discourse of humanitarianism and committed art has effectively obscured and propose a viable alternative to it.[29]

An exceptional ethnographic filmmaker who has taken such a path is Jean Rouch. Instead of claiming to neutrally record reality, as was the academic consensus of his time, Rouch repeatedly created provocative images that 'challenge his audiences to think new thoughts about Africa and Africans' (Stoller 1994: 85). In many of Rouch's films, the established order is turned upside down. In *Les Maîtres Fous* (1955), the members of a Hauka possession cult take on the identities of their colonial oppressors in order to steal their powers. In *Petit à Petit* (1970), a young Nigerien entrepreneur who plans to build a luxury hotel for Europeans travels to Paris to study the customs of his future clients. In a famous scene, he approaches several French people to measure the dimensions of their bodies, thus subverting the (post)colonial power relations. Rouch's works of 'ethnofiction' originate from a collaborative process with his protagonists that constantly disturbs the fixed distribution of roles in ethnographic filmmaking: of who is filmmaker and who is filmed; who is observer and who is observed. Accordingly, Rouch calls into question some of the basic assumptions of the anthropological discipline: who is entitled to speak about what, who is regarded as qualified to think and who is regarded as unqualified, who carries out the science and who is considered its object. For Rouch, the cinema is the privileged site where such transgressions become possible, a 'primary site for disruption and transformation' (Grimshaw 2001: 120). In the surrealist tradition, he wants to transform his audience psychologically and politically (Stoller 1994). He uses humour, defamiliarisation and unsettling juxtapositions to jolt our culturally conditioned perception.

THE RIGHTS OF THE STATELESS

Rancière's theory in many ways bears important similarities to Hannah Arendt's thoughts on the politics of visibility evoked in chapter one in order to analyse the current mass media representation of migration. There, I showed how mainstream media, but also supposedly critical documentaries, form a particular distribution of the sensible that only allows us to perceive 'illegal' migrants as an ideological category: either suggesting their criminality or their passive need for humanitarian care. These media images thus prohibit a perspective on these migrants as active agents who are in control of their own fate. As distinct individuals with an agenda, they remain invisible in public discourse. In Rancière's terms, they form the 'part that has no part' in the community. Both Arendt and Rancière generally believe in the emancipatory power of visibility. For Arendt, visibility is the basic prerequisite for political action in the common space of appearances. For Rancière, dissensual acts of visualisation can widen the frame of what can be perceived; of what counts as discourse in the prevailing sensible order. In this way both authors agree that political exclusion has to be understood foremost as a process in which those who have no part are made effectively invisible. Arendt's account in particular provides deep insights into the construction of the police consensus that prevails in the Western media: the ruling visual order in which 'illegal' migrants are exposed (as 'bare lives' who are politically abandoned) and concealed (as political subjects) at the same time. While Rancière appreciates the impact of Arendt's analysis, he takes issue with her equation of statelessness with an existence without rights. As such an existence without rights for Arendt entails the impossibility of public appearance, Rancière asks, then how could the basic human rights, the Arendtian 'right to have rights', ever be claimed by those excluded from it? How is political action possible for those who are denied public visibility? As discussed in chapter one, the aporia Arendt finds within the concept surrounding the rights of man stems from the fact that it 'broke down' in the face of those stateless refugees who had lost their citizenship and therewith their legal personhood, and consequently their existence as political beings. Accordingly for Arendt, the rights of man are the rights of those who have no other rights: the mere travesty of a right, a right that no state protects, a right that is 'granted even to savages' (1973: 300). Rancière, however, finds a similar aporia even within this argument – in that Arendt distinguishes between natural man and citizen (between a natural visibility that is merely private and a public visibility that is political) she does not offer an analysis of the experience of statelessness but rather an ontological assumption. For Arendt, the very space of appearance is only accessible for those who possess political representation and excludes those left without it. In order to demonstrate the worthlessness of human rights she sets up what Rancière terms an 'ontological trap' (2010: 67). In her account, human rights are either identical with citizenship, meaning that they are the rights of those who already have rights, which is nothing more than a tautology; or they constitute 'the rights of those who have no rights', which is an oxymoron that amounts to nothing. For Rancière, this Arendtian dilemma eventually leads to a dangerous depoliticisation of the concept: if they only remain the 'rights of the victims, the rights of those who were unable to enact any rights or even any claim in their name', then ultimately they have to be 'upheld by others, at the cost of shattering the edifice of International Rights, in the name of a new right to "humanitarian interference" – itself ultimately no more than the right to invasion' (2010: 62). In Arendt's deeply pessimistic account, human rights thus eventually become the rights of others. This leads, at best, to the depoliticized forms of

NGO humanitarianism that Renzo Martens encountered in the Congo and, at worst, to their annexation and reinterpretation as the right of intervention, as happened, for example, in the Iraq War. Rancière, however, vehemently disputes Arendt's neat distinction between the citizen who is equipped with rights and the stateless 'natural man' who lacks them. While, for Arendt, this partition is an ontological given, for Rancière it is merely subject to a political contestation about how and where this distinction is drawn. As a result he proposes a different definition of human rights; one that escapes the Arendtian quandary. For Rancière, they are 'the rights of those who have not the rights that they have and have the rights that they have not' (2010: 67). This seemingly paradoxical formulation deserves further explanation. Accordingly I will explore Rancière's conception of the political latitude of those who do not possess a legal personhood through an analysis of Sarah Vos's film *Welcome to Holland* (2003). This documentary depicts the struggle of a group of teenage migrants who have been transferred to a newly opened boarding-school-like detention centre for underage asylum seekers (termed AMAs by Dutch law). I will discuss how Vos's film offers a precise chronicle of the enactment of a political dispute in the Rancièrean sense and also constitutes a critical intervention into the consensual representation of 'illegal' migrants in the media.

PUBLIC VISIBILITY AND POLITICAL ACTION:
WELCOME TO HOLLAND

The setting of Vos's film is Campus Vught, a former military barracks that has been rebuilt to accommodate young migrants who have entered the Netherlands without their parents and with no chance to gain asylum. As they cannot be expelled under Dutch law until the age of eighteen, the camp is meant to provide them with an environment in which they can attain qualifications that will help them when they return to their home countries. The institution was created in the wake of a tightening of Dutch asylum laws. It is seen as an experiment by the Dutch government and funded with €9 million. Its claim is to offer 'humane treatment' to the young 'illegals' and to provide them with the chance to make 'positive investments in themselves' as the campus director states in the film. However, the inevitability of their future deportation is made clear to them. Thus, contact with Dutch society is kept to a minimum. The AMAs are not allowed to leave the campus as they should not develop social bonds with Dutch people or get to know the country. To further prohibit integration, no Dutch is spoken on the campus and the TVs within the institution do not show local TV channels. Instead, the minors are offered a variety of English language and computer skills courses and other activities that should 'motivate them for repatriation'. To enhance this motivation, the campus administration has come up with a complex system of social control. The AMAs, all between fifteen and seventeen years old, are separated into 'rookies' and 'seniors'. 'Rookies', who wear green clothes, have no private sphere as they share their room with up to fifteen others. Through an elaborate scoring system, they can gradually earn more and more rewards: greater privacy, increased freedom and some pocket money that they can spend in the campus shop. Scores are awarded for good behaviour, waking up independently, introducing new rookies to the campus system, and for 'accepting criticism' put forth by their coaches. At a certain level, they can become 'seniors', who are distinguished by their red t-shirts and enjoy further privileges, for example a 'club house' which they run by themselves. This reward system, however, does not run as smoothly as planned. As the coaches hand over the first red 'senior' shirts, along with some soft drinks and cookies, the receivers simply refuse to accept them. In front of all the assembled 'rookies', they choose to demand more freedom for everybody: a less rigid course schedule but, above all else, the right to leave the campus. Subsequently the group goes on strike, refusing their categorisation into 'rookies' and 'seniors' and withholding their general cooperation in the courses and activities programme (along with everything else that should distract them from their confinement). Right from the beginning, they develop a clear sense of how the presence of the film crew alters the situation on the campus and how they can directly benefit from this. The film team not only constitutes a new public that can be addressed, it also fosters a new distribution of roles inside Campus Vught: the former observers, the coaches and guards, now become observed as well. In front of Vos's camera, Théophile, who gradually becomes the spokesperson of the revolt, explicitly stages himself as the interviewer of the campus administration and uses this authority to call their rules into question. He publicly disputes the official definition of Vught as a 'campus' and redefines the place for what it is: a camp, a prison. The presence of the camera thus supports the AMAs' 'subjectification', a term Rancière (1998: 35ff) employs for the process by which political subjects deprive themselves from the police categories of identification and classification.

As the strike becomes public, the campus administration struggles to find an appropriate reaction. The campus director is replaced and his successor tries to offer some small concessions in order to keep the minors calm. Yet, instead of establishing a new consensus, this move eventually puts on the bargaining table what, throughout the film until then, appeared as non-negotiable: the right to leave the confined space. The strikers turn down the offer that a two-hour leave from the campus might be introduced as a reward within the scoring system. Instead, a group of forty youngsters leave the campus; they are not stopped by the security guards. Outside they give interviews to journalists and eventually decide to go to The Hague to demonstrate in front of the Ministry of Justice. Finally, the doors of the campus are open. The demonstrators have their pictures taken by surrounding journalists while they take their first stroll through the city. Vos underlays this highly symbolic action with a children's choir's performance of David Bowie's 'Space Oddity'. As the strike has also revealed seething conflicts between the coaches and the management about the proper reaction to the minors' demands, the campus system ultimately collapses. Campus Vught is closed and the young asylum seekers are transferred to foster families or other institutions with more freedom.

From a Rancierèan perspective, *Welcome to Holland* first of all chronicles a dispute over the given order, a dissensus about the AMAs' rights. This brings us back to the question about the 'illegal' migrants' possibilities for political action where there is lack of citizenship and so to Rancière's seemingly paradoxical definition of human rights as 'the rights of those who have not the rights that they have and have the rights that they have not'. With Rancière, we can say that in the course of their strike the young asylum seekers stage a two-fold demonstration. On the one hand, they show that they do not have the rights that they have. Through their confinement, they do not enjoy the rights that they are supposed to have according to articles 3 and 9 of the UN universal declaration of human rights that the Netherlands has agreed to and signed. As they are not convicted of a crime, they should enjoy the right to liberty and shall not be subjected to arbitrary arrest. By making their political exclusion public in front of Vos's camera, by giving interviews to journalists and by taking their protest to the street, they draw attention to the ways in which they are denied the same rights the Dutch citizens enjoy. Yet, in this way, they also show that they have the rights that they have not. Through their public actions they demonstrate their equality as speaking beings, despite their lack of legal personhood. They enact the Arendtian 'right to have rights' at the very moment they address the public, and thus speak and act *as if* they had the same rights as their audience. Hence, these rights belong to them precisely in the moment they do something with them 'to construct a dissensus against the denial of rights they suffer' (Rancière 2010: 71). Accordingly, the strength of the concept of human rights 'lies in the back-and-forth movement between the initial inscription of the right and the dissensual stage on which it is put the test' (ibid.). This is why they can be invoked even by non-citizens and even against national laws that deny their effectivity. As for Arendt the rights of man exclusively belong to definite or permanent subjects (the citizens equipped with public visibility), she must remain blind to the conflicts fought outside of the framework of the nation-state . In this way, her account ultimately prevents us from understanding 'illegal' migrants as political actors that might claim their rights. For Rancière, in contrast, human rights are precisely the subject of the social struggles that are at the heart of politics proper that, for him, is purely the staging of equality within conditions of inequality. Thus, these rights are not the precondition for politics, as Arendt argues, but politics is the dispute about their implementation. As Azoulay notes, their declaration 'has become a text in the hands of citizens and noncitizens alike, who may use it in the public arena in order to address power and who are capable of doing so independently of the logic of the market or the nation-state and its sovereign' (2008: 49).

Vos's film, however, is much more than a precise document of such a successful political subjectification, of a prolific enactment of equality. Her work is political in itself because it is the filmic demonstration of a world in which such equality eventually is possible. It subverts the distribution of roles between who has the agency to act and who is the passive object of humanitarian care, between who makes the rules and who has to follow them. In Rancièrean terminology, the film puts 'two worlds in one and the same world' (2010: 69): the world in which the camp restricts the freedom of movement and the world in which its doors can be pushed open. Thus, it makes manifest to the senses that the regime that governs migration can actually be overcome. It constitutes a redistribution of the field of experience in which new forms of emancipation, new modes of political action, seem possible. It is an intervention in the visible and the sayable as it shows its protagonists not as objects of the police regimes of exposure and concealment (like most of the examples discussed in chapter one), but as political subjects enacting their rights and claiming equality.

ANTHROPOLOGY AND THE ENACTMENT OF POSSIBILITIES

To bring the argument I have built over the course of the last chapters to a conclusion, I come back to Scheper-Hughes' demanding questions: What do we want with the images we create? What can our representations possibly achieve? I hope to have shown how important it is to intervene in the current discourse about migration, the ruling arrangement of the sensible that denies the 'illegal' migrants their part in what is common to the community. In chapter one, I have begun my analysis with an investigation of the prevailing forms of visibility that demarcate the space between the 'proper' citizens that constitute the normative subjects of political debate, and the stateless migrants that remain trapped 'in all the nakedness of their intolerable difference' (Rancière 1998: 119). I have shown how the dominant mass media representation of migration produces the exclusive categories of 'legality' and 'illegality' and further reproduces the state's modes of surveillance and control. The migrants' resulting invisibility as political actors and overexposure as 'aliens', or 'others' thus effectively reduces them to the status of non-persons in regard to the ruling law. In the following chapters, then, I have described new forms of visibility that do not merely reproduce this distribution as a given, but rather aim to intervene in the present sensible order. They search for novel ways for the artistic representation of lives that are without political representation. It is in this vein that I have explored the transformative powers of the medium of film, its ability to forge new connections between spectator and subject based on the concrete sensoriality of its modes of communication. In chapter two, I have discussed how the mimetic qualities of cinema may draw us into close sensory participation with the other's lifeworld. I have shown how film may establish a profoundly ethical engagement by opening up an intersubjective space between the filmmaker, the spectator and the filmed. In chapters three and four, I have offered a Deleuzian perspective on cinema as a form of articulating new thoughts about space and time. Departing from an understanding of migration studies as merely the study of marginalised people, I have explored how transnational human mobility produces important new spatial and temporal formations that shape our globally interconnected world. In chapter three, particularly, I have analysed how forms of temporal and spatial montage provide new possibilities for the organisation and dissemination of ethnographic knowledge in terms of multivocality and multiperspectivity and thus foster the viewer's active engagement with the contradictions and uncertainties of our deterritorialised present. Chapter four then further describes film's ability to embody its temporal complexity. The innovative cinematic approaches I have presented throughout this book thus constitute attempts to repartition the field of the visible and the audible; to offer other perspectives on migration than the economist or functionalist views that dominate political debate. Film's unique capacity to express experience as experience thus allows for a redistribution of the sensible in the Rancierèan sense. It may implement the migrant experience (that hitherto remained indiscernible and unrepresented in the prevailing order) into the common space of appearance.

With the trilogy of my own films, I have sought to create cinematic works that do exactly this, that adhere to the autonomy of migration and migrant subjects. In *Intimate Distance* I documented the manifold ways my protagonists have invented to overcome the frictions of distance by using new communication technology. As Axel and Serpil's time together is limited by the German visa regulations, they help themselves with little rituals like co-sleeping in front of the webcam in order to be close to each other. In *A Tale of Two Islands*, I sought to invent an aesthetic form that describes the contrasts but also the intimate links between two of the Comoros Islands, Mayotte and Anjouan. The work thus disarticulates the existing political partitioning of space along the EU border that forcefully keeps their inhabitants apart. In *Tell Me When...* there is an almost utopian scene that subverts, if only for one instant, the roles that migrants in Melilla's detention centre normally are assigned. In the party scene towards the end of the film, we see the African participants of the Semana Santa procession dressed up in black suits and dancing cheerily with the Spanish inhabitants of Melilla. Opara, who always tirelessly tried to achieve some public recognition for their situation, gives a speech and all the city's dignitaries listen. It is a moment that opens, if only briefly, a realm of possibility; a moment of unrealised potentiality. It possibly depicts a 'coming community' (see Agamben 1993) that has overcome political exclusion. I, therefore, am convinced that film can be a 'weapon' (and, in this way, more than 'shit') when it disputes the established consensus; when it expands the possibilities of what can be said, heard, felt and thought. I strongly believe that anthropology, and ethnographic filmmaking in particular, must constitute an important site for the formulation of such Rancierèan dissensus. Musing on the nature of the anthropological enterprise, David Graeber sees its singular quality in that it 'opens windows on other possible forms of human existence' (2007: 1). For Graeber, the discipline serves 'as a constant reminder that most of what we assume to be immutable has been, in other times and places, arranged quite differently, and therefore, that human possibilities are in almost every way greater than we ordinarily imagine' (ibid.). In a similar vein, Arjun Appadurai has distinguished between an 'ethics of probability' and an 'ethics of possibility' in humanity's orientation towards the future. The ethics of probability for Appadurai is manifest in the 'modern regimes of diagnosis, counting, and accounting' while the ethics of possibility increases our horizons of hope and 'expand(s) the field of the imagination' (2013: 295). It is this ethics of possibility on which he bases our ethical commitment as anthropologists. The present regime that governs migratory movements is a perfect example for an ethics solely concerned with probability, with managing the numbers of asylum claims, producing statistical evidence on migration routes, and equating citizenship with national belonging. Yet we can also regard migration from the perspective of the ethics of possibility as a progressive social movement that fundamentally reconfigures the political (see Heidenreich 2015: 18). In this perspective, the transnational movement of people creates spaces of potentiality through which we can challenge the probabilistic policies by which citizens and non-citizens are governed. Anthropologists who commit to an ethics of possibility, therefore, are not just neutral observers of the status quo, mere custodians of the police order. Instead, their representations might become privileged sites where two worlds can be put into one another: the world as it is, shaped by the prevailing structures of inequality, and a world that could possibly transform into something better.

NOTES

1   These are documented in the blog http://unknownrefugees.tumblr.com/ (accessed 16 November 2015).

2   During the events of summer and autumn 2015, Germany's migration politics somewhat changed. As more and more refugees from the Middle East started to enter Europe via Turkey and the Balkans, many eastern European states started to open their borders and just let people travel on towards Central Europe, thus effectively undermining the Dublin regulations. Chancellor Merkel, now unable to pass on responsibility for these people to the EU border states, suddenly expressed her willingness to accept large numbers of asylum seekers, without setting an upper limit. Interestingly, this change of politics once again became manifest in a globally circulating image, a photo showing a Syrian refugee shooting a selfie with Merkel. Conservative politicians, particularly from her own party, heavily criticized the chancellor for the symbolism of this image and its welcoming message. In the weeks that followed, German public opinion that initially applauded Merkel's decision began to shift again and the large influx of asylum seekers was met with increasing fear and rejection.

3   *Tell Me When...* (2011), *A Tale of Two Islands* (2012) and *Intimate Distance* (2015) have been screened internationally at such festivals as the Berlin International Film Festival, Jihlava IDFF, Dok.fest Munich, Rencontres Internationales Paris, Berlin, Madrid, the Kassel Documentary Film and Video Festival, World Film Festival Tartu and the Göttingen International Ethnographic Film Festival. They have been exhibited in museums such as the Hong-gah museum in Taipei (on the occasion of the Taiwan International Video Art Exhibition) and the Dresden Museum of Ethnology as well as in exhibition projects such as Vienna Art Week or the Luleå Art Biennial. They are distributed online through Doc Alliance Films (www.dafilms.com).

4   A renewed interest in montage as an analytical tool will also inform my discussion of anthropology's current spatial concepts in chapter three.

5   For Bal, 'migratory aesthetics' describes cultural expressions in a world, in which trans-national movement is not the exception but the norm, in which migration also shapes the 'host' societies. She claims that the medium of video is particularly suited to convey the aesthetics produced by migratory culture (2015: 132).

6   I contacted Dittz through fellow visual anthropologist Michaela Lola Abrera, who collaborated with me on this episode of the film. Dittz was one of the participants in Abrera's video *Virtual Balikbayan Box* (2015), a fascinating collaborative film project about the experiences of female OFWs who work as caregivers or domestic workers abroad. A 'Balikbayan box' is a kind of a care package, a corrugated box overseas Filipinos send to their loved ones containing presents and sundry goods that 'constitute a performance of diasporic intimacy' (Camposano 2012: 84). These boxes are the prime symbol for the transnational existence many Filipino families share. Abrera invited the participants of her film to contribute through mobile phone video diaries, pictures, artworks and even Facebook messages sent to the Virtual Balikbayan Box Facebook page she set up. Her aim

was to empower these migrant mothers by giving them the opportunity to share their stories on their own terms. The result is a film that makes tangibly manifest what it means to leave one's own children behind to look after the children of others.

7   In the summer of 2015, these numbers began to rise again with the increasing influx of Syrian refugees into central Europe.

8   For a comprehensive historical overview on the photographic construction of the criminal, see Regener 1999.

9   Today, these boats have to take longer and even riskier routes to Greece's Aegean Islands, Lampedusa or the Spanish Canary Islands.

10 The group consists of artist and filmmaker Charles Heller and architect and theorist Lorenzo Pezzani in collaboration with SITU studio.

11 I will explore the concept of spatial montage in further detail in chapter three.

12 Recall, for example, Maurice Bloch's famous study *From Blessing to Violence* (1986) in which he interprets a circumcision ritual of the Merina people of Madagascar as a symbolical assault on women, even though they themselves describe it as a 'blessing'.

13 See, for example, the Buenos Aires Film Festival's catalogue description of the film (BAFICI 2011: 38).

14 Merleau-Ponty terms it pre-objective experience; James, 'pure' experience.

15 Howes' negative view on vision as alienating is, for example, manifest in his formulation of 'general laws' such as: 'the more a society emphasizes the eye, the less communal it will be; the more it emphasizes the ear, the less individualistic it will be' (1991c: 177f).

16 Interestingly, newer research in neuroscience supports this view by suggesting that it might indeed be impossible (nor useful) to distinguish bodily feelings and perception from the cognitive activity of the brain (for example, see Damasio 1994). An understanding of viewing as embodied is further underpinned by studies on mirror neurons that demonstrate that the brain's premotor-cortex shows exactly the same activity both when an action is actively performed and when its performance by another is only passively observed (see Ramachandran 2000).

17 Serhat Karakayali and Vassilis Tsianos (2007: 15) have exemplified the dangers involved in taking on only one of those perspectives with regard to the political analysis of migration processes. While macro-level accounts of governmental control tend to overemphasise their power and see subjects as mere pawns in a given matrix, ethnographic micro-studies routinely remain locked in celebrating migrants' subversive practices.

18 According to Clifford, this is the magic formula by which ethnographers claim their interpretive authority (1983: 118).

19 There are some other well-known rules and techniques for establishing coherent cinematic spaces. Spatial continuity in movement-image cinema, for example, demands that all space in which the action occurs is introduced by an establishing shot. Within a once established cinematic space, the 180-degree rule defines the on-screen spatial relationship between a character and another character or an object along an imaginary axis. By keeping the camera on one side of this axis for every shot, their positions will appear consistent throughout the scene. Match on action cutting then creates a visual bridge between two shots taken from different perspectives by having a character begin an action in the first and carry it on in the next, thus making the change of angles go unnoticed. For an in-depth description of continuity editing, see Bordwell and Thompson 2010.

20 Deleuze's notion of the virtual in relation to visual anthropology is developed in chapter four.

21 In taking on such a decidedly transnational perspective, Rivera also overcomes the limitations that arise with many artists' sole fixation on the US/Mexican border as the

main site where statements on the nature of the economic and political relations between both countries could be made. Such 'border art' (for an expansive overview, see Fox 1999; Sheren 2015) often fails to account for the complexities contemporary migratory culture has brought about.

22 Kiener herself states that her reflexive mode of montage aims at a veracity of a higher order in which the concrete situation of time and place become unimportant (2008: 407).

23 On the social divide in Mayotte's labour market, see Guyot 2006: 80.

24 In the conclusion of this chapter, I will come back to this point and further explore how these new communication media have a severe impact onto their users' temporal consciousness.

25 I have already discussed this cultural trope in chapter one.

26 'Cinderella' not only alludes to Hosni's classical beauty but also to her rags-to-riches-biography.

27 Stephan's exhibition at New York's MoMA, PS1, where I first viewed the work, actually also displayed the sleeves of all the commercial VHS releases of Hosni's films.

28 A winter evening for Patricia is a summer morning for Milena – they are connected in real time, yet they live out of sync.

29 In this respect, Martens' latest (and still ongoing) project, the foundation of the 'Institute for Human Activities' (IHA), exceeds the merely cynical documentation of the process of the police. The IHA is essentially a gentrification programme that has established an art centre on the grounds of a former Unilever plantation in the DRC, about five hundred miles from Kinshasa. It wants to enable the workers to accumulate cultural, symbolic and financial capital through critical engagement with their plantation labour. While Martens has not completely abandoned his role as the paternalistic Western 'do-gooder', he now actually sets up distribution channels through which plantation workers can sell works of art (like sculptures made out of chocolate) in established Western art galleries to which they would normally never have access. Hence, the IHA's project aims at diverting economic flows in such a way that the capital accrued by artistic critiques of global inequality brings prosperity not solely to 'creative cities' like New York, Berlin, London or Venice (where such work is normally exhibited, discussed and sold), but also to those places that actually suffer from it.

FILMOGRAPHY

14 Kilometers (2007) Gerardo Olivares. 94 min. Brussels: Cooperative Nouveau Cinema.

A Tale of Two Islands (2012) Steffen Köhn and Paola Calvo. 16 min. Loop. Two-channel video installation. Prague: Doc Alliance Films (split-screen version) and Berlin: Arsenal Experimental (installation version).

Black Film (1971) Želimir Žilnik. 14 min. Novi Sad: Playground Produkcija.

Border (2004) Laura Waddington. 27 min. Paris: Péage Neutre Diffusion.

Ceuta (2006) Florian Schneider. Single-channel video installation. Loop. Distributed by the artist.

La Citadelle Europe – Lost in Transit (2004) Gilles de Maistre. 61 min. Strasbourg: Arte France.

Eat, Drink, Man, Woman (1994) Ang Lee. 124 min. Los Angeles: The Samuel Goldwyn Company.

Episode III: Enjoy Poverty (2008) Renzo Martens. 90 min. Brussels: Renzo Martens Menselijke Activiteiten.

The Fold (2011) Aryu Danusiri. 12 min. Watertown: DER (Documentary Educational Resources).

Girl from Moush (1993) Gariné Torossian. 6 min. Toronto: Canadian Filmmakers Distribution Centre.

Intimate Distance (2015) Steffen Köhn. 17 min. Prague: Doc Alliance Films.

In this World (2002) Michael Winterbottom. 88 min. London: BBC.

It Happened Just Before (2006) Anja Solomonwitz. 72 min. Wien: Autlook.

Ixok-Woman (1990) Wilma Kiener. 90 min. München: Matzka-Kiener Filmproduktion.

Kama Sutra (1996) Mira Nair. 114 min. Cologne: Pandora Filmproduktion.

The Lady from Shanghai (1947) Orson Welles. 81 min. Los Angeles: Columbia.

Les Maîtres Fous (1955) Jean Rouch. 36 min. Paris: Les Films de la Pléiade.

Liquid Traces – The The Left-to-Die Boat Case (2014) Charles Heller and Lorenzo Pezzani. 17 min. Distributed by the artists.

Measures of Distance (1988) Mona Hatoum. 15 min. A Western Front video production, Vancouver. Distributed by Mona Hatoum/White Cube Gallery London.

Mimoune (2006) Gonzalo Ballester. 12 min. Murcia: Distributed by the artist.

Mirages (2008) Olivier Dury. 46 min. Gentilly: L'Oeil Sauvage.

Passagères Clandestines – Mother's Crossing (2004) Lodet Desmet. 60 min. Paris: La Compagnie des Taxi-Brousse.

Petit à Petit (1970) Jean Rouch. 96 min. Paris: Les Films de la Pléiade.

Not Waving, But Drowning (2009) Elias Grootaers. 53 min. Ghent: Cassette for Timescapes.

The Piano (1993) Jane Campion. 121 min. Los Angeles: Miramax.

Qu'ils Reposent en Révolte (2010) Sylvain George. 150 min. Paris: Independencia Distribution.

Sahara Chronicle (2006/7) Ursula Biemann. 78 min. 12-channel video installation. Chicago: Video Data Bank.

Saphir (2006) Zineb Sedira. Two-channel video installation. 19 min. Funded and commissioned by Film and Video Umbrella and the Photographer's Gallery, London.

The Scent of the Green Papaya (1993) Tranh Anh Hung. 104 min. Paris: MKL.

The Sixth Section (2003) Alex Rivera. 27 min. New York: Subcine.

The Song of the Germans (2015) Emeka Ogboh. 1'14 min. Ten-channel sound installation. Distributed by the artist.

Speeches – Chapter 2: Words on Streets (2013) Bouchra Khalili. 18 min. Produced for "The Encyclopedic Palace", 55th Venice Biennale, 2013. From "The Speeches Series" (three digital films, 2012–2013). Courtesy of the artist and Galerie Polaris, Paris.

Sudeuropa (2007) Raphael Cuomo and Maria Iorio. 40 min. Brussels: Argos.

Tarifa Traffic – Death in the Straits of Gibraltar (2003) Joakim Demmer. 60 min. Zurich: Dschoint Ventschr.

Tell Me When… (2011) Steffen Köhn and Paola Calvo. 54 min. Prague: Doc Alliance Films.

The Three Disappearances of Soad Hosni (2011) Rania Stephan. 70 min. Beirut: JounFilms.

To Live with Herds (1972) David MacDougall. 70 min. Los Angeles: University of California/Rice University Media Center.

The Virtual Balikbayan Box (2015) Michaela Lola Abrera. 15 min. Berlin: Freie Universität. MA Visual and Media Anthropology.

Welcome to Holland (2003) Sarah Vos. 100 min. Amsterdam: VPRO.

BIBLIOGRAPHY

Agamben, Giorgio (1993) *The Coming Community*, trans. Michael Hardt. Minneapolis, MN: University of Minnesota Press.

____ (1995) 'We Refugees', trans. Michael Rocke, *Symposium*, 49, 2, 114–19.

____ (1998) *Homo Sacer: Sovereign Power and Bare Life*, trans. Daniel Heller-Roazen. Stanford, CA: Stanford University Press.

Amelina, Anna, Thomas Faist, Nina Glick Schiller and Devrimsel Nergiz (eds) (2012) *Beyond Methodological Nationalism: Research Methodologies for Cross-Border Studies*. London: Routledge.

Andrew, J. Dudley (1978) 'The Neglected Tradition of Phenomenology in Film Theory', *Wide Angle*, 2, 2, 44–9.

Andrijasevic, Rutvica (2007) 'Das zur Schau gestellte Elend: Gender, Migration und Repräsentation in Kampagnen gegen Menschenhandel', in Transit Migration Forschungsgruppe (ed.) *Turbulente Ränder. Neue Perspektiven auf Migration an den Grenzen Europas*. Bielefeld: Transcript, 7–22.

Appadurai, Arjun (1988) 'Putting Hierarchy In Its Place', *Cultural Anthropology*, 3, 1, 36–49.

____ (1996) *Modernity at Large: Cultural Dimensions of Globalization*. Minneapolis, MN: University of Minnesota Press.

____ (2013) *The Future as Cultural Fact: Essays on the Global Condition*. London: Verso.

Arendt, Hannah ([1951] 1973) *The Origins of Totalitarianism*, new edition. New York: Harcourt Brace.

____ (1958) *The Human Condition*. Chicago: University of Chicago Press.

____ (1994) *Essays in Understanding 1930–1954: Formation, Exile, and Totalitarianism*, ed. Jerome Kohn. New York: Harcourt Brace.

Armitage, John (2001) *Virilio Live: Selected Interviews*. London: Sage.

Aydemir, Murat and Alex Rotas (eds) (2008) *Migratory Settings*. Amsterdam and New York: Rodopi.

Azoulay, Ariella (2008) *The Civil Contract of Photography*. Cambridge, MA: MIT Press.

____ (2012) *Civil Imagination: A Political Ontology of Photography*. London: Verso.

Bal, Mieke (2008) 'Heterochronotopia', in Murat Aydemir and Alex Rotas (eds) *Migratory Settings*. Amsterdam and New York: Rodopi, 35–56.

____ (2012) 'Heterochrony in the Act: The Migratory Politics of Time', in Mieke Bal and Miguel Á. Hernández-Navarro (eds) *Art and Visibility in Migratory Culture: Conflict, Resistance, and Agency*. Amsterdam and New York: Rodopi, 211–39.

____ (2015) 'Documenting What?: Auto-Theory and Migratory Aesthetics', in Alexandra Juhasz and Alisa Lebow (eds) *A Companion to Contemporary Documentary Film.* Oxford: Wiley Blackwell, 124–44.

Bal, Mieke and Miguel Ángel Hernández-Navarro (2008) *2move: Video, Art, Migration.* Murcia: Cendeac.

____ (eds) (2012) *Art and Visibility in Migratory Culture: Conflict, Resistance, and Agency.* Amsterdam and New York: Rodopi.

Banks, Marcus and Howard Morphy (eds) (1997) *Rethinking Visual Anthropology.* New Haven, CT: Yale University Press.

Barbrook, Richard (2007) *Imaginary Futures: From Thinking Machines to the Global Village.* London: Pluto Press

Benjamin, Walter ([1936] 1969) 'The Work of Art in the Age of Mechanical Reproduction', in *Illuminations,* ed. Hannah Arendt, trans. Harry Zohn. New York: Schocken. 217–51.

Bergson, Henri ([1911] 1988) *Matter and Memory,* trans. Nancy Margaret Paul and W. Scott Palmer. New York: Zone.

Biemann, Ursula and Brian Holmes (eds) (2006) *The Maghreb Connection: Movements of Life Across Northern Africa.* Barcelona: Actar.

Birnbaum, Daniel (2007) *Chronology.* New York: Sternberg Press.

Bischoff, Christine, Francesca Falk and Sylvia Kafehsy (eds) (2010) *Images of Illegalized Immigration: Towards a Critical Iconology of Politics.* Bielefeld: Transcript.

Bishop, Claire (2005) *Installation Art: A Critical History.* London: Tate.

____ (2012) *Artificial Hells: Participatory Art and the Politics of Spectatorship.* London: Verso.

Black, Richard (2003) 'Breaking the Convention: Researching the "Illegal" Migration of Refugees to Europe', *Antipode,* 35, 34–54.

Bleiker, Roland (2012) *Aesthetics and World Politics.* New York: Palgrave Macmillan.

Bloch, Maurice (1986) *From Blessing to Violence.* Cambridge, MA: Cambridge University Press.

Boisadam, Philippe (2009) *Mais que faire de Mayotte? Chronologie commenté 'd'une affaire aussi dérisoire (1841–2000).* Paris: L'Harmattan.

Bordwell, David and Kristin Thompson (2010) *Film Art: An Introduction,* 9th edition. New York: McGraw-Hill.

Borren, Marieke (2008) 'Towards an Arendtian Politics of In/visibility: On Stateless Refugees and Undocumented Aliens', *Ethical Perspectives: Journal of the European Ethics Network,* 15, 2, 213–37.

____ (2010) *Amor Mundi: Hannah Arendt's Political Phenomenology of World.* Amsterdam: F & N. (Dissertation).

Buenos Aires Film Festival (2011) *Catálogo BAFICI.* Buenos Aires: Gobierno de la Ciudad Autónoma de Buenos Aires.

Bourriaud, Nicolas (1998) *Relational Aesthetics.* Dijon: Les Presses du Réel.

Brunner, Edward M. (1986) 'Experience and Its Expressions', in Victor W. Turner and Edward M. Bruner (eds) *The Anthropology of Experience.* Urbana, IL: University of Illinois Press, 3–32.

Camposano, Clement C. (2012) 'Balikbayan Boxes and the Performance of Intimacy by

Filipino Migrant Women in Hong Kong', *Asian and Pacific Migration Journal*, 21, 1, 83–103.

Casey, Edward S. (1996) 'How to Get from Space to Place in a Fairly Short Stretch of Time: Phenomenological Prolegomena', in Steven Feld and Keith H. Basso (eds) *Senses of Place*. Santa Fe: School of American Research, 13–52.

Castells, Manuel (2000a) *The Rise of the Network Society: The Information Age: Economy, Society and Culture* Vol. I, second edition. Oxford: Blackwell.

____ (2000b) *End of Millennium: The Information Age: Economy, Society and Culture* Vol. III, second edition. Oxford: Blackwell.

____ (2004) *The Power of Identity: The Information Age: Economy, Society and Culture* Vol. II, second edition. Oxford: Blackwell.

Castells, Stephen and Marc J. Miller (2009) *The Age of Migration: International Population Movements in the Modern World*, forth edition. Basingstoke: Palgrave MacMillan.

Chevrier, Jean-François (2005) 'Documentary, Document, Testimony...', in Frits Gierstberg, Martijn Verhoeven, Hans Scholten and Maartje Van Den Heuvel (eds) *Documentary Now!: Contemporary Strategies in Photography, Film and the Visual Arts*. Rotterdam: NAi Uitgevers, 46–58.

Classen, Constance (1993) *Worlds of Sense: Exploring the Senses in History and Across Cultures*. London: Routledge.

____ (1997) 'Foundations for an Anthropology of the Senses', *International Social Science Journal*, 153, 401–12.

Classen, Constance, David Howes and Anthony Synnott (eds) (1994) *Aroma: The Cultural History of Smell*. London: Routledge.

Clifford, James (1983) 'On Ethnographic Authority', *Representations*, 1, 2, 118–46.

____ (1988) 'On Ethnographic Surrealism', in *The Predicament of Culture*. Cambridge, MA: Harvard University Press, 117–51.

____ (1997) *Routes: Travel and Translation in the Late Twentieth Century*. Cambridge, MA: Harvard University Press.

Cole, Simon (2001) *Suspect Identities: A History of Fingerprinting and Criminal Identification*. Cambridge, MA: Harvard University Press.

Coles, Alex (ed.) (2001) *Site-Specificity – The Ethnographic Turn (De-, Dis-, Ex-, Volume 4)*. London: Black Dog.

Coutin, Susan Bibler (1993) *The Culture of Protest: Religious Activism and the U.S. Sanctuary Movement*. Boulder, CO: Westview Press.

____ (2000) *Legalizing Moves: Salvadoran Immigrants' Struggle for U.S. Residency*. Ann Arbor, MI: University of Michigan Press.

Cresswell, Tim (2002) 'Introduction: Theorizing Place', in Tim Cresswell (ed.) *Placing Mobility, Mobilizing Place*. Amsterdam and New York: Rodopi, 11–32.

Csordas, Thomas J. (1990) 'Embodiment as a Paradigm for Anthropology', *Ethos*, 18, 1, 5–47.

____ (ed.) (1994) 'Introduction: The Body as Representation and Being-in-the-World', in Thomas J. Csordas (ed.) *Embodiment and Experience: The Existential Ground of Culture and Self*. Cambridge, MA: Cambridge University Press, 1–24.

Damasio, Antonio R. (1994) *Descartes' Error: Emotion, Reason and the Human Brain*.

New York: Avon Books.

Dasgupta, Sudeep (2008) 'The Visuality of the Other: The Place of the Migrant between Derrida's Ethics and Ranciere's Aesthetics in *Calais: The Last Border*', in Murat Aydemir and Alex Rotas (eds) *Migratory Settings*. Amsterdam and New York: Rodopi.

Davis, Mike (2001) *Magical Urbanism: Latinos Reinvent the U.S. City*. London: Verso.

De Genova, Nicolas P. (2002) 'Migrant "Illegality" and Deportability in Everyday Life', *Annual Review of Anthropology*, 31, 1, 419–47.

——(2009) 'Conflicts of Mobility, and the Mobility of Conflicts: Rightlessness, Presence, Subjectivity, Freedom', *Subjectivity*, 29, 445–66.

Deleuze, Gilles (1986) *Cinema 1: The Movement-Image*, trans. Hugh Tomlinson and Barbara Habberjam. London: The Athlone Press.

—— (1989) *Cinema 2: The Time-Image*, trans. Hugh Tomlinson and Robert Galeta. London: The Athlone Press.

Deleuze, Gilles and Felix Guattari (1987) *A Thousand Plateaus: Capitalism and Schizophrenia*, trans. Brian Massumi. Minneapolis, MN: University of Minnesota Press.

Demos, T. J. (2010) 'Another World, and Another… Notes on Uneven Geographies', in Alex Farquharson and Jim Waters (eds) *Uneven Geographies*, Exhibition catalogue. Nottingham: Nottingham Contemporary, 11–19.

—— (2012a) *Return to the Postcolony: Specters of Colonialism in Contemporary Art*. Berlin: Sternberg Press.

——(2012b) 'Toward a New Institutional Critique: A Conversation with Renzo Martens', *Atlántica*, 52, 90–103.

—— (2013) *The Migrant Image: The Art and Politics of Documentary During Global Crisis*. Durham, NC: Duke University Press.

Derrida, Jacques (1976) *Of Grammatology*, trans. Gayatri Chakravorty Spivak. Baltimore, MD: Johns Hopkins University Press.

Desjarlais, Robert R. (1992) *Body and Emotion: The Aesthetics of Illness and Healing in the Nepal Himalayas*. Philadelphia: University of Pennsylvania Press.

Desjarlais, Robert R. and C. Jason Throop (2011) 'Phenomenological Approaches in Anthropology', *Annual Review of Anthropology*, 40, 87–102.

Doy, Gen (2005) 'Visualising the Invisible?: Images of Migrants and Refugees in the New Europe', in Graham Coulter-Smith and Maurice Owen (eds) *Art in the Age of Terrorism*. London: Paul Holberton, 60–79.

Düvell, Franck (2001) 'Grundzüge des europäischen Migrationsregimes', *Flüchtlingsrat – Zeitschrift für Flüchtlingspolitik in Niedersachsen*, 75/76, 32–7.

Enwezor, Okwui, Mélanie Bouteloup, Abdellah Karroum, Émilie Renard and Claire Staebler (eds) (2012) *Intense Proximity: An Anthology of the Near and the Far*. Paris: Editions ArtLys.

Fabian, Johannes (1983) *Time and the Other: How Anthropology Makes Its Object*. New York: Columbia University Press.

Falk, Francesca (2010) 'Invasion, Infection, Invisibility: An Iconology of Illegalized Immigration', in Christine Bischoff, Francesca Falk and Sylvia Kafehsy (eds) *Images of Illegalized Immigration: Towards a Critical Iconology of Politics.* Bielefeld: Transcript, 83–100.

___ (2011) *Eine gestische Geschichte der Grenze. Wie der Liberalismus an der Grenze an seine Grenzen kommt.* Munich: Fink.

Falzon, Mark-Anthony (ed.) (2009) *Multi-Sited Ethnography: Theory, Praxis and Locality in Contemporary Research.* Aldershot: Ashgate.

Feld, Steven (1982) *Sound and Sentiment: Birds, Weeping, Poetics, and Song in Kaluli Expression.* Philadelphia: University of Pennsylvania Press.

Ferguson, James (2002) 'Global Disconnect: Abjection and the Aftermath of Modernism', in Jonathan Xavier, Inda Rosaldo and Renato Rosaldo (eds) *The Anthropology of Globalization, A Reader.* London: Blackwell, 136–53.

Foster, Hal (1996) *The Return of the Real: The Avant-garde at the End of the Century.* Cambridge, MA: MIT Press.

Foucault, Michel (1970) *The Order of Things: An Archaeology of the Human Sciences.* New York: Vintage.

Fox, Claire (1999) *The Fence and the River: Culture and Politics at the U.S.-Mexico-Border.* Minneapolis, MN: University of Minnesota Press.

Geertz, Clifford (1973) *The Interpretation of Cultures.* New York: Basic Books.

Gell, Alfred (1992) *The Anthropology of Time: Cultural Constructions of Temporal Maps and Images.* Oxford: Berg.

Geurts, Kathryn L. (2003) 'On Embodied Consciousness in Anlo-Ewe Worlds: A Cultural Phenomenology of the Fetal Position', *Ethnography*, 4, 3, 363–95.

Glick Schiller, Nina, Linda Basch and Christina Blanc-Szanzon (eds) (1992) *Towards a Transnational Perspective on Migration.* New York: New York Academy of Science.

___ (1995) 'From Immigrant to Transmigrant: Theorizing Transnational Migration', *Anthropological Quarterly*, 68, 1, 48–63.

Glick Schiller, Nina and Noel B. Salazar (2013) 'Regimes of Mobility Across the Globe', *Journal of Ethnic and Migration Studies*, 39, 2, 183–200.

Godfrey, Mark, T. J. Demos, Eyal Weizman and Ayesha Hameed (2010) 'Rights of Passage. Migration.' *Tate Etc.* 19, http://www.tate.org.uk/context-comment/articles/rights-passage (accessed 16 November 2015).

Gordon, Anna Pegler (2006) 'Chinese Exclusion, Photography, and the Development of U.S. Immigration Policy', *American Quarterly*, 58, 1, 51–77.

Gordon, Avery F. (2008) *Ghostly Matters: Haunting and the Sociological Imagination.* Minneapolis, MN: University of Minnesota Press.

Graeber, David (2007) *Possibilities: Essays on Hierarchy, Rebellion and Desire.* Oakland: AK Press.

Grimshaw, Anna (2001) *The Ethnographer's Eye: Ways of Seeing in Anthropology.* Cambridge, MA: Cambridge University Press.

Grimshaw, Anna and Amanda Ravetz (eds) (2005) *Visualizing Anthropology.* Bristol: Intellect.

___ (2009) *Observational Cinema: Anthropology, Film, and the Exploration of Social Life.* Bloomington, IN: Indiana University Press.

Grossman, Alan and Àine O'Brien (eds) (2007) *Projecting Migration: Transcultural*

Documentary Practice. London and New York: Wallflower Press.

Guha, Ranajit (2011) 'The Migrant's Time', in Saloni Mathur (ed.) *The Migrant's Time: Rethinking Art History and Diaspora*. New Haven, CT: Yale University Press, 3–9.

Gutberlet, Marie-Hélène and Sissy Helff (eds) (2011) *Die Kunst der Migration: Aktuelle Positionen zum europäisch-afrikanischen Diskurs*. Bielefeld: Transcript.

Guyot, David (2006) *Travailleurs immigrés à Mayotte*. Pamandzi: ISM.

Habermas, Jürgen ([1962] 1989) *The Structural Transformation of the Public Sphere: An Inquiry into a Category of Bourgeois Society*, trans. Thomas Burger. Cambridge, MA: MIT Press.

Hannerz, Ulf (1996) *Transnational Connections – Culture, People, Places*. London: Routledge.

Hastrup, Kirsten (1992) 'Anthropological Visions: Some Notes on Visual and Textual Authority', in Peter I. Crawford and David Turton (eds) *Film as Ethnography*. Manchester: Manchester University Press, 8–25.

Heidenreich, Nanna (2015) *V/Erkennungsdienste, das Kino und die Perspektive der Migration*. Bielefeld: Transcript.

Heller, Charles (2006) 'Crossroads at the Edge of Worlds: Sub-Saharan Transit Migration in Morocco', in Ursula Biemann and Brian Holmes (eds) *The Maghreb Connection: Movements of Life Across Northern Africa*. Barcelona: Actar, 107–35.

Henley, Paul (2004) 'Putting Film to Work: Observational Cinema as Practical Ethnography', in Sarah Pink, Laszlo Kurti and Ana Isabel Afonso (eds) *Working Images: Visual Research and Representation in Ethnography*. London and New York: Routledge, 109–30.

Hernández-Navarro, Miguel Á. (2012) 'Out of Synch: Visualizing Migratory Times through Video Art', in Mieke Bal and Miguel Á. Hernández-Navarro (eds) *Art and Visibility in Migratory Culture: Conflict, Resistance, and Agency*. Amsterdam and New York: Rodopi, 191–208.

Herzfeld, Michael (2001) *Anthropology: Theoretical Practice in Culture and Society*. Oxford: Blackwell.

Hess, Sabine and Bernd Kasparek (eds) (2010) *Grenzregime. Diskurse, Praktiken, Insitutionen in Europa*. Berlin: Assoziation A.

Holert, Tom (2007) 'Das Überleben der Anderen. Zur Repräsentation von Flüchtlingen und MigrantInnen im aktuellen Dokumentarfilm', *Springerin*, 13, 2, 32–5.

Howes, David (ed.) (1991a) *Varieties of Sensory Experience*. Toronto: University of Toronto Press.

_____ (1991b) 'Introduction: To Summon All the Senses', in David Howes (ed.) *Varieties of Sensory Experience*. Toronto: University of Toronto Press, 3–24.

_____ (1991c) 'Sensorial Anthropology', in David Howes (ed.) *Varieties of Sensory Experience*. Toronto: University of Toronto Press, 167–91.

_____ (ed.) (2003) *Sensual Relations: Engaging the Senses in Culture and Social Theory*. Ann Arbor, MI: University of Michigan Press.

_____ (ed.) (2005) *Empire of the Senses: The Sensual Culture Reader*. Oxford: Berg.

_____ (2011a) 'Reply to Tim Ingold', *Social Anthropology*, 19, 3, 318–22.

_____ (2011b) 'Reply to Tim Ingold 2', *Social Anthropology*, 19, 3, 328–31.

Howes, David and Constance Classen (1991) 'Sounding Sensory Profiles', in David Howes (ed.) *The Varieties of Sensory Experience*. Toronto: University of Toronto Press, 257–88.

Howes, David and Sarah Pink (2010) 'The Future of Sensory Anthropology/The Anthropology of the Senses', *Social Anthropology*, 18, 3, 331–40.

Husserl, Edmund ([1928] 1991) *On the Phenomenology of the Consciousness of Internal Time (1893–1917)*, trans. John B. Brough. Dordrecht: Kluver.

Hymes, Dell (ed.) (1972) *Reinventing Anthropology*. New York: Pantheon Books.

Hyndman-Rizk, Nelia (2014) 'At Home With Skype: New Media Technologies and Social Change Between Lebanon and the Diaspora', in Trevor Batrouney, Tobias Boos, Anton Escher and Paul Tabar (eds) *Palestinian, Lebanese and Syrian Communities in the World: Theoretical Frameworks and Empirical Studies*. Heidelberg: Winter Universitätsverlag, 87–100.

Ingold, Tim (2000) *The Perception of the Environment: Essays on Livelihood, Dwelling and Skill*. London and New York: Routledge.

_____ (ed.) (2011a) *Redrawing Anthropology: Materials, Movements, Lines*. Farnham/ Burlington: Ashgate.

_____ (2011b) 'Worlds of Sense and Sensing the World: A Response to Sarah Pink and David Howes', *Social Anthropology*, 19, 3, 313–17.

_____ (2011c) 'Reply to David Howes', *Social Anthropology*, 19, 3, 323–27.

Institut national de la statistique et des études économiques (INSEE) (2010) Tableau Économique de Mayotte. Édition 2010, http://www.insee.fr/fr/insee_regions/ mayotte/themes/dossiers/tem/tem2010.pdf (accessed 16 November 2015).

Jackson, Michael (1989) *Paths Towards a Clearing: Radical Empiricism and Ethnographic Enquiry*. Bloomington, IN: Indiana University Press.

_____ (ed.) (1996) *Things as They Are: New Directions in Phenomenological Anthropology*. Bloomington, IN: Indiana University Press.

_____ (2005) *Existential Anthropology: Events, Exigencies, and Effects*. New York: Berghahn.

_____ (2006) *The Politics of Storytelling: Violence, Transgression and Intersubjectivity*. Copenhagen: Museum Tusculanum Press.

_____ (2011) *Life Within Limits: Wellbeing in a World of Want*. Durham, NC: Duke University Press.

Jackson, Peter, Phillip Crang and Claire Dwyer (eds) (2004) *Transnational Spaces*. London: Routledge.

Jameson, Fredric (1991) *Postmodernism, or The Cultural Logic of Late Capitalism*. Durham, NC: Duke University Press.

_____ (1992) *The Geopolitical Aesthetic: Cinema and Space in the World System*. Bloomington, IN: Indiana University Press.

Kafehsy, Sylvia (2010) 'Images of Victims in Trafficking in Women: The Euro 08 Campaign Against Trafficking in Women in Switzerland', in Christine Bischoff, Francesca Falk and Sylvia Kafehsy (eds) *Images of Illegalized Immigration. Towards a Critical Iconology of Politics*. Bielefeld: Transcript, 71–81.

Kapferer, Bruce (2013) 'Montage and Time: Deleuze, Cinema and a Buddhist Sorcery Rite', in Christian Suhr and Rane Willerslev (eds) *Transcultural Montage*. New

York: Berghahn, 20–39.

Karakayali, Serhat (2008) *Gespenster der Migration*. Bielefeld: Transcript.

Karakayali, Serhat and Vassilis Tsianos (2007) 'Movements that Matter', in Transit Migration Forschungsgruppe (ed.) *Turbulente Ränder. Neue Perspektiven auf Migration an den Grenzen Europas*. Bielefeld: Transcript, 7–22.

Katz, Jack and Thomas J. Csordas (2003) 'Phenomenological Ethnography in Sociology and Anthropology', *Ethnography*, 4, 3, 275–88.

Kauffman, Linda S. (1986) *Discourses of Desire: Gender, Genre, and Epistolary Fictions*. Ithaca, NY: Cornell University Press.

Kiener, Wilma (2008) 'The Absent and the Cut', *Visual Anthropology*, 21, 5, 393–409.

Klein, Naomi (2007) *The Shock Doctrine: The Rise of Disaster Capitalism*. New York: Metropolitan Books.

Knibbe, Kim and Peter Versteeg (2008) 'Assessing Phenomenology in Anthropology: Lessons from the Study of Religion and Experience', *Critique of Anthropology*, 28, 47–62.

Knox, Paul L. and Sallie Marston (2012) *Human Geography: Places and Regions in Global Context*, sixth edition. Upper Saddle River: Pearson Prentice Hall.

Korsmeyer, Carolyn (ed.) (2005) *The Taste Culture Reader: Experiencing Food and Drink*. Oxford: Berg.

Kuster, Brigitta (2007) 'Die Grenze filmen', in Transit Migration Forschungsgruppe (ed.) *Turbulente Ränder. Neue Perspektiven auf Migration an den Grenzen Europas*. Bielefeld: Transcript, 187–201.

Kwon, Miwon (1997) 'One Place after Another: Notes on Site Specificity', *October*, 80, 85–110.

Larkin, Brian (2008) *Signal and Noise: Media, Infrastructure, and Urban Culture in Nigeria*. Durham, NC: Duke University Press.

Lefebvre, Henri (1991) *The Production of Space*, trans. Donald Nicholson-Smith. Oxford: Basil Blackwell.

Lévi-Strauss, Claude (1973) *Tristes Tropiques*. New York: Atheneum.

Levitt, Peggy and Nina Glick Schiller (2004) 'Conceptualizing Simultaneity: A Transnational Social Field Perspective on Society', *International Migration Review*, 38, 1002–39.

Lind, Maria and Hito Steyerl (2008) *The Greenroom: Reconsidering the Documentary and Contemporary Art*. Berlin: Sternberg Press.

Longhurst, Robyn (2013) 'Using Skype to Mother: Bodies, Emotions, Visuality, and Screens', *Environment and Planning D: Society and Space*, 31, 4, 664–79.

Low, Setha M. and Sally Engle Merry (2010) 'Engaged Anthropology: Diversity and Dilemmas: An Introduction to Supplement 2', *Current Anthropology*, 51, S2, 203–26.

Lucht, Hans (2011) *Darkness Before Daybreak: African Migrants Living on the Margins in Southern Italy Today*. Berkley, CA: University of California Press.

Lyotard, Jean-François (1984) *The Postmodern Condition: A Report on Knowledge*, trans. Geoffrey Bennington and Brian Massumi. Minneapolis: University of Minnesota Press.

MacDougall, David (1998) *Transcultural Cinema*. Princeton, NJ. Princeton University

Press.

____ (2006) *The Corporeal Image: Film, Ethnography, and the Senses*. Princeton, NJ: Princeton University Press.

Madianou, Mirca and Daniel Miller (2012) *Migration and New Media: Transnational Families and Polymedia*. London: Routledge.

Malinowski, Bronislaw (1967) *A Diary in the Strict Sense of the Term*. Stanford, CA: Stanford University Press.

Malkki, Liisa (1992) 'National Geographic: The Rooting of Peoples and the Territorialization of National Identity among Scholars and Refugees', *Cultural Anthropology*, 7, 1, 24–44.

Manovich, Lev (2001) *The Language of New Media*. Cambridge, MA: MIT Press.

Marcus, George (1994) 'The Modernist Sensibility in Recent Ethnographic Writing and the Cinematic Metaphor of Montage', in Lucien Taylor (ed.) *Visualizing Theory Selected Essays from VAR 1990–1994*. New York: Routledge, 2–12.

____ (1995) 'Ethnography In/Of the World System: The Emergence of Multi-Sited Ethnography', *Annual Review of Anthropology*, 24, 95–117.

Marcus, George and Fred Myers (eds) (1995) *The Traffic in Culture: Refiguring Art and Anthropology*. Los Angeles: University of California Press.

Marcus, George and Michael M. J. Fischer (1986) *Anthropology as Cultural Critique*. Chicago: University of Chicago Press.

Marks, Laura (2000) *The Skin of the Film: Intercultural Cinema, Embodiment, and the Senses*. Durham, NC: Duke University Press.

Massey, Doreen (2005) *For Space*. London: Sage.

Mathur, Saloni (ed.) (2011) *The Migrant's Time: Rethinking Art History and Diaspora*. New Haven, CT: Yale University Press.

Mattingly, Cheryl (1998) *Healing Dramas and Clinical Plots: The Narrative Structure of Experience*. Cambridge: Cambridge University Press.

McLagan, Meg and Yates McKee (2012) *Sensible Politics: The Visual Culture of Nongovernmental Activism*. New York: Zone.

McNevin, Anne (2011) *Contesting Citizenship: Irregular Migrants and New Frontiers of the Political*. New York: Columbia University Press.

Melitopoulos, Angela and Maurizio Lazzarato (2006) 'Timescapes/ B-Zone', in Ursula Biemann, Imre Szeman and Angela Melitopoulos (eds) *Political Typographies: Visual Essays on the Margins of Europe*. Barcelona: Fundacio Antoni Tapies, 71–85.

Merleau-Ponty, Maurice (1962) *The Phenomenology of Perception*, trans. Colin Smith. London and New York: Routledge.

____ (1964) *Signs*, trans. Richard McCleary. Evanston, IL: Northwestern University Press.

____ (1968) *The Visible and the Invisible*, trans. Claude Lefort. Evanston, IL: North-western University Press.

Mezzadra, Sandro (2011) 'The Gaze of Autonomy: Capitalism, Migration and Social Struggles', in Victoria Squire (ed.) *The Contested Politics of Mobility: Borderzones and Irregularity*. London: Routledge, 121–43.

Miller, Daniel (2011) *Tales from Facebook*. Cambridge: Polity Press.

Miller, Daniel and Jolynna Sinanan (2014) *Webcam*. Cambridge: Polity Press.

Mitchell, W. J. T. (1986) *Iconology: Image, Text, Ideology.* Chicago: University of Chicago Press.

＿＿ (1994) *Picture Theory: Essays on Verbal and Visual Representation.* Chicago: University of Chicago Press.

＿＿ (2004) 'Migrating Images: Totemism, Fetishism, Idolatry', in Petra Stegmann and Peter C. Seel (eds) *Migrating Images.* Berlin: Haus der Kulturen der Welt, 14–24.

Mitry, Jean (1965) *Esthetique et Psychologie du Cinema.* Vol. 2. Paris: Editions Universitaires.

Mondloch, Kate (2010) *Screens: Viewing Media Installation Art.* Minneapolis, MN: University of Minnesota Press.

Morse, Margaret (1998) *Virtualities: Television, Media Art, and Cyberculture.* Bloomington, IN: Indiana University Press.

Muenger, Laura (2011) *Im Kwassa-Kwassa nach Mayotte. Migrationsprozesse und sozialer Wandel in einem (post-)kolonialen Kontext.* Working Paper 53, Institute for Social Anthropology. Bern: University of Bern.

Munn, Nancy (1992) 'The Cultural Anthropology of Time: A Critical Essay', *Annual Review of Anthropology*, 21, 93–123.

Naficy, Hamid (1993) *The Making of Exile Cultures: Iranian Television in Los Angeles.* Minneapolis, MN: University of Minnesota Press.

＿＿ (2001) *An Accented Cinema: Exilic and Diasporic Filmmaking.* Princeton, NJ: Princeton University Press.

＿＿ (2012) *A Social History of Iranian Cinema, Vol. 4: The Globalizing Era, 1984–2010.* Durham, NC: Duke University Press.

Ots, Thomas (1994) 'The Silenced Body – The Expressive Leib: On the Dialectic of Mind and Life in Chinese Cathartic Healing', in Thomas Csordas (ed.) *Embodiment and Experience: The Existential Ground of Culture and Self.* Cambridge, MA: Cambridge University Press, 116–36.

Pandolfo, Stefania (2007) '"The Burning": Finitude and the Politico-Theological Imagination of Illegal Migration', *Anthropological Theory*, 7, 329–63.

Papadopoulos, Dimitris and Vassilis Tsianos (2007) 'The Autonomy of Migration: The Animals of Undocumented Mobility', in Anna Hickey-Moody and Peta Malins (eds) *Deleuzian Encounters: Studies in Contemporary Social Issues.* New York: Palgrave Macmillan, 223–35.

Papastergiadis, Nikos (2000) *The Turbulence of Migration. Globalization, Deterritorialization and Hybridity.* Cambridge: Polity Press.

Pink, Sarah (2009) *Doing Sensory Ethnography.* London: Sage.

Rajchmann, John (2008) 'Deleuze's Time, or How the Cinematic Changes Our Idea of Art', in Tanya Leighton (ed.) *Art and the Moving Image.* London: Tate, 307–27.

Ramachandran, V. S. (2000) 'Mirror Neurons and Imitation Learning as the Driving Force behind "The Great Leap Forward" in Human Evolution', *Edge*, 69; http://edge.org/conversation/mirror-neurons-and-imitation-learning-as-the-driving-force-behind-the-great-leap-forward-in-human-evolution (accessed 16 November 2015).

Rancière, Jacques (1998) *Disagreement: Politics and Philosophy*, trans. Julie Rose. Minneapolis, MN: University of Minnesota Press.

＿＿ (2006) *The Politics of Aesthetics: The Distribution of the Sensible*, trans. Gabriel

Rockhill. New York: Continuum.

____ (2009) *The Emancipated Spectator*, trans. Gregory Elliott. London: Verso.

____ (2010) *Dissensus: On Politics and Aesthetics*, trans. Steven Corcoran. New York: Continuum.

Ray, Manas (2006) 'Chalo Jahaji: Bollywood in Diaspora – in the Tracks of Indenture to Globalization', in Preben Kaarsholm (ed.) *City Flicks: Indian Cinema and the Urban Experience*. London: Seagull, 138–79.

Rees, A. L., David Curtis, Duncan White and Steven Ball (2011) *Expanded Cinema: Art, Performance, Film*. London: Tate.

Regener, Susanne (1999) *Fotografische Erfassung. Zur Geschichte medialer Konstruktionen des Kriminellen*. München: Fink.

Reichert, Ramon (2011) 'Das Geschlecht der Grenze. Genderrepräsentationen von der Berliner Mauer bis zur EU-Aussengrenze', in Bettina Dennerlein and Elke Frietsch (eds) *Identitäten in Bewegung. Migration im Film*. Bielefeld: Transcript, 35–56.

Rodman, Margaret C. (2003) 'Empowering Place: Mulilocality and Multivocality', in Setha M. Low and Denise Lawrence-Zúñiga (eds) *Anthropology of Space and Place: Locating Culture*. Malden, MA: Blackwell, 204–23.

Rosello, Mireille (1998) 'Representing Illegal Immigrants in France: From Clandestins to L'affaire des Sans-Papiers de Saint-Bernard', *Journal of European Studies*, 28, 137–51.

Russell, Catherine (1999) *Experimental Ethnography*. Durham, NC: Duke University Press.

Sacks, Oliver (1995) 'To See and Not See', in *An Anthropologist on Mars*. London: Picador, 108–52.

Said, Edward W. (1978) *Orientalism*. New York: Vintage.

____ 1993. *Culture and Imperialism*. New York: Vintage.

Samers, Michael (2009) *Migration*. New York: Routledge

Sassen, Saskia (1998) *Globalization and Its Discontents: Essays on the New Mobility of People and Money*. New York: New Press.

Scheper-Hughes, Nancy (1995) 'The Primacy of the Ethical: Propositions for a Militant Anthropology', *Current Anthropology*, 36, 3, 409–40.

Schmid, Antonia (2011) 'Visual Discourse Analysis: A Methodological Attempt to Take the Pictorial Turn Seriously', in Michael Gubo, Martin Kypta and Florian Öchsner (eds) *Kritische Perspektiven: 'Turns', Trends und Theorien*. Münster: Lit, 301–27.

Schneider, Arnd (2011) 'Expanded Visions: Rethinking Anthropological Research and Representation through Experimental Film', in Tim Ingold (ed.) *Redrawing Anthropology. Materials, Movements, Lines*. Farnham: Ashgate, 177–94.

Schneider, Arnd and Caterina Pasqualino (2014) *Experimental Film and Anthropology*. London and New York: Bloomsbury.

Schneider, Arnd and Christopher Wright (eds) (2006) *Contemporary Art and Anthropology*. Oxford: Berg.

____ (eds) (2010) *Between Art and Anthropology. Contemporary Ethnographic Practice*. Oxford: Berg.

____ (eds) (2013) *Anthropology and Art Practice*. London: Bloomsbury Academic.

Schneider, Florian (2011) 'Enklaven, Ausnahmezustände und die Camps als Gegenlabore', in Marie-Hélène Gutberlet and Sissy Helff (eds) *Die Kunst der Migration: Aktuelle Positionen zum europäisch-afrikanischen Diskurs*. Bielefeld: Transcript, 137–45.

Seremetakis, C. Nadia (1994) *The Senses Still: Perception and Memory as Material Culture in Modernity*. Boulder, CO: Westview.

Sivandandan, Ambalavaner (2000) 'Casualties of Globalism', *The Guardian*, 8 August, 13.

Sheller Mimi and John Urry (2006) 'The New Mobilities Paradigm', *Environment and Planning A*, 38, 2, 207–26.

Sheren, Ira (2015) *Portable Borders: Performance Art and Politics on the U.S. Frontera Since 1984*. Austin, TX: University of Texas Press.

Skype (2013) 'Skype Celebrates a Decade of Meaningful Conversations!', http://blogs.skype.com/2013/08/28/skype-celebrates-a-decade-of-meaningful-conversations/ (accessed 16 November 2015).

Smith, Michael Peter (2001) *Transnational Urbanism: Locating Globalization*. Malden, MA: Blackwell.

Sobchack, Vivian (1992) *The Address of the Eye: Phenomenology and Film Experience*. Princeton, NJ: Princeton University Press.

____ (2004) *Carnal Thoughts: Embodiment and Moving Image Culture*. Berkeley, CA. University of California Press.

Soja, Edward W. (1996) *Thirdspace: Journeys to Los Angeles and Other Real-and-Imagined Places*. Oxford: Basil Blackwell.

Sontag, Susan (2003) *Regarding the Pain of Others*. New York: Farrar, Straus and Giroux.

Spivak, Gayatri Chakravorty (1988) 'Can the Subaltern Speak?', in Cary Nelson and Lawrence Grossberg (eds) *Marxism and the Interpretation of Culture*. Chicago: University of Illinois Press, 271–313.

Stallabras, Julian (2013) 'Introduction', in Julian Stallabras (ed.) *Documentary (Documents on Contemporary Art)*. London: Whitechapel Gallery/Cambridge, MA: MIT Press, 12–21.

Stoller, Paul (1989) *The Taste of Ethnographic Things: The Senses in Anthropology*. Philadelphia: University of Pennsylvania Press.

____ (1994) 'Artaud, Rouch, and the Cinema of Cruelty', in Lucien Taylor (ed.) *Visualizing Theory: Selected Essays from VAR [Visual Anthropology Review]*. New York: Routledge, 84–98.

____ (1997) *Sensuous Scholarship*. Philadelphia: University of Pennsylvania Press.

____ (2004) 'Sensuous Ethnography, African Persuasions, and Social Knowledge', *Qualitative Inquiry*, 10, 6, 817–35.

Stoller, Paul and Cheryl Olkes (1987) *In Sorcery's Shadow: A Memoir of Apprenticeship among the Songhay of Niger*. Chicago: University of Chicago Press.

Strecker, Ivo (2013) 'Co-presence, Astonishment and Evocation in Cinematography', in Ivo Strecker and Marcus Verne (eds) *Astonishment and Evocation: The Spell of Culture in Art and Anthropology*. New York: Berghahn, 52–62.

Suhr, Christian and Rane Willerslev (2012) 'Can Film Show the Invisible?: The Work of Montage in Ethnographic Filmmaking', *Current Anthropology*, 53, 3, 282–301.

____ (eds) (2013) *Transcultural Montage*. New York: Berghahn.

Taussig, Michael T. (1987) *Shamanism, Colonialism, and the Wild Man: A Study in Terror and Healing.* Chicago: University of Chicago Press.

____ (2004) *My Cocaine Museum.* Chicago: University of Chicago Press.

Taylor, Lucien (1996) 'Iconophobia', *Transition*, 69, 64–88.

Telegeography (2014) 'Skype Traffic Continues to Thrive', https://www.telegeography. com/products/commsupdate/articles/2014/01/15/skype-traffic-continues-to-thrive/ (accessed 16 November 2015).

Telesca, Jennifer E. (2013) 'Preface: What Is Visual Citizenship?', *Humanity: An International Journal of Human Rights, Humanitarianism, and Development.* 4, 3, 339–43.

Thompson, Nato (2012) *Living as Form: Socially Engaged Art from 1991–2011.* Cambridge, MA: MIT Press.

Throop, Jason (2003) 'Articulating Experience', *Anthropological Theory*, 3, 2, 219–41.

Transit Migration Forschungsgruppe (2007) *Turbulente Ränder: Neue Perspektiven auf Migration an den Grenzen Europas.* Bielefeld: Transcript.

Tsianos, Vassilis, Sabine Hess and Serhat Karakayali (2009) 'Transnational Migration Theory and Method of an Ethnographic Analysis of Border Regimes', in *Working Paper 55.* University of Sussex: Sussex Centre for Migration Research.

Tsianos, Vasilis and Serhat Karakayali (2010) 'Transnational Migration and the Emergence of the European Border Regime: An Ethnographic Analysis', *European Journal of Social Theory*, 13, 3, 373–87.

Turner, Victor W. (1986) 'Dewey, Dilthey, and Drama: An Essay in the Anthropology of Experience', in Victor W. Turner and Edward M. Brunner (eds) *The Anthropology of Experience.* Urbana, IL: University of Illinois Press, 33–44.

Turner, Victor W. and Edward M. Brunner (eds) (1986) *The Anthropology of Experience.* Urbana, IL: University of Illinois Press.

Tyler, Stephen (1987) *The Unspeakable: Discourse, Dialogue and Rhetoric in the Postmodern World.* Madison, WI: University of Wisconsin Press.

UNCDF (2013) 'UNCDF in Comoros Islands', http://www.uncdf.org/en/Comoros-Islands (accessed 16 November 2015).

UNHCR (2015) 'World Refugee Day takes place against backdrop of worsening global crisis', http://www.unhcr.org/55842cb46.html (accessed 16 November 2015).

Urry, John (2003) *Global Complexity.* Cambridge: Polity Press/Oxford: Blackwell.

Van Assche, Christine (2006) 'Zineb Sedira in Conversation with Christine Van Assche', in Claire Grafik and Mériadek Caraës (eds) *Zineb Sedira: Saphir.* London and Paris: The Photographers' Gallery, Kamel Mennour and Paris Musées, 56–63.

Vertovec, Steven (2004) 'Cheap Calls: The Social Glue of Migrant Transnationalism', *Global Networks*, 4, 219–24.

____ (ed.) (2010) *Migration: Critical Concepts in the Social Sciences* (five volumes). London: Routledge/Max-Planck Institute.

Vigh, Henrik (2009) 'Wayward Migration: On Imagined Futures and Technological Voids', *Ethnos*, 74, 1, 91–109.

Virilio, Paul (2000) *Polar Inertia.* London: Sage.

Weber, Cynthia (2008) 'Popular Visual Language as Global Communication: The Remediation of United Airlines Flight 93', *Review of International Studies*, 34,

137–53.

Weizman, Eyal (2014) 'Introduction: Forensis', in Forensic Architecture (ed.) *Forensis: The Architecture of Public Truth.* Berlin: Sternberg Press, 9–32.

Wenk, Silke and Rebecca Krebs (2007) *Analysing the Migration of People and Images: Perspectives and Methods in the Field of Visual Culture,* http://www.york.ac.uk/res/researchintegration/Integrative_Research_Methods/Wenk%20Visual%20Culture%20April%202007.pdf (accessed 16 November 2015).

Willerslev, R. and Olga Ulturgashewa (2007) 'The Sable Frontier: The Siberian Fur Trade as Montage', *Cambridge Anthropology,* 26, 2, 79–100.

World Policy Institute (2011) 'The Newest French Department', http://www.worldpolicy.org/blog/2011/04/14/newest-french-department (accessed 16 November 2015).

Wright, Terence (2002) 'Moving Images: The Media Representation of Refugees', *Visual Studies,* 17, 1, 53–66.

Žižek, Slavoj (2015) 'The Non-Existence of Norway', *London Review of Books Online,* http://www.lrb.co.uk/2015/09/09/slavoj-zizek/the-non-existence-of-norway (accessed 16 November 2015).

INDEX

activism 12, 21, 35, 49–50; media activist
14; art activist 16; filmmaker activist
138
aesthetics: aestheticisation of politics 18;
aesthetic practice 20–1, 87; aesthetics-
political ontologies 23; critical aesthetic
services 12; of empathy 141–2, 144; of
ethnographic filmmaking 29; migratory
aesthetics 14, 154n.4; of observational
film 100; politico-aesthetic space 18; of
politics 18–19; relational aesthetics 16,
23; space of 18; of surveillance 45–6, 48
Africa: decolonisation movements 101;
East Africa 50; illegal migrants 18,
37–8, 43, 46, 59, 101, 113; North Africa
14, 26, 38–9, 96, 113, 128; and Ceuta and
Melilla; sub-Saharan Africa 5, 44, 59,
80, 89–90; victimisation of Africans 141;
West Africa 91; see also Comoros Islands
Agamben, Giorgio 34, 44, 153
Algeria 64, 91, 127–8
All the World's Futures 15, 18
Aloua, Mehdi 41
Alys, Francis 14
AMAs 148–50
Anjouan 24, 27, 98, 100–4, 152; see also
Comoros Islands
Antonioni, Michelangelo 121
Appadurai, Arjuan 4, 9, 85, 92, 117, 130, 153
Arab Spring 38
Arendt, Hannah 17, 20, 23–5, 30, 33–5, 37,
41–4, 52, 58, 82–3, 139, 146–8, 150–1;
and visibility and in/visibility
asylum seekers 1–3, 5, 10, 32, 35, 37, 39,
95, 120, 138, 148, 153; underage asylum
seekers 148, 150; see also migration
A Tale of Two Islands 24, 27, 84, 98, 100,
106–7, 152, 154n.3
audience 15, 19, 23, 25, 27, 47, 49, 53, 65,
69, 73, 75–7, 86, 92, 103, 105, 119–20,
134, 145–6, 150; art audience 18;
diasporic audience 117; European
audience 39; migrant audience 117;
Western audience 140

avant-garde 12, 23; avant-garde
constructivism 87
Azoulay, Ariella 16–19, 23–4, 35, 145, 151

Ballester, Gonzalo 131–2, 136
barbed-wire 46–7; see also Ceuta and
Melilla
Bataille, George 13
Benedict, Ruth 139
Benjamin, Walter 18, 107
Bergson, Henri 74, 110, 124–5, 136–7
Berlin: borders of 1; Berlin Wall 13; see
also Germany
Biemann, Ursula 11, 14–15, 89–93, 105–6
Birnbaum, Daniel 111, 119, 129
Bischoff, Christine 30–1
Black Film 138
Boas, Franz 139
Bollywood 76, 117, 123
Border 48
Borren, Marieke 34, 35, 37, 41

Calais 6, 48, 63, 65, 95
Calvo, Paola 102
Campion, Jane 62
Cartesian dualism 70
Casey, Edward 78, 80
Castaing-Taylor, Lucien 12, 18, 60
Center for Political Beauty 1–2, 21
Centro de Estancia Temporal de Inmigrantes;
see CETI
CETI 79, 80–2
Ceuta 47
Ceuta 6, 95; border fences 37, 46, 80;
see also Spain and System of External
Vigilance (SIVE)
Christianity 32, 82, 89
Cinema 2: The Time Image 121
Citadelle Europe – Lost in Transit, La 48
citizenship 16, 18, 21–2, 34–5, 43, 101, 147,
150, 153; full citizenship 96; nation-state
18; non-citizenship 96; visual citizenship
19; weak citizenship 96
civil space 19